Chivalry and the Crusades

CEREMONY OF CONFERRING KNIGHTHOOD

Chivalry and the Crusades
A History of the European Knights at War

G. P. R. James

LEONAUR

Chivalry and the Crusades
A History of the European Knights at War
by G. P. R. James

First published under the title
The History of Chivalry

Leonaur is an imprint of Oakpast Ltd

Copyright in this form © 2012 Oakpast Ltd

ISBN: 978-1-78282-038-3 (hardcover)
ISBN: 978-1-78282-039-0 (softcover)

http://www.leonaur.com

Publisher's Notes

Contents

Preface

In writing the pages which follow this preface, I have had to encounter the difficulty of compressing very extensive matter into an extremely limited space. As the subject was, in my eyes, a very interesting one, and every particular connected with it had often been food for thought and object of entertainment to myself, the task of curtailing was the more ungrateful: nor should I have undertaken it, had I not been convinced by my publisher that one volume would be as much as the public in general would be inclined to read. I wished to write upon chivalry and the Crusades, because I fancied that in the hypotheses of many other authors I had discovered various errors and misstatements, which gave a false impression of both the institution and the enterprise; and I have endeavoured, in putting forth my own view of the subject, to advance no one point, however minute, which cannot be justified by indisputable authority.

A favourite theory is too often, in historical writing like the bed of the ancient Greek; and facts are either stretched or lopped away to agree with it: but to ensure as much accuracy as possible, I have taken pains to mark in the margin of the pages the different writers on whose assertions my own statements are founded, with a corresponding figure, by which each particular may be referred to its authority.

In regard to these authors themselves, it seems necessary here to give some information, that those persons who are inclined to inquire beyond the mere surface may know what credit is to be attached to each.

On the first crusade we have a whole host of contemporary writers, many of whom were present at the events they describe. Besides these are several others, who, though they wrote at an after-period, took infinite pains to render their account as correct as possible. The authors I have principally cited for all the earlier facts of the Holy War are, William of Tyre, Albert of Aix, Fulcher of Chartres, Raimond of Agiles, Guibert of Nogent, Radulph of Caën, and Robert, surnamed the Monk.

William of Tyre is, beyond all doubt, the most illustrious of the many historians who have written on the crusades. Born in Palestine, and though both educated for the church and raised step by step to its highest dignities, yet mingling continually in the political changes of the Holy Land—the preceptor of one of its kings—frequently employed in embassies to Europe, and ultimately Archbishop of Tyre and Chancellor of the kingdom of Jerusalem, William possessed the most extensive means of gathering materials for the great work he has left to posterity. He brought to his task, also, a powerful mind, as well as considerable discrimination; and was infinitely superior in education and every intellectual quality to the general chroniclers of his age. He was not born, however, at the time of the first crusade; and consequently, where he speaks of the events of that enterprise, we may look upon him as an historian, clear, talented, elegant, and not extremely credulous; but we must not expect to find the vivid identity of contemporaneous writing. In regard to the history of his own days he is invaluable, and in respect to that of the times which preceded them, his work is certainly superior, as a whole, to anything that has since been written on the subject.

A much more vivid and enthusiastic picture of the first crusade is to be found in Albert of Aix, from whom William of Tyre borrowed many of his details; but the Syrian archbishop, living long after, saw the events he recounted as a whole, rejected much as false that Albert embraced as true, and softened the zealous fire which the passions and feelings of the moment had lighted up in the bosom of the other. Albert himself was not one of the crusaders; but living at the time, and conversing continually with those who returned from the Holy Land, he caught, to an extraordinary extent, the spirit of the enterprise, and has left behind him a brilliant transcript of all the passed-by dreams and long-extinguished enthusiasms of his day.

Thus, as a painting of manners and customs, the *Chronicon Hierosolymitanum* is one of the most valuable records we possess, and the account there given of Peter the Hermit and *Gautier sans avoir* is in many points more full and comprehensive than any other.

Fulcher of Chartres set out for the Holy Land with Stephen, Count of Blois, one of the first crusaders. He soon after became chaplain to Baldwin, the brother of Godfrey de Bouillon, and ended his days a canon of the Holy Sepulchre. His relation is useful in many respects, especially in regard to the march of the crusaders through Italy—the proceedings of Baldwin at Edessa, and the history of Jerusalem for several years after its conquest. His style, however, is tumid and circumlocutory, and his credulity equal to that of Raimond d'Agiles.

Raimond d'Agiles accompanied the Count of Toulouse on the first crusade, in quality of chaplain. Superstitious to the most lamentable degree, and as bigoted in party politics as in religion, he wrote as he lived, like a weak and ignorant man. Nevertheless there is, in his account, much excellent information, detailed with simplicity; and very often, through the folly of the historian, we arrive at truths which his prejudices concealed from himself.

Guibert of Nogent did not visit the Holy Land; but he lived during the first crusade, and, in common with all Europe, felt deeply interested in the fate of that expedition. He examined and noted with accuracy all the anecdotes which reached Europe, and painted, with great vivacity, scenes that he had not himself witnessed. In his account of the crusade many circumstances, evincing strongly the spirit of the age, are to be met with which do not appear elsewhere; and, as we have every reason to feel sure of his general accuracy, it is but fair to suppose that these are well founded.

Radulph, or Raoul, of Caën, is inflated in style, and often inexact; but he is perhaps less superstitious than any other chronicler of the crusades. By poetical exaggeration, he often renders his narrative doubtful; yet, as the biographer of Tancred, he tends to elucidate much that would otherwise have remained in darkness. Robert, called the Monk, was present at the council of Clermont, at which the first crusade was determined; and, though he did not immediately take the Cross, he set out for the Holy Land not long after, and was present at the siege of Jerusalem. He is, in general, accurate and precise; and, though not a little credulous in regard to visions, apparitions, and such imaginations of the day, he is on the whole more calm, clear, and exact than any other contemporary author.

Besides these writers, I have had occasion to cite several others of less authority. Of these, Baldric bears the highest character; and, notwithstanding the fact of his not having been present at the crusade, he is in general accurate. Tudebodus is both brief and imperfect. Matthew of Edessa deserves little or no credit; and the part of the Alexiad which refers to the first crusade is far more likely to mislead than to assist. The most important part, of the whole work, as it is published at present, consists in the notes of Ducange. William of Malmsbury is more useful, but still his account is merely a repetition of what we find in other sources. For all the affairs of Normandy, I have consulted Orderic, Vital, and William of Jumieges.

The history of William of Tyre was afterward continued by several writers, the chief of whom is an author taking the title of Bernard the Treasurer. A Latin version of his book was published by Muratori: Martenne, however, has since printed a work from an old French manuscript, the identity of which with the account of Bernard the Treasurer has been proved by Mansi. This work is one of the most interesting extant; for although it wants entirely either the power or the grace of William of Tyre's composition, and is full of errors, in respect to every thing beyond the immediate limits of the Holy Land, yet there is a simple and interesting minuteness—an individuality of tone through the whole, where it relates to the affairs of Syria, which could not have been given but by an eyewitness. Even the old French in which it is written, slightly different from the exact language of France at the same period, gives it a peculiar character, and stamps it as the work of a Syrian Frank.

Another continuation of William of Tyre is extant, by a Suabian of the name of Herold. This, however, is a much later composition, and possesses few of the qualities of the other. The Cardinal de Vitry also wrote an abbreviated history of the Crusades, bringing it down to his own time *A. D.* 1220. His work is principally to be consulted for the account it gives of the events which passed under the author's own eyes, while Bishop of Acre, and for a great many curious particulars concerning the manners and customs of the Saracens, which are to be found in no other work. The second book of the Cardinal de Vitry's History has been omitted, I cannot conceive why, in the Gesta Dei per Francos. It is, nevertheless, infinitely valuable, as showing the horrible state of the Christians of Palestine, and displaying those vices and weaknesses which eventually brought about the ruin of the Latin kingdom.

The authorities for the second crusade are lamentably few, and by their very paucity show what a change had come over the spirit of the age in the short space of fifty years. The only eyewitnesses who have written on the subject, as far as I can discover, are Odo, a priest of Deuil, or Diagolum, in the neighbourhood of Paris, and Otho, Bishop of Freysinghen. The first of these authors followed Louis VII. to the Holy Land as his chaplain, and his account is, more properly speaking, an epistle to the famous Suger, Abbot of St. Denis, than a chronicle.

Otho of Freysinghen was nearly related to the emperor Conrad, whom he accompanied on his unfortunate expedition. Both these authors, therefore, had the best means of obtaining information; and in the writings of each there is an air of truth and sincerity, which does much towards conviction. I have had occasion in speaking of this crusade to cite casually a number of authors, of whom it is not necessary to give any very detailed account. Their works are to be found in the admirable collections of Dom Bouquet, Duchesne, Martenne, or Muratori.

Wherever I have been obliged to quote from any of the Arabian writers, I am indebted to the extracts of Monsieur Reinaud.

In regard to the crusade of Richard Cœur de Lion and Philip Augustus; for the history of the first, I have borrowed from Benedict of Peterborough, from Hovedon, and especially from Vinesauf, whose work is inestimable. These, with the other English authorities I have cited, are too well known to need comment. Having some time ago written a romance, not yet published, on the history of Philip Augustus, I had previously studied almost all the old chroniclers who speak of that monarch. The most important treatise on his reign is the work of Rigord, who was at once monk, physician, and historiographer at the court of Philip. William the Breton, one of the king's chaplains, continued his history in prose, from the period where Rigord abandoned the task. He also wrote a bombastic poem on the reign of his patron, which, however exaggerated and absurd, is useful as an historical document, and a painting of the manners and customs of the time.

On the taking of Constantinople by the French, I have found no want of authorities. Villehardouin,[1] one of the principal actors in the scenes he describes, has been my chief source of information. I have also met with much in Nicetas, who was present; and I have confirmed the evidence of other writers, by the chronicle in the Rouchy dialect, published by Monsieur Buchon, and by the metrical chronicle of Philippe Mouskes in the same collection. I need hardly say that the works of Ducange have proved invaluable in every part of my inquiry, and that his history of Constantinople under its French monarchs

---

1. *Knights of the Cross* by Geoffrey de Villehardouin & Jean de Joinville (*Chronicle of the Fourth Crusade and The Conquest of Constantinople* by Geoffrey de Villehardouin and *Chronicle of the Crusade of St. Louis* by Jean de Joinville) also published by Leonaur.

both gave me facts and led me to authorities.

Joinville is the principal writer on the crusade of St. Louis. He was an eyewitness, a sufferer, and a principal actor in the scenes he describes. Of all old chroniclers, with the exception, perhaps, of Froissart, Joinville offers the most original, simple, and delightful painting of times and manners long gone by. With the notes of Ducange, his work is an erudite repertory for antique manners and usages, and may be read and reread with gratification, and studied deeply with advantage.

The folio edition in my own library comprises the *Observations, and Dissertations* of Ducange, and the *Commentaries* of Claud Menard; together with the *Establishments of St. Louis,* and a curious treatise upon the ancient law of France, by Pierre de Fontaines. All these works afford a great insight into the spirit of that day; and many other particulars are to be found in the *Branche aux royaux Lignages,* and in the Sermon of Robert de Sainceriaux. Besides the authors I have here particularized, I have had occasion to cite casually a great number of others, whose names, with some account of the works of each, may be found in the *Manuel* of Brunet. Vertot also has furnished us with much information concerning the Knights of St. John; and Dupuy, Raynouard, &c. have spoken largely of the Templars.

I cannot close the enumeration of authors to whom I am under obligations for information or instruction without mentioning M. Guizot, one of the most clearsighted and unprejudiced of all modern historians. His views of causes I have often adopted, sometimes with very slight modifications, and sometimes with none; and, in all instances to which his writings extend, I have been indebted to him for light to conduct me through the dark sanctuary of past events, to the shrine of Truth, even where he has not unveiled the deity herself. I can only regret that his essays did not embrace more of the very comprehensive subject on which I was called to treat.

Several motives have impelled me to give this long account of my authorities; one of which motives was, that often, in reading works on history, I have myself wished that the sources from which facts were derived had been laid open to my examination; but still, my principal view in the detail was, to show the ground on which I had fixed opinions directly opposed to those of several other authors. In many cases, the aspect under which I have seen the events of the Crusades has been entirely different from that under which Mills has regarded them, and I felt myself called upon not to attack any position of a clever writer and a learned man, without justifying myself as completely as possible.

In regard to my own work I shall say nothing, but that I have spared neither labour nor research to make it as correct as if it had appeared under a much more imposing form. In space, I have been confined; and in time, I have been hurried: but I have endeavoured to remedy the one inconvenience, by cutting off all superfluous matter; and to guard against evil consequences from the other, by redoubling my own exertions. Whether I have succeeded or not the world must judge; and if it does judge with the same generous lenity which it has extended to my other productions, I shall have every reason to be both satisfied and grateful.

CHAPTER 1

An Inquiry Into the Origin
of Chivalry

The first principles of whatever subject we may attempt to trace in history are ever obscure, but few are so entirely buried in darkness as the origin of chivalry. This seems the more extraordinary, as we find the institution itself suddenly accompanied by regular and established forms, to which we can assign no precise date, and which appear to have been generally acknowledged before they were reduced to any written code.

Although definitions are dangerous things—inasmuch as the ambiguity of language rarely permits of perfect accuracy, except in matters of abstract science—it is better, as far as possible, on all subjects of discussion, to venture some clear and decided position, that the subsequent reasoning may be fixed upon a distinct and unchanging basis.

If the position itself be wrong, it may be the more speedily proved so from the very circumstance of standing forth singly, uninvolved in a labyrinth of other matter; and if it be right, the arguments that follow may always be more easily traced, and afford greater satisfaction by being deduced from a principle already determined. These considerations lead me to offer a definition of chivalry, together with some remarks calculated to guard that definition from the consequences of misapprehension on the part of others, or of obscurity on my own.

When I speak of chivalry I mean a military institution, prompted by enthusiastic benevolence, sanctioned by religion, and combined with religious ceremonies, the purpose of which was to protect the weak from the oppression of the powerful, and to defend the right cause against the wrong.

Its military character requires no proof; but various mistaken opinions, which I shall notice hereafter, render it necessary to establish the fact, that religious ceremonies of some kind were always combined with the institutions of chivalry.

All those written laws and regulations affecting knighthood,[1] which were composed subsequent to its having taken an acknowledged form, prescribed, in the strictest manner, various points of religious ceremonial, which the aspirant to chivalry was required to perform before he could be admitted into that high order.

What preceded the regular recognition of chivalry as an institution is entirely traditional; yet in all the old romances, *fabliaux, sirventes*, ballads, &c. not one instance is to be found in which a squire becomes a knight, without some reference to his religious faith. If he be dubbed in the battlefield, he swears to defend the right, and maintain all the statutes of the noble order of chivalry, upon the *cross* of his sword; he calls *heaven* to witness his vow, and the *saints* to help him in its execution. Even in one of the most absurd fables[2] of the chivalrous ages, wherein we find Saladin himself receiving the order of chivalry from the hands of the Count de Tabarie, that nobleman causes the infidel sultan to be shaved, and to bathe as a symbol of baptism, and then to rest himself upon a perfumed bed, as a type of the repose and joy of Paradise. These tales are all fictitious, it is true; and few of them date earlier than the end of the twelfth century: but at the same time, as they universally ascribe religious ceremonies to the order of knighthood, we have every reason to suppose that such ceremonies formed a fundamental part of the institution.

Before proceeding to inquire into the origin of chivalry, I must be permitted to make one more observation in regard to my definition; namely, that there was a great and individual character in that order, which no definition can fully convey. I mean the spirit of chivalry; for, indeed, it was more a spirit than an institution; and the outward forms with which it soon became invested, were only, in truth, the signs by which it was conventionally agreed that those persons who had proved in their initiate they possessed the spirit, should be distinguished from the other classes of society. The ceremonial was merely the public declaration, that he on whom the order was conferred was worthy to exercise the powers with which it invested him; but still, *the spirit was the chivalry.*

In seeking the source of this order through the dark mazes of the

---

1. *La Père Menestrier, Ordres de Chevalerie*; Jouvencel; Favin Théâtre.
2. *Fabliau de l'ordene de Chevalerie dans les fabliaux de Le Grand d'Aussi.*

history of modern Europe, it appears to me that many writers have mistaken the track; and, by looking for the mere external signs, have been led into ages infinitely prior to the spirit of chivalry.

Some have supposed that the institution descended to more modern times, from the equestrian order of the ancient Romans; but the absence of all but mere nominal resemblance between the two, has long placed this theory in the dusty catalogue of historical dreams.

Others again have imagined that the Franks, and the rest of the German nations, who, on the fall of the Roman Empire, subdued and divided Gaul, brought with them the seeds of chivalry, which spontaneously grew up into that extraordinary plant which has flourished but once in the annals of the world. This opinion they support by citing the customs of the German tribes [3] who, not only at particular periods invested their youth with the shield and the javelin, but also (especially towards the period of the conquest of Gaul) chose from the bravest of the tribe a number of warriors, to be the companions and guards of the chief. These were termed *Leudes*, and we find them often mentioned under the whole of the first race of French kings.

They served on horseback, while the greater part of each German nation fought on foot only; and they were bound to the chief by an oath of fidelity.[4] The reception of an aspirant into the body of *Leudes* was also marked with various ceremonies; but in this, if we examine correctly, we find neither the spirit nor the forms of chivalry. The oath of the Frank was one of service to his prince; that of the knight, to his God and to society: the one promised to defend his leader; the other to protect the oppressed, and to uphold the right. The *Leudes* were in fact the nobility of the German tribes, though that nobility was not hereditary; but they were in no respect similar to the knights of an after-age, except in the circumstance of fighting on horseback.

A third opinion supposes the origin of chivalry to be found among the ancient warlike tribes of Northmen, or Normans, who, towards the ninth century, invaded in large bodies the southern parts of Europe, and established themselves principally in France; and certainly, both in their traditions, and even in their actions, as recorded by Abbon, an eyewitness to their deeds in the siege of Paris, there is to be found an energetic and romantic spirit, not unlike that which animated chivalry at the rudest period of its existence. Still, there is much wanting. The great object of chivalry, the defence of the weak, was absent, as well as

---

3. *Tacit. de Mor.* Germ.
4. Marculfus.

every form and ceremony. The object of the Northman's courage was plunder; and all that he had in common with the knight was valour, contempt of death, and a touch of savage generosity, that threw but a feint light over his dark and stormy barbarities.

Many persons again have attributed the foundation of all the chivalrous institutions of Europe to the bright and magnificent reign of Charlemagne; and as this opinion has met with much support, among even the learned, it is worth while more particularly to inquire upon what basis it is raised. Of the reign of Charlemagne we have not so many authentic accounts as we have romances, founded upon the fame of that illustrious monarch. Towards the tenth, eleventh, and twelfth centuries, when chivalry was in its imaginative youth, a thousand tales of wild adventure were produced, in which Charlemagne and his warriors were represented with all the qualities and attributes of those knights, whose virtues and courage had by that time wrought deeply on the heart and fancy of the people. We should be as much justified, however, in believing that Virgil was a celebrated necromancer, or that Hercules was a *Preux Chevalier*—characters which have been assigned to them by the very same class of fables—as in giving any credit to the distorted representations that those romances afford of the days of Charlemagne.

In regard to the tales of King Arthur, I am perfectly inclined to use the energetic words of Menestrier, who, in speaking of the famous knights of the round table, says, without hesitation, *"All that they tell of King Arthur and that fictitious chivalry of which they represent him as the author, is nothing but a lie;"*[5] for, though beyond all doubt the romances of chivalry afford a great insight into the manners of the times wherein they were written, they are, nevertheless, quite worthless as authority concerning the ages which they pretend to display, and which had preceded their composition by nearly three centuries.

After rejecting the evidences of such tales, we find nothing in the authentic records of Charlemagne which gives the slightest reason to suppose that chivalry was known, even in its most infant state, during his reign. Though his great system of warfare had that in common with chivalry which all warfare must have—feats of daring courage, heroic valour, bursts of feeling and magnanimity, and as much of the sublime as mighty ambition, guided by mighty genius, and elevated by a noble object can achieve—yet the government of Charlemagne was, in fact, anything but a chivalrous government. Too powerful a hand held the

---

5. *Menestrier de la Chevalerie et ses preuves.*

reins of state for chivalry either to have been necessary or permitted; and in reading the annals of Eginhard, his life of Charlemagne, or the account, given by the monk of St. Gall, we find a completely different character from that which is visible in every page of the history of the knightly ages. We find, indeed, that Charlemagne, according to the immemorial custom of his German [6] ancestors, solemnly invested his son Lewis with the arms of a man.

A thousand years before, in the forests of the North, his predecessors had done the same: and Charlemagne, one of whose great objects ever was, to preserve both the habits and the language of the original country [7] free from amalgamation with those of the conquered nations, not only set the example of publicly receiving his son into the ranks of manhood and warfare, but strictly enjoined that the same should be done by his various governors in the provinces. But this custom of the Franks, as I have before attempted to show, had no earthly relation to knighthood. Were nothing else a proof that chivalry was perfectly unknown in the days of Charlemagne, it would be sufficient that the famous capitularies of that monarch, which regulate everything that can fall under the eye of the law, even to the details of private life, make no mention whatever of an institution which afterward exercised so great an influence on the fate of Europe.

Nor can we trace in the annals of the surrounding countries, a mark of chivalry having been known at that period to any other nation more than to the Franks. Alfred, it is true, invested Athelstan with a purple garment and a sword; but the Saxons were from Germany as well as the Franks, and no reason exists for supposing that this ceremony was in any degree connected with the institutions of chivalry. There have been persons, indeed, who supposed that Pharaoh conferred knighthood upon Joseph, when he bestowed upon him the ring and the golden chain, and probably the Egyptian king had fully as much knowledge of the institution of chivalry as either Charlemagne or Alfred.

Of the annals that follow the period of Charlemagne, those of Nithard, Hincmar, and Thegan, together with those called the Annals of St. Bertinus and of Metz, are the most worthy of credit; and in these, though we often meet with the word *miles*, which was afterward the name bestowed upon a knight, it is used simply in the signification of a soldier, or one of the military race.[8] No mention whatever is made

---

6. *Tacitus de Morib.* German.
7. *Eginhard Ann.*
8. See Notes 1.

of anything that can fairly be looked upon as chivalrous, either in feeling or institution. All is a series of dark conflicts and bloodthirsty contentions, among which the sprouts of the feudal system, yet young and unformed, are seen springing up from seeds sown long before. In the picture of those times, a double darkness seemed to cover the earth, which, a chaos of unruly passions, showed no one general institution for the benefit of mankind except the Christian religion: and that, overwhelmed by foul superstitions and guarded chiefly by barbarous, ignorant, selfish, and disorderly priests, lay like a treasure hidden by a miser, and watched by men that had not soul to use it. This was no age of knighthood.

Up to this period, then, I fully believe that chivalry did not exist; and having attempted to show upon some better ground than mere assertion, that the theories which assign to it an earlier origin are wrong, I will now give my own view of its rise, which possibly may be as erroneous as the rest.

Charlemagne expired like a meteor that, having broken suddenly upon the night of ages, and blazed brilliantly over a whole world for a brief space, fell and left all in darkness, even deeper than before. His dominions divided into petty kingdoms—his successors waging long and inveterate wars against each other—the nations he had subdued shaking off the yoke—the enemies he had conquered avenging themselves upon his descendants—the laws he had established forgotten or annulled—the union he had cemented scattered to the wind—in a lamentably brief space of time, the bright order which his great mind had established throughout Europe was dissolved. Each individual, who, either by corporeal strength, advantageous position, wealth, or habit, could influence the minds of others, snatched at that portion of the divided empire which lay nearest to his means, and claimed that power as a gift which had only been intrusted as a loan.

The custom of holding lands by military service had come down to the French from their German ancestors, and the dukes, the marquises, the counts, as well as a whole herd of inferior officers, who in former days had led the armies, or commanded in the provinces as servants of the crown, now arrogated to themselves hereditary rights in the charges to which they had been intrusted; and, in their own behalf, claimed the feudal service of those soldiers to whom lands had been granted, instead of preserving their allegiance for their sovereigns. The weak monarchs, who still retained the name of kings, engaged in ruinous wars with each other and in vain attempts to repel the invasions of the Northmen or Normans, first tolerated these encroachments, because they had at the time no power of resisting, and then gradually recognised them as rights, upon the condition that those who committed them should assist the sovereign in his wars, and acknowledge his title in preference to that of any of his competitors.

Thus gradually rose the feudal system from the wrecks of Charlemagne's great empire. But still all was unstable and unconfirmed; the limits of the different powers in the state undecided and variable, till the war of Paris, the incompetence of the successors of Charlemagne, and the elevation of Hugues Capet, the Count of Paris, to the throne, showed the barons the power they had acquired, and crowned the feudal compact by the creation of a king whose title was found in it alone.

Great confusion, however, existed still. The authority of the sovereign extended but a few leagues round the city of Paris; the Normans ravaged the coast; the powerful and the wicked had no restraint imposed upon their actions, and the weak were everywhere oppressed and wronged. Bands of plunderers raged through the whole of France and Germany, property was held by the sword, cruelty and injustice reigned alone, and the whole history of that age offers a complete medley of massacre, bloodshed, torture, crime, and misery.

Personal courage, however, had been raised to the highest pitch by the very absence of everything like security. Valour was a necessity and a habit, and Eudes and his companions, who defended Paris against the Normans, would have come down as demigods to the present day, if they had but possessed a Homer to sing their deeds. The very Normans themselves, with their wild enthusiasm and supernatural daring, their poetical traditions, and magnificent superstitions, seemed to bring a new and extraordinary light into the very lands they desolated. The plains teemed with murder, and the rivers flowed with blood; but the world was weary of barbarity, and a reacting spirit of order was born from the very bosom of confusion.

It was then that some poor nobles, probably suffering themselves from the oppression of more powerful lords, but at the same time touched with sincere compassion for the wretchedness they saw around them, first leagued together with the holy purpose of redressing wrongs and defending the weak.[9] They gave their hands to one another in pledge that they would not turn back from the work, and called upon St. George to bless their righteous cause. The church

9. Charles Nodier on St. Palaye.

readily yielded its sanction to an institution so noble, aided it with prayers, and sanctified it with a solemn blessing. Religious enthusiasm became added to noble indignation and charitable zeal; and the spirit of chivalry, like the flame struck forth from the hard steel and the dull flint, was kindled into sudden light by the savage cruelty of the nobles, and the heavy barbarity of the people.

The spirit spread rapidly, and the adoration of the populace, who almost deified their heroic defenders, gave both fresh vigour and purity to the design. Every moral virtue became a part of knightly honour, and the men whose hands were ever ready to draw the sword in defence of innocence—who in their own conduct set the most brilliant example—whose sole object was the establishment of right, and over whom no earthly fear or interested consideration held sway, were readily recognised as judges, and appealed to as arbitrators. Public opinion raised them above all other men, even above kings themselves; so much so, indeed, that we find continually repeated, in the writings of the chivalrous ages, such passages as the following:—

Chevaliers sont de moult grant pris,
Ils ont de tous gens le pris,
Et le los et le seignorie.

Thus gradually chivalry became no longer a simple engagement between a few generous and valiant men, but took the form of a great and powerful institution; and as each knight had the right of creating others without limit, it became necessary that the new class thus established in society should be distinguished by particular signs and symbols, which would guard it against the intrusion of unworthy or disgraceful members.

The time at which fixed regulations first distinguished chivalry from every other order in the state cannot be precisely determined; certainly it was not before the eleventh century. Then, however, it is probable, that this was done more from a general sense of its necessity, and by slow and irregular degrees, than by any one law or agreement. Everything in that age was confusion, and though the spirit of chivalry had for its great object the restoration of order, it is not likely that its own primary efforts should be very regular, amid a chaos of contending interests and unbridled passions, which rendered general communication or association difficult, if not impossible. Each knight, in admitting another to the noble order of which he himself was a member, probably added some little formality, as he thought fit, till the

22

mass of these customs collected by tradition formed the body of their ceremonial law.

The first point required of the aspirants to chivalry, in its earliest state, was certainly a solemn vow, "*To speak the truth, to succour the helpless and oppressed, and never to turn back from an enemy.*"[10]

This vow, combined with the solemn appeal to Heaven in witness thereof, was the foundation of chivalry; but, at the same time, we find, that in all ages, only one class of people was eligible to furnish members to the institution; namely, the military class, or, in other words, the northern conquerors of the soil; for, with very few exceptions, the original inhabitants of Europe had been reduced to the condition of serfs, or slaves of the glebe. Some few, indeed, had held out till they forced the invaders to permit their being incorporated with themselves upon more equal terms; but this was very rare, and the *race rustique*, as it was called, though it furnished archers to the armies, was kept distinct from the military race by many a galling difference. This lower race, then, could not be invested with the honours of chivalry; and one of the first provisions we find in any written form, respecting the institution of knighthood, is designed to mark this more particularly. *Ad militarem honorem nullus accedat qui non sit de genere militum*, says a decree of the twelfth century. We may therefore conclude that this was the first requisite, and the vow the first formality of chivalry.

It is more than probable that the ceremony next in historical order, attached to the admission of an aspirant into the ranks of knighthood, was that of publicly arming him with the weapons he was to use, in pursuance of his vow. This is likely, from many circumstances. In the first place, to arm him for the cause was naturally the next preceding to his vowing himself to that cause, and also by his receiving those arms in the face of the public, the new defender that the people had gained became known to the people, and thus no one would falsely pretend to the character of a knight without risking detection. In the second place, as I have before said, the arming of the German youth had been from the earliest ages, like the delivery of the virile robe to young Romans, an occasion of public solemnity; and it was therefore natural that it should be soon incorporated with the ceremonial of the new military institution which now took the lead of all others.

The church of course added her part to secure reverence for an order which was so well calculated to promote all the objects of religion, and vigils, fasts, and prayers speedily became a part of the initiation to

---

10. *Ordene de Chevalerie Fabliaux.*

knighthood. Power is ever followed by splendour and display; but to use the energetic words of a learned and talented writer of the present day,[11] the knights for long after the first institution of chivalry, were "simple in their clothing, austere in their morals, humble after victory, firm under misfortune."

In France, I believe, the order first took its rise; and, probably, the disgust felt by some pure minds at the gross and barbarous licentiousness of the times, infused that virtuous severity into the institutions of chivalry which was in itself a glory. If we may give the least credit to the picture of the immorality and luxury of the French, as drawn by Abbon in his poem on the siege of Paris, no words will be found sufficient to express our admiration for the men who first undertook to combat not only the tyranny but the vices of their age; who singly went forth to war against crime, injustice, and cruelty who defied the whole world in defence of innocence, virtue, and truth; who stemmed the torrent of barbarity and evil; and who, from the wrecks of ages, and the ruins of empires, drew out a thousand jewels to glitter in the star that shone upon the breast of knighthood.

For long the Christian religion had struggled alone, a great but shaded light through the storms of dark and barbarous ages. Till chivalry arose there was nothing to uphold it; but from that moment, with a champion in the field to lead forth the knowledge that had been imprisoned in the cloister, the influence of religion began to spread and increase. Though worldly men thereunto attached the aggrandizement of their own temporal power, and knaves and villains made it the means of their avarice, or the cloak of their vice, still the influence of the divine truth itself gradually wrought upon the hearts of men, purifying, calming, refining, till the world grew wise enough to separate the perfection of the Gospel from the weakness of its teachers, and to reject the *errors* while they restrained the *power* of the Roman church.

In the meantime chivalry stood forth the most glorious institution that man himself ever devised. In its youth and in its simplicity, it appeared grand and beautiful, both from its own intrinsic excellence, and from its contrast with the things around. In its after-years it acquired pomp and luxury; and to pomp and luxury naturally succeeded decay and death; but still the legacy that it left behind it to posterity was a treasure of noble feelings and generous principles.

There cannot be a doubt that chivalry, more than any other insti-

11. Charles Nodier.

tution (except religion) aided to work out the civilization of Europe. It first taught devotion and reverence to those weak, fair beings, who but in their beauty and their gentleness have no defence. It first raised love above the passions of the brute, and by dignifying woman, made woman worthy of love. It gave purity to enthusiasm, crushed barbarous selfishness, taught the heart to expand like a flower to the sunshine, beautified glory with generosity, and smoothed even the rugged brow of war.

For the mind, as far as knowledge went, chivalry itself did little; but by its influence it did much. For the heart it did everything; and there is scarcely a noble feeling or a bright aspiration that we find among ourselves, or trace in the history of modern Europe, that is not in some degree referable to that great and noble principle, which has no name but the *Spirit of Chivalry*.

CHAPTER 2

Of Chivalrous Customs

Although the customs which I am about to detail at once grew gradually up under the various circumstances of different centuries, and were for the most part unknown to the infancy of chivalry, I think it right to notice here the principal peculiarities of the institution, rather than to interrupt the course of my narrative afterward, when the history of knighthood may be traced continuously down to its final extinction. We have already seen that each individual member of the order possessed the power of admitting any other person to its honours without restraint; but it did not by any means follow that all previous trial and education was dispensed with.

Very soon after the first institution of chivalry every one became covetous of the distinction, and it naturally followed that the object of each boy's aspirations, the aim of every young man's ambition, was one day to be a knight. Those, however, who had already received the order, were scrupulously careful to admit none within its fellowship who might disgrace the sword that dubbed them; and knighthood gradually became as much the reward of a long and tedious education, as the bonnet of the doctor or the stole of the clerk.

The feudal system had now reached its acme; and each individual lord, within his own domain, assumed the state and importance of a prince. With the vain spirit of ostentatious imitation which unhappily is common to all climes and all centuries, the great feudatories of the crown copied the household of the sovereign, and the petty barons imitated them. Each had his crowd of officers, and squires, and pages, and varlets. Even the monasteries and the abbeys affected the same pomp and ceremonial, so that we find the abbot of St. Denis riding[1] forth accompanied by his chamberlain and marshal, whose offices

1. Felibien, *Hist. St. Denis.*

were held as feoffs.

The manor or the castle of each feudal chieftain, however, soon became the school of chivalry, and any noble youth whose parents were either dead or too poor to educate him to the art of war was willingly received in the dwelling of a neighbouring baron, who took care that his pupil should be instructed in all military exercises, glad to attach to his own person as large a body of armed retainers as his circumstances would permit.

Till they reached the age of seven years the youths, afterward destined to arms, were left to the care of the females of the household, who taught them the first principles of religion and of chivalry. They were then in general sent from home, those fathers even, who possessed the means of conducting their education themselves, preferring to intrust it to some other noble knight who could be biased [2] by no parental tenderness to spare the young aspirant to chivalry any of those trials and hardships absolutely necessary to prepare him for his after-career.

On entering the household of another knight, the first place filled by the youths, then fresh from all the soft kindnesses of home, was that of page or varlet, which, though it implied every sort of attendance on the person of their new lord, was held as honourable, not degrading.

Here they still remained [3] much among the women of the family, who undertook to complete their knowledge of their duty to God and their lady, instilling into their infant minds that refined and mystic idea of love, which was so peculiar a trait in the chivalry of old. In the meanwhile the rest of their days were passed in the service of their lord, accompanying him in his excursions, serving him at table, pouring out his drink; all of which offices being shared in by the children and young relations of the baron himself,[4] were reckoned, as I have said, highly honourable, and formed the first step in the ascent to chivalry.

At the same time infinite pains were bestowed upon the education of these pages. They were taught all sorts of gymnastic exercises which could strengthen the body; and, by continually mingling with the guests of the castle, receiving them on their arrival, offering them every sort of service, and listening respectfully to the conversation of their elders, they acquired that peculiar grace of manner which, under

---

2. *Coutumes de Beauvoisis.*

3. St. Palaye.

4. *Vie de Bayard.*

the name of courtesy, formed a principal perfection in the character of the true knight.

At fourteen the page was usually admitted to the higher grade of squire, and exchanged his short dagger for the manly sword. This, however, was made a religious ceremony; and the weapon which he was in future to wear was laid upon the altar, from whence it was taken by the priest, [5] and after several benedictions, was hung over the shoulder of the new squire, with many a sage caution and instruction as to its use.

His exercises now became more robust than they had ever been before; and, if we are to believe the old biographer of the celebrated Boucicaut, they were far more fatiguing than any man of the present age could endure. To spring upon horseback armed at all pieces, without putting a foot in the stirrup; to cast somersets in heavy armour[6] for the purpose of strengthening the arms; to leap upon the shoulders of a horseman from behind, without other hold than one hand laid upon his shoulder—such, and many others, were the daily exercises of the young noble, besides regular instruction in riding and managing his arms. Though it would seem at first that few constitutions could undergo for any length of time such violent exertions, we must remember the effects produced—we must call to mind that these very men in their after-life, are found bearing a weight, that few persons of the present times could lift, through the heat of a whole summer's day, under the burning sun of Palestine. We must remember the mighty feats of strength that these men performed; and, when we see a Boemond fighting from noon to sunset cased from head to foot in thick iron, or in long after-days a Guise swimming against a torrent armed *cap-a-pie,* we must naturally conclude that no ordinary course of training could produce such vigour and hardihood.

Several degrees of squires or esquires are mentioned in the ancient chronicles; and it is difficult to distinguish which class included the young noble—which was filled by an inferior race. That there was a distinction is evident; for in the life of Bayard[7] we find an old squire mentioned more than once, from whom he received instructions, but who never appears to have aspired to any higher degree. Nevertheless it is equally certain that many services which we should consider menial, were performed by the squires of the highest race about the

5. Favin Théâtre.
6. Vie de Boucicaut, *Coll. Pelitot et Momerque.*
7. *Vie de Bayard.*

persons of their lords.

Nor was this confined to what might be considered military services; for we learn that they not only held the stirrup for their lord to mount, and then followed, carrying his helm, his lance, his shield, or his gauntlets; but they continued to serve him at table, to clean his armour, to dress his horses, and to fulfil a thousand other avocations, in which they were aided, it is true, by the *gros varlets* or common servants, but which they still had their share in accomplishing with their own hands.[8] The highest class of esquires, however, was evidently the *écuyer d'honneur*, who, from the manner of Froissart's mention of many at the court of the Count de Foix, appears to have had in charge the reception and entertainment of guests and strangers.

The squires of course had often more important duties to perform. It was for them to follow their lords to the battlefield; and, while the knights, formed in a long line, fought hand to hand against their equals, the squires remained watching eagerly the conflict, and ready to drag their master from the *mêlée*, to cover him if he fell, to supply him with fresh arms, and, in short, to lend him every aid; without, however, presuming to take an active part against the adverse knights, with whose class it was forbidden for a squire to engage.

St. Palaye limits to these defensive operations the services of the squires in the field of battle,[9] and it is possible that the strict laws of chivalry might justify such a restriction. Nevertheless there can be no earthly doubt that they were often much more actively engaged, even in the purest days of chivalry. In all the wars between Richard Cœur de Lion and Philip Augustus,[10] we find them often fighting bravely; and at the Battle of Bovine, a squire had nearly taken the life of the famous Count de Boulogne.

These services in the field perfected the aspirant to chivalry in the knowledge of his profession; and the trials of skill which, on the day that preceded a tournament, were permitted to squires, in the lists, gave him an opportunity of distinguishing himself in the eyes of the people, and of gaining a name among the heralds and chroniclers of knightly deeds.

If a noble squire had conducted himself well during the period of his service, it seldom occurred that his lord refused to bestow upon him the honour of knighthood at the age of twenty-one; and sometimes, if he

---

8. Froissart.

9. St. Palaye, *liv.* i.

10. Guillaume Guiart.; *Guill, Amoric.; Rigord; Philipeid.*

had been distinguished by any great or gallant feat, or by uniform talent and courage,[11] he was admitted into the order before he had reached that age. This, nevertheless, was rare, except in the case of sovereign princes; and, on the contrary, it occasionally happened that a knight who did not choose to part so soon with a favourite squire would delay on various pretences a ceremony which almost always caused some separation between the young knight and his ancient master.[12]

The squire, however, had always the right to claim the knighthood from the hand of another, if his lord unjustly refused to bestow it; and that high sense of honour which was their great characteristic prevented the knights thus applied to from ever refusing, when the aspirant was fully justified in his claim.

The times chosen for conferring knighthood were generally either those of great military ceremony,[13] as after tournaments, *cours plénières*, the muster or *monstre*, as it was called, of the army, or on days consecrated by the church to some peculiar solemnity, as Easter-day, the day of Pentecost, or even Christmas-day.[14]

This was, nevertheless, by no means imperative; for we have already seen that knighthood was often conferred on any particular emergency, and even on the field of battle.[15] On these occasions the forms were of course abridged to suit the necessity of the case, but the knighthood was not the less valid or esteemed.

The more public and solemn the ceremony could be made, the more it appeared to the taste of the nobles of the middle ages. Nor was the pomp and display without its use, raising and dignifying the order in the eyes of the people, and impressing deeply upon the mind of the young knight the duties which he had voluntarily taken upon himself. We all know how much remembrance depends upon external circumstance, and it is ever well to give our feelings some fixed resting-place in the waste of life, that in after-years memory may lead us back and refresh the resolutions and bright designs of youth by the aid of the striking scenes and solemn moments in which those designs and resolutions were first called into activity. Nothing could be better calculated to make a profound impression on the mind than the ceremonies of a knight's reception in the mature times of chivalry.

---

11. Brantome.
12. See Notes 2.
13. Charles Nodier's *Annotations on St. Palaye.*
14. Ducange, *Dissert.* xxii. Menestrier, chap. 2; St. Palaye.
15. *Roman de Garin,* Fabliaux, vol. ii.

On the day appointed, [16] all the knights and nobles at that time in the city where the solemnity was to be performed, with the bishops and clergy, each covered with the appropriate vestments of his order, the knight in his coat-of-arms, and the bishop in his stole, conducted the aspirant to the principal church of the place. There, after the high mass had been chanted, the novice approached the altar and presented the sword to the bishop or priest, who, taking it from his hand, blessed and consecrated it to the service of religion and virtue.

It often happened that the bishop himself then solemnly warned the youth of the difficulties and requisites of the order to which he aspired. Said the Bishop of Valenciennes to the young Count of Ostrevant on one of these occasions:—[17]

> He who seeks to be a knight, he who wishes to be a knight should have great qualities. He must be of noble birth, liberal in gifts, high in courage, strong in danger, secret in council, patient in difficulties, powerful against enemies, prudent in his deeds. He must also swear to observe the following rules: To undertake nothing without having heard mass fasting; to spare neither his blood nor his life in defence of the Catholic faith; to give aid to all widows and orphans; to undertake no war without just cause; to favour no injustice, but to protect the innocent and oppressed; to be humble in all things; to seek the welfare of those placed under him; never to violate the rights of his sovereign, and to live irreprehensibly before God and man.

The bishop, then taking his joined hands in his own, placed them on the missal, and received his oath to follow the statutes laid down to him, after which his father advancing dubbed him a knight.

At other times it occurred, that when the sword had been blessed, the novice[18] carried it to the knight who was to be his godfather in chivalry, and kneeling before him plighted his vow to him. After this the other knights, and often the ladies present, advanced, and completely armed the youth, sometimes beginning with one piece of the armour, sometimes another. St. Palaye declares that the spurs were always buckled on before the rest, but in the history of Geoffrey, Duke of Normandy, we find the corslet and the greaves mentioned first, and the spear and sword last.

---

16. Menestrier, chap. 2. and 9.
17. Menestrier, chap. 9.
18. St. Palaye.

After having been armed, the novice still remained upon his knees before his godfather in arms, who then, rising from his seat, bestowed upon him the *accolade*, as it was called, which consisted generally of three blows of the naked sword upon the neck or shoulder. Sometimes it was performed by a blow given with the palm of the hand upon the cheek of the novice, which was always accompanied by some words, signifying that the ceremony was complete, and the squire had now become a knight.

The words which accompanied the accolade were generally, when the kings of France bestowed the honour, "In the name of God, St. Michael, and St. George, I make thee knight; be loyal, bold, and true."

Sometimes to the blow were joined the words, [19] "Bear this blow and never bear another," and sometimes was added the more Christian admonition to humility, "Remember that the Saviour of the world was buffeted and scoffed."[20]

Whatever was its origin the custom was a curious one, and bore a strong resemblance to the ceremony of manumission among the Romans, who, on freeing a slave, struck him a slight blow, which Claudian happily enough terms *felicem injuriam*. I do not, however, intend to insinuate that the one custom was derived from the other, though, perhaps, the fact of a serf becoming free if his lord struck him with any instrument, [21] except such as were employed in his actual labour, may have been, in some degree, a vestige of the Roman law in this respect, which we know descended entire to many of the barbarous nations.

However that may be, after having submitted to the blow which ended his servitude as a squire, the new knight was decorated with his casque, which had hitherto been held beside him, and then proceeding to the door of the church, or of the castle, where his knighthood had been bestowed, he sprang upon his horse and showed himself armed in the principal places of the city, while the heralds proclaimed his name and vaunted his prowess. [22]

As long vigils, fast, prayers, and confessions had preceded and accompanied the admission of the new knight, festivals, banquets, and tournaments followed.[23] The banquets and the festivals, as common to

---

19. Hartknoch, lib. ii. c. 1.
20. Existing Orders of Knighthood
21. Cappefigue.
22. Menestrier, ix.; St. Palaye.
23. Adré Favin Théât.

all ages, though differing in each, I will pass over: suffice it, that one of the strictest laws of chivalry forbade gluttony and intemperance.

The tournament, as a purely chivalrous institution, I must mention; though so much has been already written on the subject, that I could have wished to pass it over in silence. The most complete description ever given of a tournament is to be found in the writings of one whose words are pictures; and if I dared but copy into this place the account of the passage of arms in Ivanhoe, I should be enabled to give a far better idea of what such a scene really was, than all the antiquarian researches in my power will afford.

All military nations, from the earliest antiquity, have known and practised various athletic games in imitation of warfare; and we of course find among the Franks various exercises of the kind from the very first records which we have of that people. Nithard, [24] however, gives an elaborate picture of these mock-fights as practised in the reigns succeeding Charlemagne; and we find but little resemblance to the tournament. Four equal bands of Saxons, Gascons, Austrasians, and Armoricans (or Britons, [25] as they are there called) met together in an open place, and, while the populace stood round as spectators, pursued each other, in turn, brandishing their arms, and seeming fiercely to seek the destruction of their adversaries. When this had proceeded for some time, Louis and Charles (the two monarchs in whose history the description is given) suddenly rushed into the field with all their choice companions, and, with quivering lances and loud cries, followed, now one, now another, of the parties, who took care to fly before their horses.

The first authentic mention of a tournament [26] is to be found in the Chronicle of Tours, which records the death of Geoffrey de Priuli in 1066; adding the words *qui torneamenta invenit*—who invented tournaments. From the appearance [27] of these exercises in Germany [28] about the same time, we may conclude that this date is pretty nearly correct; and that if tournaments were not absolutely invented at that precise period, they were then first regulated by distinct laws.

---

24. Nithard, lib. iii.

25. *Britannarum* is the word.

26. *Ducange apud Chron. Tur. an.* 1066.

27. Munster. *Geogr.* lib. iii.

28. Ducange, in his sixth dissertation, has satisfactorily overturned the assertion made by Modius, that tournaments were known in Germany at a much earlier period than here stated.

In England[29] they did not appear till several years later, when the Norman manners introduced after the conquest had completely superseded the customs of the Saxons.

Thus much has seemed necessary to me to say concerning the origin of tournaments, as there are so many common fables on the subject which give far greater antiquity to the exercise than that which it is entitled to claim.

The ceremonies and the splendour of the tournament of course differed in different ages and different countries; but the general principle was the same. It was a chivalrous game, originally instituted for practising those exercises, and acquiring that skill which was likely to be useful in knightly warfare.

A tournament was usually given upon the occasion of any great meeting, for either military or political purposes. Sometimes it was the king himself who sent his heralds through the land to announce to all noblemen and ladies, that on a certain day he would hold a grand tournament, where all brave knights might try their prowess. At other times a tournament was determined on by a body of independent knights; and messengers were often sent into distant countries to invite all gallant gentlemen to honour the passage of arms.

The spot fixed upon for the lists was usually in the immediate neighbourhood of some abbey or castle, where the shields of the various[30] cavaliers who purposed combating were exposed to view for several days previous to the meeting. A herald was also placed beneath the cloisters to answer all questions concerning the champions, and to receive all complaints against any individual knight. If, upon investigation, the kings of arms and judges of the field found that a just accusation was laid against one[31] of the knights proposing to appear, a peremptory command excluded him from the lists; and if he dared in despite thereof to present himself, he was driven forth with blows and ignominy.

Round about the field appointed for the spectacle were raised galleries, scaffoldings, tents,[32] and pavilions, decorated with all the magnificence of a luxurious age. Banners and scutcheons, and bandrols, silks and cloth of gold, covered the galleries and floated round the field; while all that rich garments and precious stones, beauty and youth, could do to outshine the inanimate part of the scene, was to

---

29. Ducange, *Dissert.* vii.
30. Menestrier *Origine.*
31. Favin Théâtre.
32. St. Palaye.

be found among the spectators. Here too was seen the venerable age of chivalry—all those old knights whose limbs were no longer competent to bear the weight of arms, surrounding the field to view the prowess of their children and judge the deeds of the day. Heralds and pursuivants, in the gay and many-coloured garments which they peculiarly affected, fluttered over the field, and bands of warlike music were stationed near to animate the contest and to salute the victors.

The knights, as they appeared in the lists, were greeted by the heralds and the people [33] according to their renown; but the approbation of the female part of the spectators was the great stimulus to all the chivalry of the field. Each knight, as a part of his duty, either felt or feigned himself in love; and it was upon these occasions that his lady might descend from the high state to which the mystic adoration of the day had raised her, and bestow upon her favoured champion a glove, a riband, a bracelet,[34] a jewel, which, borne on his crest through the hard-contested field, was the chief object of his care, and the great excitement to his valour.

Often, too, in the midst of the combat, if accident or misfortune deprived the favoured knight of the gage of his lady's affection, her admiration or her pity won her to supply another token, sent by a page or squire, to raise again her lover's resolution, and animate him to new exertions.

The old romance of Perce-forest gives a curious picture of the effects visible after a tournament, by the eagerness with which the fair spectators had encouraged the knights. The writer says:—

> At the close of the tournament, the ladies were so stripped of their ornaments, that the greater part of them were bareheaded. Thus they went their ways with their hair floating on their shoulders more glossy than fine gold; and with their robes without the sleeves, for they had given to the knights to decorate themselves, wimples and hoods, mantles and shifts, sleeves and bodies. When they found themselves undressed to such a pitch, they were at first quite ashamed; but as soon as they saw everyone was in the same state, they began to laugh at the whole adventure, for they had all bestowed their jewels and their clothes upon the knights with so good a will, that they had not perceived that they uncovered themselves.

---

33. St. Palaye.
34. *Vie de Bayard.*

This is probably an exaggerated account of the enthusiasm which the events of a tournament excited in the bosom of the fair ladies of that day: but still, no doubt can be entertained, that they not only decorated their knights before the tournament with some token of their approbation, but in the case of its loss, often sent him even a part of their dress in the midst of the conflict.

The other spectators, also, though animated by less thrilling interests, took no small share in the feelings and hopes of the different parties. Each blow of the lance or sword, struck well and home, was greeted with loud acclamations; and valour met with both its incitement and its reward, in the expecting silence and the thundering plaudits with which each good champion's movements were waited for and seen.

In the meanwhile, without giving encouragement to any particular knight, the heralds strove to animate all by various quaint and characteristic exclamations, such as "The love of ladies!" "Death to the horses!" "Honour to the brave!" "Glory to be won by blood and sweat!" "Praise to the sons of the brave!"

It would occupy too much space to enter into all the details of the tournament, or to notice all the laws by which it was governed. Every care was taken that the various knights should meet upon equal terms; and many a precaution was made use of to prevent accidents, and to render the sports both innocent and useful. But no regulations could be found sufficient to guard against the dangerous consequences of such furious amusements; and Ducange gives a long list of princes and nobles who lost their lives in these fatal exercises. The church often interfered, though in vain, to put them down; and many monarchs forbade them in their dominions; but the pomp with which they were accompanied, and the excitement they afforded to a people fond of every mental stimulus, rendered them far more permanent than might have been expected.

The weapons in tournaments were, in almost all cases, restrained to blunted swords and headless spears, daggers, and battle-axes; but, as may well be imagined, these were not to be used without danger; so that even those festivals that passed by without the absolute death of any of the champions, left, nevertheless, many to drag out a maimed and miserable existence, or to die after a long and weary sickness. And yet the very peril of the sport gave to it an all-powerful interest, which we can best conceive, at present, from our feelings at some deep and thrilling tragedy.

After the excitement, and the expectation, and the suspense, and the eagerness, came the triumph and the prize—and the chosen queen of the field bestowed upon the champion whose feats were counted best, that reward, the value of which consisted more in the honour than the thing itself. Sometimes it was a jewel,[35] sometimes a coronet[36] of flowers or of laurel; but in all cases the award implied a right to one kiss from the lips of the lady appointed to bestow the prize. It seems to have been as frequent a practice to assign this prize on the field, as in the *chateau* [37] or palace whither the court retired after the sports were concluded; and we often find that the female part of the spectators were called to decide upon the merits of the several champions, and to declare the victor[38] as well as confer the reward. Mirth and festivity ever closed the day of the tournament, and song and sports brought in the night.

Everything that could interest or amuse a barbarous age was collected on the spot where one of these meetings was held. The minstrel or *menestrier*, the juggler, the saltimbank, the story-teller, were present in the hall to soothe or to entertain; but still the foundation of tale and song was Chivalry;—the objects of all praise were noble deeds and heroic actions; and the very voice of love and tenderness, instead of seducing to sloth and effeminacy, was heard prompting to activity, to enterprise, and to honour—to the defence of virtue, and the search for glory.

It may be here necessary to remark, that there were several sorts of tournaments, which differed essentially from each other; but I shall not pause upon these any longer than merely to point out the particular differences between them. The joust, which was certainly a kind of tournament, was always confined to two persons, though these persons encountered each other with blunted arms.[39]

The combat at *outrance* was, in fact, a duel, and only differed from the trial by battle in being voluntary, while the other was enforced by law. This contest was often the event of private quarrels, but was, by no means, always so; and, to use the language of Ducange, "though mortal, it took place ordinarily between persons who most frequently did not know each other, or, at least, had no particular misunderstanding,

---

35. *Vie de Bayard.*
36. Olivier de la Marche.
37. Ducange, *Dissert.* vi.
38. St. Palaye.
39. Ducange, *Dissert.* vii.

but who sought alone to show forth their courage, generosity, and skill in arms."Sometimes, however, the combat at *outrance* was undertaken by a number of knights[40] together, and often much blood was thus shed, without cause.

The *pas d'armes* or passage of arms, differed from general tournaments, inasmuch as a certain number of knights fixed their shields and tents in a particular pass, or spot of ground, which they declared their intention to defend against all comers.[41] The space before their tents was generally listed in, as for a tournament; and, during the time fixed for the defence of the passage, the same concourse of spectators, heralds, and minstrels were assembled.

The round table was another distinct sort of tournament,[42] held in a circular amphitheatre, wherein the knights invited jousted against each other. The origin of this festival, which was held, I believe, for the last time by Edward III., is attributed to Roger Mortimer,[43] who, on receiving knighthood, feasted a hundred knights and a hundred ladies at a round table. The mornings were spent in chivalrous games, the prize of which was a golden lion, and the evenings in banquets and festivities. This course of entertainments continued three days with the most princely splendour; after which Mortimer, having won the prize himself, conducted his guests to Warwick, and dismissed them.

From this account, taken from the *History of the Priory of Wigmore*, Menestrier deduces that those exercises called "round tables" were only tournaments, during which the lord or sovereign giving the festival entertained his guests at a table which, to prevent all ceremony in respect to precedence, was in the form of a circle. Perhaps, however, this institution may have had a different and an earlier origin, though I find it mentioned in no author previous to the year 1279.[44]

Chivalry, which in its pristine purity knew no reward but honour, soon—as it became combined with power—appropriated to itself various privileges which, injuring its simplicity, in the end brought about its fall. In the first place, the knight was, by the fact of his chivalry, the judge of all his equals, and consequently of all his inferiors.[45] He

---

40. Mat. *Paris, Ann.* 1241
41. Colombiere.
42. Menestrier, vi.
43. Mat. *Westmonas.*
44. Should anyone be tempted to investigate further, he will find the subject discussed at length in the seventh dissertation of Ducange. See also the *Chronique de Molinet*.
45. St. Palaye; *Ribeiro, lib. x.*

was also, in most cases, the executor of his own decree, and it would indeed have required a different nature from humanity to secure such a jurisdiction from frequent perversion. The knight[46] also took precedence of all persons who had not received chivalry, a distinction well calculated to do away with that humility which was one of knighthood's strictest laws.[47]

Added to this was the right of wearing particular dresses and colours, gold and jewels, which were restrained to the knightly class, by very severe ordinances. Scarlet and green were particularly reserved for the order of knighthood, as well as ermine, minever, and some other furs. Knights also possessed what was called privilege of clergy, that is to say, in case of accusation, they could claim to be tried before the ecclesiastical judge.[48] Their arms were legally forbidden to all other classes, and the title of Sire, Monseigneur, Sir, Don, &c., were applied to them alone, till the distinction was lost in the course of time.

Though these privileges changed continually, and it is scarcely possible to say what age gave birth to any one of them, yet it is evident that monarchs, after they had seen the immense influence which chivalry might have on their own power, and had striven to render it an engine for their own purposes, took every care to secure all those rights and immunities to the order which could in some degree balance the hardships, fatigues, and dangers inevitably attendant upon it, and supply the place of that enthusiasm which of course grew fainter as the circumstances which excited it changed, and the objects which it sought were accomplished.

It is probable that there would always have been many men who would have coveted chivalry for the sole purpose of doing good and protecting the innocent; but monarchs sought to increase the number of knights as a means of defending their realms and extending their power, and, consequently, they supplied other motives and external honours as an inducement to those persons of a less exalted mind.

Chivalry was indeed a distinction not to be enjoyed without many and severe labours. The first thing after receiving knighthood was generally a long journey[49] into foreign countries, both for the purpose of jousting with other knights, and for instruction in every sort of chivalrous knowledge. There the young knight studied carefully the

---

46. Menestrier.
47. *Ordonances des Rois de France, ann.* 1294.
48. Pasquier *Recherches*.
49. *Vie de Bayard sur Jean d'Arces.*

demeanour of every celebrated champion he met, and strove to glean the excellencies of each. Thus he learned courtesy and grace, and thus he heard all the famous exploits of the day which, borne from court to court by these chivalrous travellers, spread the fame of great deeds from one end of the world to the other.[50]

It cannot be doubted that this practice of wandering armed through Europe gave great scope to licentiousness in those who were naturally ill-disposed; and many a cruelty and many a crime was assuredly committed by that very order instituted to put down vice and to protect innocence. To guard against this the laws of chivalry were most severe;[51] and as great power was intrusted to the knight, great was the shame and dishonour if he abused it. The oath taken in the first place was as strictly opposed to every vice, as any human promise could be, and the first principle of chivalrous honour was never to violate an engagement. I must here still repeat the remark, that it was the spirit which constituted the chivalry, and as that spirit waned, chivalry died away.

One of the most curious institutions of chivalry was that which required a knight, on his return from any expedition,[52] to give a full and minute account to the heralds, or officers of arms, of all his adventures during his absence, without reserve or concealment; telling as well his reverses and discomfitures, as his honours and success. To do this he was bound by oath; and the detail thus given was registered by the herald, who by such relations learned to know and estimate the worth and prowess of each individual knight. It served also to excite other adventurers to great deeds in imitation of those who acquired fame and honour; and it afforded matter of consolation to the unfortunate, who in those registers must ever have met with mishaps to equal or surpass their own.

The spirit of chivalry, however, led to a thousand deeds and habits not required nor regulated by any law. Were two armies opposed to each other, or even encamped in the neighbourhood of each other, though at peace,[53] the knights would continually issue forth singly from the ranks to challenge any other champion to come out, and break a lance in honour of his lady. Often before a castle, or on the eve of a battle, a knight would vow to some holy saint never to quit

---

50. See Notes 3.
51. Colombiere.
52. La Colombiere.
53. Froissart *Olivier de la Marche.*

the field, or abandon the siege, till death or victory ended his design. Frequently, too, we find that in the midst of some great festival, where all the chivalry of the land was assembled, a knight would suddenly appear, bearing in his hands [54] a peacock, a heron, or some other bird. Presenting it in turn to each noble in the assembly, he would then demand their oath upon that bird to do some great feat of arms against the enemy. No knight dared to refuse, and the vow so taken was irrevocable and never broken.

One of the most extraordinary customs of chivalry, and also one of the most interesting, was the adoption of a brother in arms.[55]

This custom[56] seems to have taken its rise in England, and was in common use especially among the Saxons. After the Conquest, however, it rapidly spread to other nations, and seems to have been a favourite practice with the crusaders. Esteem and long companionship were the first principles of this curious sort of alliance, which bound one knight to another by ties more strict than those of blood itself.

It is true the brotherhood in arms was often contracted but for a time, or under certain circumstances,[57] which once passed by, the engagement was at an end; but far oftener it was a bond for life, uniting interests and feelings, and dividing dangers and successes. The brothers in arms [58] met all perils together, undertook all adventures in company, shared in the advantage of every happy enterprise, and partook of the pain or loss of every misfortune. If the one was attacked in body, in honour, or in estate, the other sprang forward to defend him. Their wealth and even their thoughts were in common; so that the news which the one received, or the design that he formed, he was bound to communicate to the other without reserve. Even if the one underlay a wager of battle[59] against any other knight, and was cut off by death before he could discharge himself thereof, his brother in arms was bound to appear in the lists, in defence of his honour, on the day appointed.

Sometimes[60] this fraternity of arms was contracted by a solemn deed; sometimes by a vow ratified by the communion and other cer-

---

54. See the *Vœu du Heron* and the *Vœu du Paon*. cited in St. Palaye.
55. See Notes 4.
56. Ducange, *Dissert*, xxi.
57. Monstrelet.
58. *Juvenal des Ursius.*
59. *Hardouin de la Jaille.*
60. See deed between Du Guesclin and Clisson. Ducange, *Dissert*, xxi.

emonies of the church. In many cases, [61] however, the only form consisted in the mutual exchange of arms, which implied the same devotion to each other, and the same irrevocable engagement.

I have now said sufficient concerning the habits and customs of the ancient knights, to give a general idea of the rules by which chivalry was governed, and the spirit by which it was animated. That spirit waxed fainter, it is true, as luxury and pomp increased, and as the barbarities of an early age merged into the softer licentiousness that followed.

But the rules of the order themselves remained unchanged, and did far more than any other institution to restrain the general incontinence [62] of the age. Even in those days when chivalrous love was no longer pure, and chivalrous religion no longer the spring of the noblest morality, the spirit of the days of old lingered amid the ruins of the falling institution. An Edward, a Du Guesclin, a Bayard, a Sidney, would rise up in the midst of corrupted times, and shame the vices of the day by still showing one more true knight; and even now, when the order has altogether passed away, we feel and benefit by its good effects.

So complete a change has come over manners and customs, so rapid has been our late progress, and so many and vast have been the events of latter years, that to trace the remains of chivalry in any of our present feelings or institutions, seems but a theoretical dream. The knights of old are looked upon as things apart, that have neither kin nor community with ourselves; their acts are hardly believed; and their very existence is doubted. Let him who would make historical remembrance more tangible, and see how nearly the days of chivalry approach to our own, run his eye over one short page in the chronology of the world, and he will find that no more than three centuries have passed since Bayard himself died, a knight without reproach.

---

61. Ducange, *Gloss. Lat. Mutare Armas.*
62. See the Chevalier de la Tour, as cited by St. Palaye.

CHAPTER 3

The Progress of Chivalry in Europe

The picture which I have just attempted to draw of the various customs of chivalry must be looked upon rather as a summary of its institutions and feelings, as they changed through many ages and many nations, than as a likeness of chivalry at any precise period, or in any one country.

Previous to the age of the crusades, to which I now propose to turn as speedily as possible, the state of chivalry in Europe had made but little progress. It had spread, however, as a spirit, to almost all the nations surrounding the cradle of its birth. In Spain Alphonso VI.[1] was already waging a completely chivalric war against the Moors, and many of the knights of France, who afterward distinguished themselves in the Holy Land, had, in the service of one or other of the Spanish princes, tried their arms against the Saracens.

In England we have seen that there is reason to suppose the institution of knighthood was known to the Saxons,[2] though the indiscriminate manner in which the word *miles* is used in the Latin chronicles of the day renders it scarcely possible to ascertain at what period the order was introduced. The same difficulty indeed occurs in regard to the Normans, though from various circumstances connected with the accounts given by William of Jumieges,[3] of the reigns of William I. and Richard I., Dukes of Normandy, we are led to believe that chivalry was very early introduced among that people. At all events it seems certain that after the accession of Richard to the ducal dignity, *A. D.* 960, knightly feelings made great progress among the Normans, and in 1003, we find an exploit so purely chivalrous, performed by a

---

1. Vertot.
2. Sharon Turner.
3. *William of Jumieges*, lib. iv.

body of forty gentlemen from Normandy, that we cannot doubt the spirit of knighthood in its purest form had already spread through that country.

Vertot says:—

Forty Norman gentlemen, all warriors, who had distinguished themselves in the armies of the Duke of Normandy, returning from a pilgrimage to the Holy Land, disembarked in Italy without arms. Having learned that the town of Salerno was besieged by the Saracens, their zeal for religion caused them instantly to throw themselves into that place. Guimard, the Prince of Salerno, had shut himself up in the town, to defend it to the last against the *infidels*; and he immediately caused arms and horses to be given to the Norman gentlemen, who made so many vigorous and unexpected sallies upon the Saracens, that they compelled them to raise the siege.

In Italy we find many traces of chivalry at an early date, and it would appear that the institution which took its rise in France was no sooner known than adopted by most other nations. The Normans, whom we have seen above succouring the Prince of Salerno in his necessity, did not remain a sufficient length of time in Italy to spread the chivalrous spirit; but it is said that Guimard, after using every effort to induce them to stay, sent deputies after them to Normandy, praying for aid from the nobles of that country against the Saracens. Several large bodies of Norman adventurers, in consequence of his promises and persuasions, proceeded to establish themselves in Apulia and Calabria, defeated the Saracens, cleared the south of Italy and part of Greece of those locust-like invaders, and re-established the Greek and Italian princes in their dominions.

These princes, however, soon became jealous of their new allies, and employed various base means to destroy them. They, on the other hand, united for mutual defence, and under the famous Robert Guiscard, one of twelve brothers who had left Normandy for Italy together, they speedily conquered for themselves the countries which they had restored to ungrateful lords. Guiscard was now universally acknowledged as their chief, and thus began the chivalrous Norman empire in Italy.

Nothing, perhaps, more favoured the general progress of chivalry than the state of religion in that day; which, overloaded with superstitions, and decked out with every external pomp and ornament, appealed to the imagination through the medium of the senses, and woke a thousand enthusiasms which could find no such fitting career as in the pursuits of knighthood. The first efforts of the feudal system, too, gradually extending themselves to every part of Europe, joined to make chivalry spread through the different countries where they were felt, by raising up a number of independent lords who—each anxious to reduce his neighbours to vassalage, and to preserve his own separate lordship—required continual armed support from others, to whom he offered in return honour and protection.

Thus, for about a century, or perhaps a little more, after the first institution of knighthood, chivalry slowly gained ground, and by each exploit of any particular body of knights (such, for instance, as we have recorded of the Normans) the order became more and more respected, and its establishment more firm, decided, and regular. It wanted but one great enterprise commenced and carried through upon chivalrous principles alone to render chivalry, combined as it was with religion and the feudal system, the great master power of Europe—and that enterprise was at hand.

The natural reverence for those countries, sanctified and elevated by so many miracles, and rendered sublimely dear to the heart of every Christian, as the land in which his salvation was brightly but terribly worked out, had from all ages rendered Palestine an object of pilgrimage. In the earliest times, after the recognition of the Christian faith by Constantine, the subjects of the Roman Empire had followed the example of the empress Helena, and had deemed it almost a Christian duty to visit the scenes of our Saviour's mortal career. For many ages while the whole of Judea remained under the sway of the Cesars, the journey was an easy one. Few difficulties waylaid the passenger, or gave pilgrimage even the merit of dangers encountered and obstacles overcome.

Towards the seventh century, the eastern provinces of the Roman Empire, already weakened by many invasions, had to encounter the exertions of another adversary, who succeeded in wresting them from their Christian possessors. The successors of Mahomet, who from a low station had become a great legislator, a mighty conqueror, and a pretended prophet, carried on the conquest which he had begun in Arabia, and one by one made themselves masters of Syria, Antioch, Persia, Medea, and in fact the greater part of the rich continent of Asia.

It is not here my purpose to trace the progress of these conquerors, or to examine for a moment the religion they professed. Suffice it, that in the days of Charlemagne the fame of that great prince produced from the *calif* Haroun al Raschid many liberal concessions in favour of the Christian pilgrims to Jerusalem, now in the hands of the unbelievers.

Particular ages seem fertile in great men; and it is very rare to find one distinguished poet, monarch, or conqueror standing alone in his own century. Nay more;—we generally discover—however different the country that produces them, and however opposite the circumstances under which they are placed—that there is a similarity in the character of the mind, if I may so express myself without obscurity, of the eminent persons produced in each particular age. This was peculiarly the case in the age of Charlemagne. It seemed as if the most remote corners of the earth had made an effort, at the same moment, to produce from the bosom of barbarism and confusion a great and intelligent monarch—an Alfred, a Haroun, and a Charlemagne.

The likeness seemed to be felt by the two great emperors of the east and the west; and a reciprocation of courtesy[4] and friendship appears to have taken place between them, most rare in that remote age. Various presents were transmitted from one to the other; and the most precious offering that the Christian monarch could receive, the keys of the Holy City, were sent from Bagdad to Aix, together with a standard, which has been supposed to imply the sovereignty of Jerusalem resigned by Haroun to his great contemporary. Nothing could afford a nobler proof of a great, a liberal, and a delicate mind, than the choice evinced by the *calif* in his gift. Charlemagne took advantage so far of Haroun's liberality, [5] as to establish an hospital and a library for the Latin pilgrims.

The successors of Haroun, and more particularly Monstacer Billah, continued to yield tolerance at least, if not protection, to the Christians of Jerusalem. The pilgrims also were more or less protected during the reigns that followed, both from motives of liberal feeling and of interest, as the great influx of travellers, especially from Italy, brought much wealth and commerce into Syria.

Under the *califs* of the Fatemite race several persecutions took place; and when at length the invasion of the Turkish hordes had brought the whole of Palestine under the dominion of a wild and barbarous race, Jerusalem was taken and sacked; and while the Christian inhabit-

---

4. Eginhard. *Annal.*
5. Mabillon.

ants were treated with every sort of brutal cruelty, the pilgrims were subject to taxation [6] on their arrival, as well as liable to plunder by the way.

A piece of gold was exacted for permission to enter the Holy City; and at that time, when the value of the precious metals was infinitely higher than in the present day, few, if any, of the pilgrims on their arrival possessed sufficient to pay the cruel demand.

Thus, after having suffered toils unheard of—hunger, thirst, the parching influence of a burning sky, sickness, danger, and often robbery, and wounds; when the weary wanderer arrived at the very entrance of the city, with the bourn of all his long pilgrimage before him, the enthusiastic object of all his hopes in sight, the place of refuge and repose for which he had longed and prayed within his reach—unless he could pay the stipulated sum, he was driven by the barbarians from the gates, and was forced to tread back all his heavy way unfurnished with any means, and unsupported by any hope, or to die by the roadside of want, weariness, and despair.

The pilgrimages nevertheless continued with unremitting zeal; and the number of devotees increased greatly in the tenth and eleventh centuries. In the tenth, indeed, the custom of pilgrimage became almost universal, from a misinterpretation [7] of a prophecy in the Apocalypse. A general belief prevailed that at the end of the tenth century, the thousand years being concluded, the world was to be judged; and crowds of men and women, in the frantic hope of expiating their sins by the long and painful journey to the Holy Land, flocked from all parts of Europe towards Jerusalem.

Many of the more clear-sighted and sensible of the Christian prelates had from time to time attempted to dissuade the people from these dangerous and fatal pilgrimages; but the principle of bodily infliction being received as a mark of internal penitence and a means of obtaining absolution, had been so long inculcated by the church of Rome, that the current of popular opinion had received its impulse, and it was no longer possible to turn it from its course. No penance could be more painful or more consistent with the prejudices of the multitude, than a pilgrimage to the Holy Land; and thus the priests continued often to enforce the act, while the heads of the church themselves, as religion became corrupted, learned to see this sort of penitence in the same light as the people, and encouraged its execution.

6. William of Tyre, *lib.* i.
7. Voltaire, *Essai sur les Mœurs.*

They found the great efficacy of external excitements in stimulating the populace to that superstitious obedience on which they were fast building up the authority of the Roman church, and probably also were not without a share in the bigoted enthusiasm which they taught. Thus in the tenth century the pilgrimages which fear lest the day of judgment should be approaching induced many to undertake in expiation of their sins, met but little opposition; while various meteoric phenomena, of a somewhat awful nature, earthquakes, hurricanes, &c., contributed to increase the general alarm.

When these had passed by, and the dreaded epoch had brought forth nothing, the current still continued to flow on in the course that it had taken; and during the eleventh century several circumstances tended to increase it. Among others the terror spread through France by the Papal Interdict, called forth by the refractory adherence of Robert I. to his queen [8] Bertha, brought more pilgrims than usual from that country.

Of many thousands who passed into Asia,[9] a few isolated individuals only returned; but these every day, as they passed through the different countries of Europe on their journey back, spread indignation and horror by their account of the dreadful sufferings of the Christians in Judea. Various [10] letters are reported as having been sent by the emperors of the east to the different princes of Europe, soliciting aid to repel the encroachments of the infidel; and if but a very small portion of the crimes and cruelty attributed to the Turks by these epistles were believed by the Christians, it is not at all astonishing that wrath and horror took possession of every chivalrous bosom.

Pope Sylvester II. had made an ineffectual appeal to Christendom towards the end of the tenth century, bringing forward the first idea of a crusade;[11] but the age was not then ripe for a project that required a fuller development of chivalrous feelings. Gregory VII. revived the

---

8. Guibert de Nogent.

9. *Will. Tyr. lib.* i.

10. Mills mentions one from Manuel VII. to Pope Gregory VII., and Guibert of Nogent speaks of another which, though he cautiously avoids naming the emperor who wrote it, lest he should mislead from want of correct information, could only have been sent, under some of the circumstances he mentions, by Isaac Comnenus. Mills supposes it to have been the same with a letter written by Alexius, though it differs in many parts from the usual version of that epistle. Probably, however, this opinion is correct, as a letter is stated to have been addressed to Robert of Flanders, who was in his extreme youth in the time of Isaac Comnenus.

11. Murator. *Script. Ital.*

idea, and made it the subject of a very pompous epistle; but he himself was one of the first to forget the miseries of his fellow-Christians in Palestine, in the pursuit of his own aggrandizement.

Still, the persecution of the Christians in Palestine, and the murder and pillage of the pilgrims continued; still the indignation of Europe was fed and renewed by repeated tales of cruel barbarity committed in the Holy Land—sufferings of the church—insults to religion—and merciless massacres of countrymen and relations: still, also, the spirit of chivalry was each day spreading further and rising more powerfully, so that all was preparing for some great and general movement. The lightning of the crusade was in the people's hearts, and it wanted but one electric touch to make it flash forth upon the world.

At this time a man, of whose early days we have little authentic knowledge, but that he was born at Amiens, and from a soldier had become a priest,[12] after living for some time the life of a hermit, became seized with the desire of visiting Jerusalem. He was, according to all accounts,[13] small in stature and mean in person; but his eyes possessed a peculiar fire and intelligence, and his eloquence was powerful and flowing. The fullest account of his manners and conduct is to be found in Robert the Monk, who was present at the council of Clermont, and in Guibert of Nogent, who speaks in the tone of one who has beheld what he relates.

The first of these authors describes Peter the Hermit,[14] of whom we speak, as esteemed among those who best understand the things of earth, and superior in piety to all the bishops or abbots of the day. He fed upon neither flesh nor bread, says the same writer, though he permitted himself wine and other aliments, finding nevertheless his pleasure in the greatest abstinence.

Guibert, or Gilbert, of Nogent, speaks still more fully of his public conduct.[15] Says the writer:—

He set out from whence I know not, nor with what design; but we saw him at that time passing through the towns and villages, preaching everywhere, and the people surrounding him in crowds, loading him with presents, and celebrating his sanctity with such high eulogiums, that I never remember to have seen such honours rendered to any other person. He showed him-

---

12. Albert of Aix; William of Tyre.
13. *Ibid.*
14. *Robert, lib.* i.
15. Guib. *Nogent, lib.* ii.

49

self very generous, however, in the distribution of the things given to him. He brought back to their homes the women that had abandoned their husbands, not without adding gifts of his own, and re-established peace between those who lived unhappily, with wonderful authority. In everything he said or did, it seemed as if there was something of divine; so much so, that people went to pluck some of the hairs from his mule, which they kept afterward as relics; which I mention here not that they really were so, but merely served to satisfy the public love of anything extraordinary. While out of doors he wore ordinarily a woollen tunic, with a brown mantle, which fell down to his heels. He had his arms and his feet bare, ate little or no bread, and lived upon fish and wine.

Such was his appearance after his return: prior to that period it is probable that this hermit had made himself remarkable for nothing but his general eloquence and his ascetic severity. Great and extraordinary men are often long before opportunity gives scope for the display of the particular spirit whose efforts are destined to distinguish them. I mean not to class Peter the Hermit among great men; but certainly he deserves the character of one of the most extraordinary men that Europe ever produced, if it were but for the circumstance of having convulsed a world—led one continent to combat to extermination against another, and yet left historians in doubt whether he was madman or prophet, fool or politician.

Peter, however, accomplished in safety his pilgrimage to Jerusalem,[16] paid the piece of gold demanded at the gates, and took up his lodging in the house of one of the pious Christians of the Holy City. Here his first emotion[17] seems to have been indignant horror at the barbarous and sacrilegious brutality of the Turks. The venerable prelate of Tyre represents him as conferring eagerly with his host upon the enormous cruelties of the *infidels*, even before visiting the general objects of devotion. Doubtless the ardent, passionate, enthusiastic mind of Peter had been wrought upon at every step he took in the Holy Land, by the miserable state of his brethren, till his feelings and imagination became excited to almost frantic vehemence.

After performing the duties of the pilgrimage, visiting each object of reputed holiness,[18] and praying in those churches which had the

16. *Hist. Hieros. abrev.* Jacob. *Vit. lib.* i.
17. Will. Tyr. lib. i.; *Albert. Chron. Hieros.*
18. Will. Tyr.; *Hist. Hieros.; Jacob. Vit. lib.* i.

fame of peculiar sanctity, Peter, with his heart wrung at beholding the objects of his deepest veneration in the hands of the church's enemies, demanded an audience of the patriarch, to whom some Latin friend presented him.

Simeon the patriarch, though a Greek, and consequently in the eyes of Peter a heretic, was still a Christian, suffering in common with the rest of the faithful in the Holy Land, and the hermit saw in him that character alone. The union—the overflowing confidence with which the hermit and the prelate appear to have treated each other—raises them both in our estimation; but it also throws an historical light upon the character of Peter, which places him in a more elevated situation than modern historians have been willing to concede to him. The patriarch Simeon, a man as famous for his good sense as for his piety, would not, surely, have opened his inmost thoughts to a wandering pilgrim like Peter, and intrusted to him a paper sealed with his own seal, which, if taken by the Turks, would have ensured death to himself and destruction to Christianity in Palestine, had he not recognised in the hermit "a man," [19] to use the words of William of Tyre, "full of prudence and experience in the things of this world."

This, however, was the case; and after long conversations, wherein many a tear was shed over the hapless state of the Holy Land, it was determined, at the suggestion of Peter, that the patriarch should write to the pope and the princes of the west, setting forth the miseries of Jerusalem and of the faithful people of the Holy City, and praying for aid and protection against the merciless sword of the Saracen. Peter, on his part, promised to seek out each individual prince, and to show, with his whole powers of language, the ills of the Christians of Palestine.

From these conversations Peter went again and again to pray in the church of the Resurrection, petitioning ardently for aid in the great undertaking before him. On one of these occasions it is said that he fell asleep,[20] and beheld the Saviour in a vision, who exhorted him to hasten on his journey, and persevere in his design.

Without searching for anything preternatural, the vision is not at all difficult to believe, though the place of its occurrence seems to have been fictitious. Nothing could be more natural than for Peter the Hermit, with his mind full of the mission he was about to undertake, to dream that the Being in whose cause he believed himself engaged

---

19. Will. Tyr. lib. i.
20. Albert. *Aquensis; Hist. Hieros.; Jacobi Vitr.*; Will. *Tyr.*

appeared to encourage him, and to hasten his enterprise; and it is easy to conceive that, with full confidence in this manifestation of heavenly favour, he should set forth upon his journey with enthusiastic zeal.

Bearing the letter of the patriarch, Peter now returned in haste to Italy, and sought out the pope, to declare the miseries of the church in the Holy Land, and to propose the means of its deliverance. Urban II., who then occupied the apostolic chair, had inherited from Gregory wars and contestations with the emperor Henry IV., and was at the same time embroiled with the weak and luxurious Philip I. of France, on the subject of that king's adulterous intercourse with Bertrade. He, as well as Gregory, had taken refuge in Apulia and Calabria, and had thrown himself upon the protection of the famous Robert Guiscard, who readily granted him the aid of that powerful mind which made the utmost parts of the earth tremble.[21]

It does not correctly appear at what place Urban sojourned at the time of Peter's arrival in Italy.[22] His whole support was, evidently, still in the family of Guiscard; and it seems that with Boemond, Prince of Tarentum, the gallant and chivalrous son of Robert, he first held council upon the hermit's[23] great and interesting proposal, before he determined on the line of conduct to be pursued.

One of the historians of the crusades,[24] attributing perhaps somewhat too much the spirit of modern politics to an age whose genius was of very different quality, supposes that the course determined on by the pope and his ally was, in fact, principally a shrewd plot to fix Urban firmly in the Vatican, and to forward Boemond's ambitious views in Greece. It seems to me, however, that such a supposition is perfectly irreconcilable with the subsequent conduct of either. The pope shortly after threw himself into the midst of his enemies, to hold a council on the subject of the crusades; and Boemond abandoned everything in Europe to carry on the holy war in Palestine. It is much more natural to imagine that the spirit of their age governed both the prelate and the warrior—the enthusiasm of religion the one, and the enthusiasm of chivalry the other.

However that may be, Peter the Hermit met with a most encouraging reception from the pope. The sufferings of his fellow-Christians

---

21. See Notes 5.
22. William of Tyre says that he was wandering from place to place under the protection of Guiscard. This opinion I have adopted, although Albert of Aix declares that Peter joined him at Rome.
23. Will. of Malmsbury.
24. Mills.

brought tears from the prelate's eyes; the general scheme of the crusade was sanctioned[25] instantly by his authority; and, promising his quick and active concurrence, he sent him on, the pilgrim to preach the deliverance of the Holy Land through all the countries of Europe. Peter wanted neither zeal nor activity[26]—from town to town, from province to province, from country to country, he spread the cry of vengeance on the Turks, and deliverance to Jerusalem! The warlike spirit of the people was at its height; the genius of chivalry was in the vigour of its early youth; the enthusiasm of religion had now a great and terrible object before it, and all the gates of the human heart were open to the eloquence of the preacher. That eloquence was not exerted in vain; nations rose at his word and grasped the spear; and it only wanted someone to direct and point the great enterprise that was already determined.

In the meantime the pope did not forget his promise; and while Peter the Hermit spread the inspiration throughout Europe,[27] Urban called together a council at Placentia, to which deputies were admitted from the emperor of Constantinople, who displayed the progress of the Turks, and set forth the danger to all Christendom of suffering their arms to advance unopposed. The opinion of the assembly was universally favourable to the crusade; and trusting to the popularity of the measure, and the indications of support which he had already met with, the pope determined to cross the Alps and to hold a second council in the heart of Gaul.

The ostensible object of this council was to regulate the state of the church, and to correct abuses; but the great object was, in fact, the crusade. It is useless to investigate the motives which gave Urban II. courage to summon a council, destined, among other things, to solemnly reprobate the dissolute conduct of Philip of France, in the midst of dominions, if not absolutely feudatory to the crown[28] of that monarch, at least bound to it by friendship and alliance. Whether it arose from fortitude of a just cause, or from reliance on political calculation, the prelate's judgment was proved by the event to be right. After one or two changes in regard to the place of meeting, the council was assembled at Clermont, in Auvergne,[29] and was composed of

---

25. Will. Tyr. lib. i.
26. Guibertus; Gesta Dei.
27. A. D. 1095.
28. Mills, chap. ii.
29. Will. Tyr. lib. i.

an unheard-of multitude of priests, princes, and nobles, both of France and Germany, all willing and eager to receive the pope's injunctions with reverence and obedience.

After having terminated the less important affairs which formed the apparent business of the meeting, and which occupied the deliberation of seven days, Urban, one of the most eloquent men of the age, came forth from the church[30] in which the principal ecclesiastics were assembled, and addressed the immense concourse which had been gathered into one of the great squares, no building being large enough to contain the number.

The prelate[31] then, with the language best calculated to win the hearts of all his hearers, displayed the miseries of the Christians in the Holy Land. He addressed the multitude as a people peculiarly favoured by God, in the gift of courage, strength, and true faith. He told them that their brethren in the east were trampled under the feet of *infidels*, to whom God had not granted the light of his Holy Spirit—that fire, plunder, and the sword had desolated completely the fair plains of Palestine—that her children were led away captive, or enslaved, or died under tortures too horrible to recount—that the women of their land were subjected to the impure passions of the pagans, and that God's own altar, the symbols of salvation, and the precious relics of the saints were all desecrated by the gross and filthy abomination of a race of heathens.

To whom, then, he asked—to whom did it belong to punish such crimes, to wipe away such impurities, to destroy the oppressors, and to raise up the oppressed? To whom, if not to those who heard him, who had received from God strength, and power, and greatness of soul; whose ancestors had been the prop of Christendom, and whose kings had put a barrier to the progress of *infidels?* He cried:—

Think of the sepulchre of Christ our Saviour possessed by the foul heathen!—think of all the sacred places dishonoured by

30. Robertus Monachus, lib. i.

31. I have followed as nearly as possible the account of Robertus Monachus, who was present. Having found in no book of any authenticity the speech attributed by more modern writers to Peter the Hermit, I have rejected it entirely as supposititious. Neither Robert, nor Albertus Aquensis, nor William of Tyre, nor Guibert of Nogent, nor James of Vitry, the most authentic historians of the crusade, some of whom were present at the council of Clermont, and most of whom lived at the time, even mention the appearance of Peter at that assembly. That he might be there, I do not attempt to deny, but that he addressed the people I believe utterly unfounded.

their sacrilegious impurities!—O brave knights, offspring of invincible fathers, degenerate not from your ancient blood! remember the virtues of your ancestors, and if you feel held back from the course before you by the soft ties of wives, of children, of parents, call to mind the words of our Lord himself: *'Whosoever loves father or mother more than me, is not worthy of me. Whosoever shall abandon for my name's sake his house, or his brethren, or his sisters, or his father, or his mother, or his wife, or his children, or his lands, shall receive an hundredfold, and shall inherit eternal life.'*

The prelate then went on to point out the superior mundane advantages which those might obtain who took the Cross. He represented their own country as poor and arid, and Palestine as a land flowing with milk and honey; and, blending the barbarous ideas of a dark age with the powerful figures of enthusiastic eloquence, he proceeded:—

"Jerusalem is in the centre of this fertile land; and its territories, rich above all others, offer, so to speak, the delights of Paradise. That land, too, the Redeemer of the human race rendered illustrious by his advent, honoured by his residence, consecrated by his passion, repurchased by his death, signalized by his sepulture. That royal city, Jerusalem—situated in the centre of the world—held captive by *infidels*, who deny the God that honoured her—now calls on you and prays for her deliverance. From you—from you above all people she looks for comfort, and she hopes for aid; since God has granted to you, beyond other nations, glory and might in arms. Take, then, the road before you in expiation of your sins, and go, assured that, after the honour of this world shall have passed away, imperishable glory shall await you even in the kingdom of heaven!"

Loud shouts of "God wills it! God wills it!" pronounced simultaneously by the whole people, in all the different dialects and languages of which the multitude was composed, here interrupted for a moment the speech of the prelate: but, gladly seizing the time, Urban proceeded, after having obtained silence:—

Dear brethren, today is shown forth in you that which the Lord has said by his evangelist—*'When two or three shall be assembled in my name, there shall I be in the midst of them;'* for if the Lord God had not been in your souls, you would not all have pronounced the same words; or, rather, God himself pronounced them by your lips, for he it was that put them in your hearts. Be they, then, your war-cry in the combat, for those words came forth

55

from God.—Let the army of the Lord, when it rushes upon his enemies, shout but that one cry, 'God wills it! God wills it!' [32]

Remember, however, that we neither order nor advise this journey to the old, nor to the weak, nor to those who are unfit to bear arms. Let not this way be taken by women, without their husbands, or their brothers, or their legitimate guardians, for such are rather a burden than an aid. Let the rich assist the poor, and bring with them, at their own charge, those who can bear arms to the field. Still, let not priests nor clerks, to whatever place they may belong, set out on this journey without the permission of their bishop; nor the layman undertake it without the blessing of his pastor, for to such as do so their journey shall be fruitless. Let whoever is inclined to devote himself to the cause of God, make it a solemn engagement, and bear the cross of the Lord either on his breast or on his brow till he set out; and let him who is ready to begin his march place the holy emblem on his shoulders, in memory of that precept of the Saviour—'He who does not take up his cross and follow me, is not worthy of me.'

The *pontiff* thus ended his oration, and the multitude prostrating themselves before him, repeated the *Confiteor*[33] after one of the cardinals. The pope then pronounced the absolution of their sins, and bestowed on them his benediction; after which they retired to their homes to prepare for the great undertaking to which they had vowed themselves.

Miracles are told of the manner in which the news of this council, and of the events that distinguished it, spread to every part of the world; but nevertheless it did spread, as may easily be conceived, with great quickness, without any supernatural aid; and, to make use of the words of him from whom we have sketched the oration of the pope:—

Throughout the earth, the Christians glorified themselves and were filled with joy, while the Gentiles of Arabia and Persia trembled and were seized with sadness: the souls of the one race were exalted, those of the others stricken with fear and stupor.

Great, certainly, was the influence which the zeal and eloquence of Urban gave him over the people. Some authors, with a curious sort

---

32. See Notes 6.
33. Robertus Monachus.

56

of historical puritanism, which leads them to judge of ages past only by the principles of the day in which they themselves exist, have reproached the pope with not using the means in his hands for purposes which would have needed the heart of a Fenelon to conceive properly, and the head of a Napoleon to execute. They say that, with the powers which he did possess, he might have reformed a world! It is hardly fair, methinks, to require of a man in a barbarous, ignorant, corrupted age the enlightened visions of the nineteenth century.

Pope Urban II., at the end of the eleventh century, showed a great superiority to the age in which he lived, and at the council of Clermont evinced qualities of both the heart and the mind which have deservedly brought his name down to us with honour. His first act in the council was to excommunicate, for adulterous profligacy, Philip, monarch of the very ground on which he stood; and, in so doing, he made use of the only acknowledged authority by which the kings of that day could be checked in the course of evil. Whether the authority itself was or was not legitimate, is not here the question; but, being at the time undisputed, and employed for the best of objects, its use can in no way fairly be cited as an instance either of pride or ambition.

The pope's conduct in preaching the crusade is equally justifiable. His views were of course those of the age in which he lived, and he acted with noble enthusiasm in accordance with those views. He made vast efforts, he endangered his person, he sacrificed his ease and comfort, to accomplish what no churchman of his day pretended to doubt was a glorious and a noble undertaking. In thus acting, he displayed great qualities of mind, and showed himself superior to the century in powers of *conducting*, if he was not so in the powers of *conceiving* great designs.

It would be very difficult to prove, also, that the pope, had he even possessed the will, could, by the exertion of every effort, have produced the same effect in any other cause that he did in favour of the crusades. I have already attempted to show that all things were prepared in Europe for the expedition to the Holy Land, by the spirit of religious and military enthusiasm; and the task was light, to aid in pouring on the current of popular feeling in the direction which it had already begun to take, when compared with the labour necessary to have turned that current into another channel. He who does not grasp the spirit of the age on which he writes, but judges of other days by the feelings of his own, is like one who would adapt a polar dress to the climate of the tropics.

Before closing this chapter, one observation also must be made respecting the justice of the crusade, which enterprise it has become somewhat customary to look upon as altogether cruel and unnecessary. Such an opinion, however, is in no degree founded on fact. The crusade was not only as just as any other warfare of the day, but as just as any that ever was waged. The object was, the protection and relief of a cruelly oppressed and injured people—the object was, to repel a strong, an active, and an encroaching enemy—the object was, to wrest from the hands of a bloodthirsty and savage people territories which they themselves claimed by no right but the sword, and in which the population they had enslaved was loudly crying for deliverance from their yoke—the object was, to defend a weak and exposed frontier from the further aggression of a nation whose boast was conquest.

Such were the objects of the crusades; and though much of superstition was mingled with the incitements, and many cruelties committed in its course, the evils were not greater than ordinary ambition every day produces; and the motives were as fair as any of those that have ever instigated the many feuds and warfares of the world.

CHAPTER 4

The Effects of the Council of Clermont

The immediate effects of the council of Clermont are detailed with so much animation by Guibert of Nogent, that I shall attempt to trace them nearly in his own words, merely observing, that previous to his departure from France, Urban II., having taken every means in his power to secure the property of the crusaders during their absence, committed the chief direction of the expedition to Adhemar, Bishop of Puy, in Auvergne.[1]

Says the historian:—

As soon as the council of Clermont was concluded a great rumour spread through the whole of France, and as soon as fame brought the news of the orders of the *pontiff* to anyone, he went instantly to solicit his neighbours and his relations to engage with him in the *way of God*, for so they designated the purposed expedition.

The Counts Palatine[2] were already full of the desire to undertake this journey; and all the knights of an inferior order felt the same zeal. The poor themselves soon caught the flame so ardently, that no one paused to think of the smallness of his wealth, or to consider whether he ought to yield his house and his fields, and his vines; but each one set about selling his property, at as low a price as if he had been held in some horrible captivity, and sought to pay his ransom without loss of time.

At this period, too, there existed a general dearth. The rich even

---

1. Fulcher of Chartres; Guibert of Nogent; William of Tyre.
2. See Notes 7.

felt the want of corn; and many, with everything to buy, had nothing, or next to nothing, wherewithal to purchase what they needed. The poor tried to nourish themselves with the wild herbs of the earth; and, as bread was very dear, sought on all sides food heretofore unknown, to supply the place of corn. The wealthy and powerful were not exempt; but finding themselves menaced with the famine which spread around them, and beholding every day the terrible wants of the poor, they contracted their expenses, and lived with the most narrow parsimony, lest they should squander the riches now become so necessary.

The ever insatiable misers rejoiced in days so favourable to their covetousness; and casting their eyes upon the bushels of grain which they had hoarded long before, calculated each day the profits of their avarice. Thus some struggled with every misery and want, while others revelled in the hopes of fresh acquisitions. No sooner, however, had Christ inspired, as I have said, innumerable bodies of people to seek a voluntary exile, than the money which had been hoarded so long was spread forth in a moment; and that which was horribly dear while all the world was in repose, was on a sudden sold for nothing, as soon as everyone began to hasten towards their destined journey. Each man hurried to conclude his affairs; and, astonishing to relate, we then saw—so sudden was the diminution in the value of everything—we then saw seven sheep sold for five *deniers*. The dearth of grain, also, was instantly changed into abundance; and every one, occupied solely in amassing money for his journey, sold everything that he could, not according to its real worth, but according to the value set upon it by the buyer.

In the meanwhile, the greater part of those who had not determined upon the journey, joked and laughed at those who were thus selling their goods for whatever they could get; and prophesied that their voyage would be miserable, and their return worse. Such was ever the language one day; but the next— suddenly seized with the same desire as the rest—those who had been most forward to mock, abandoned everything for a few crowns, and set out with those whom they had laughed at but a day before. Who shall tell the children and the infirm that, animated with the same spirit, hastened to the war? Who shall count the old men and the young maids who hurried forward to the fight?—not with the hope of aiding, but for the crown of martyrdom to be won amid the swords of the *infidels.* 'You, warriors,' they cried, 'you shall vanquish by the spear and brand; but let us, at least, conquer Christ by our sufferings.'

At the same time, one might see a thousand things springing from the same spirit, which were both astonishing and laughable: the poor shoeing their oxen, as we shoe horses, and harnessing them to two-wheeled carts, in which they placed their scanty provisions and their young children; and proceeding onward, while the babes, at each town or castle that they saw, demanded eagerly whether that was Jerusalem.

Such is the picture presented, by an eyewitness, of the state of France after the first promulgation of the crusade; and a most extraordinary picture it is. The zeal, the enthusiasm, the fervour of the spirit, the brutal ignorance and dark barbarity of the people, are the objects that catch the eye from the mere surface; but underneath may be seen a hundred fine and latent tints which mingle in the portrait of the age. There may be found the hope of gain and the expectation of wealth in other lands, as well as the excitement of devotion; and there also may be traced the reckless, daring courage of a period when comfort was unknown, and when security was scarcely less to be expected among the swords of the Saracens, than in the fields of France and Germany. While the thirst of adventure, the master-passion of the middle ages, prompted to any change of scene and circumstances, imagination portrayed the land in view with all that adventitious splendour which none—of all the many betrayers of the human mind—so well knows how to bestow as hope.

The same land, when the Jews marched towards it from the wilderness, had been represented to them as a land flowing with milk and honey,—rich in all gifts; and doubtless that inducement moved the stubborn Hebrews, as much as the command of him they had so often disobeyed. Now the very same prospect was held out to another host of men, as ignorant of what lay before them as the Jews themselves; and it may be fairly supposed that, in their case too, imaginary hopes, and all the gay phantasma of ambition, shared powerfully with religion in leading them onward to the promised land.

Still zeal, and sympathy, and indignation, and chivalrous feeling, and the thirst of glory, and the passion for enterprise, and a thousand vague but great and noble aspirations, mingled in the complicated motive of the crusade. It increased by contagion; it grew by communion; it spread from house to house, and from bosom to bosom; it became a universal desire—an enthusiasm—a passion—a madness.

In the meanwhile, the crusade was not without producing a sensible benefit even to Europe. The whole country had previously been desolated by feuds[3] and pillage, and massacre. Castle waged war with castle: baron plundered baron; and from field to field, and city to city, the traveller could scarcely pass without injury or death. No sooner,[4] however, had the crusade been preached at the council of Clermont, than the universal peace, which was there commanded, called the *Truce*[5] *of God*, was sworn throughout the country, the plunder ceased and the feuds disappeared. The very fact of the wicked, the infamous, and the bloodthirsty having embraced the crusade, either from penitence or from worse motives, was a positive good to Europe. That not alone the good, [6] the religious, the zealous, or the brave, filled the ranks of the Cross is admitted on all hands; yet those who had once assumed that holy sign were obliged, in some degree, to act as if their motives had been pure, and their very absence was a blessing to the land they left.

Still the crusade went on; and the imagination of the people being once directed towards a particular object found, even in the phenomena which in former days would have struck nations with fear and apprehension, signs of blessing and omens of success. An earthquake itself [7] was held as good augury; and scarcely a meteor shot across the sky without affording some theme for hope.

The sign of the Cross was now to be seen on the shoulder of every one; and being generally cut in red [8] cloth, was a conspicuous and remarkable object. As these multiplied, the hearts even of the fearful grew strong, and the contagion of example added to the number every hour. Peter the Hermit, indefatigable in his calling, though his mind seems day by day[9] to have become more excited, till enthusiasm grew nearly akin to madness, gathered a vast concourse of the lower orders, and prepared to set out by the way of Hungary. But the real and serviceable body of crusaders was collected from among another

---

3. Guibert of Nogent.
4. Fulcher of Chartres; William of Tyre.
5. Guibert; Gesta Dei.
6. Albert. Aquensis; Will. Tyr.; Guibert
7. Albert of Aix.
8. See Ducange in Sig. Cruc.
9. Albert of Aix; James of Vitry; Robert the Monk; Guibert.

class, whose military habits and chivalrous character were well calculated to effect the great object proposed.

In France, Hugh, the brother of King Philip, Robert, Count of Flanders, Stephen, Count of Chartres and Blois, Adhemar, Bishop of Puy, William, Bishop of Orange, Raimond, Count of Toulouse, and many others of the highest station, assumed the Cross, and called together all the knights and retainers that their great names and influence could bring into the field. Robert, Duke of Normandy, son of William the Conqueror of England, accompanied by a number of English barons, prepared also for the crusade. Godfrey of Loraine, and his brothers were added to the number; and Boemond, Prince of Tarento, the valiant son of Robert Guiscard, cast from him the large possessions which his sword and that of his father had conquered, and turned his hopes and expectations towards the east.

The immense multitudes thus assembled are said to have amounted to nearly six millions of souls; [10] and one of the most astonishing proofs of the rapidity with which the news of the crusade must have spread, and the enthusiasm with which it was received, is to be found in the fact, that the council of Clermont was held in the November of the year 1095, and that early in the spring of 1096 a large body of the crusaders was in motion towards Palestine.

The historians of the day are not at all agreed in regard to which was the multitude that led the way towards the Holy Land. It appears [11] almost certain, however, that *Gautier sans avoir*, or Walter the Penniless, a Burgundian gentleman, without fortune, who had assembled a considerable band of the lower classes under the banner of the Cross, was the first who set out in compliance with the general vow. He was, according to all accounts, a complete soldier of fortune, renowned for his poverty even to a proverb, but by no means, as has been asserted, without military fame. All[12] the contemporary writers designate him by his cognomen of poverty; but all at the same time describe him as an illustrious warrior.

Nevertheless, the host that he led was rather an ill-governed crowd of men on foot than an army; and but eight knights accompanied the leader on his expedition. The difficulties of the undertaking were incalculable; and the followers of Walter had provided but little for the

---

10. Fulcher.

11. Albert of Aix; William of Tyre. Mills follows this opinion; Guibert of Nogent and James of Vitry are opposed to it, and Fulcher gives a different account also.

12. Fulcher; Will. Tyr.; Albert Aquen.

necessities of the way. It showed, however, no small skill in that leader to conduct the disorderly rabble by which he was followed, so far as he did in safety.

Passing through Germany [13] he entered into Hungary; where, entangled among the marshes and passes of that kingdom, his whole followers must have perished inevitably, had he not met with the greatest kindness and assistance from the king and people of the country, who, professing the Christian religion, understood and venerated the motives of the crusade.

Thus the host of Walter swept on till their arrival at Semlin, where some stragglers were attacked and plundered by a party of Hungarians less humane than their brethren. The arms and crosses of the crusaders who had thus been despoiled, were fixed upon the walls of the city as a sort of trophy; but Walter, though strongly urged by his followers to seek vengeance for the insult, wisely forbore and passing forward, entered into Bulgaria. Here the champions of the Cross met with no further aid. The people regarded them with jealous suspicion; the cities shut their gates upon them; all commerce was prohibited, and all supplies denied.

Famine now imperiously urged them to violence; and having taken possession of whatever flocks and herds they could find, the crusaders soon found themselves attacked by the Bulgarians, by whom considerable numbers were cut off and destroyed.

Walter himself, with great wisdom[14] and resolution, forced his way through innumerable difficulties, till he had left behind him the inhospitable country of the Bulgarians; and at length brought his army, infinitely wasted by both famine and the sword, to the neighbourhood of Constantinople. Here he obtained permission to refresh his forces, and wait the arrival of Peter the Hermit himself, who followed close upon his steps.

The multitude which had been collected by the Hermit was even of a less uniform and regular description than that which had followed *Gautier sans avoir*. Men, women, and children,—all sexes, ages, and professions,—many and distinct languages—a quantity of baggage and useless encumbrance, rendered the army of Peter as unwieldy and dangerous an engine as ever was put in motion. Notwithstanding its bulk and inconsistency, it also proceeded in safety, and without much reproach, through Germany and Hungary; but at Semlin, the sight of

13. Will. Tyr.
14. Albert of Aix; William of Tyre.

the crosses and vestments which had been stripped from[15] the stragglers of Walter's host roused the anger of the multitude. The town was attacked and taken by assault, with all the acts of savage ferocity which usually follow such an occurrence; and the crusaders, without remorse, gave themselves up to every barbarity that dark and unrestrained passions could suggest.[16]

The news of this event soon reached the King of Hungary; who, calling together a considerable force, marched to avenge the death and pillage of his subjects. His approach instantly caused Peter to decamp from Semlin; but the passage of the Morava was opposed by a tribe of savage Bulgarians: few boats were to be procured; those that were found were of small dimensions; and the rafts that could be hastily constructed were but little manageable in a broad and rapid river. Some of the crusaders thus perished in the water, some fell by the arrows of the enemy; but the tribe that opposed the passage being defeated and put to flight, the rest of Peter's followers were brought over in safety.

The Hermit now, after having sacrificed the prisoners to what was then considered a just resentment, pursued his way to Nissa, in which town the Duke of Bulgaria had fortified himself, having abandoned Belgrade at the approach of the army of the Cross. Finding, however, that Peter did not at all contemplate taking vengeance for the inhospitality shown to *Gautier sans avoir*, the duke wisely permitted his subjects to supply the crusaders with necessaries.

Thus all passed tranquilly under the walls of Nissa, till Peter and his host had absolutely departed, when some German stragglers, remembering a controversy of the night before with one of the Bulgarian merchants, set fire to several mills and houses without the walls of the town.

Enraged at this wanton outrage, the armed people of the city rushed out upon the aggressors, and, not contented with sacrificing them to their fury, fell upon the rear of the Hermit's army, glutted their wrath with the blood of all that opposed them, and carried off the baggage, the women, the children, and all that part of the multitude whose weakness at once caused them to linger behind, and left them without defence.

The moment that Peter heard of this event, he turned back; and, with a degree of calmness and moderation that does high honour

15. Albert of Aix.
16. Guibert.

to his memory, he endeavoured to investigate the cause of the disaster, and conciliate by courtesy and fair words. This negotiation was highly successful; the duke, appeased with the vengeance he had taken, agreed to return the prisoners and the baggage, and everything once more assumed a peaceful aspect; when suddenly, a body of a thousand imprudent men, fancying that they saw an opportunity of seizing on the town, passed the stone bridge, and endeavoured to scale the walls. A general conflict ensued; the ill-disciplined host of the crusaders was defeated and dispersed, and Peter himself, obliged to fly alone, took refuge, like the rest, in the neighbouring forests.

For some time he pursued his way over mountains, [17] and wastes, and precipices; and it may easily be conceived that his heart—so lately elated with honour, and command, and gratified enthusiasm—now felt desolate and crushed, to find the multitude his voice had gathered dispersed or slain, and himself a wandering fugitive in a foreign land, without shelter, protection, or defence. At length, it is said, he met by chance several of his best and most courageous knights at the top of a mountain, where they had assembled with no more than five hundred men, which seemed at first all that remained of his vast army. [18] He caused, however, signals to be made and horns to be sounded in the different parts of the forest, that any of the scattered crusaders within hearing might be brought to one spot.

These and other means which were put in practice to call together the remnants of his army, proved so successful, that before night seven thousand men were collected, and with this force he hastened to march on towards Constantinople. As he went, other bands, which had been separated from him in the confusion of the flight, rejoined him, and the only difficulty, as the host advanced, was to procure the necessaries of life.

The news of Peter's adventures flew before them, and reached even Constantinople. Alexius, the emperor, who had not yet learned to fear the coming of the crusaders, sent deputies to meet the Hermit, and to hasten his journey; and at Philippopoli the eloquent display of his sufferings, which Peter addressed to the assembled people, moved their hearts to compassion and sympathy. The wants of the host were plentifully supplied, and, after reposing for some days in the friendly city, the whole body, now again amounting to thirty thousand men, set out for Constantinople, where they arrived in safety, and joined the troops

17. Albert of Aix.
18. *Ibid.*

which Walter the Penniless had conducted thither previously.

Here they found a considerable number of Lombards and Italians; but these, also, as well as the troops which they had themselves brought thither were not only of the lowest, but of the most disorderly classes of the people. It is no wonder therefore—although Alexius supplied them with money and provisions, and tried to secure to them the repose and comfort that they needed in every respect—that these ruffian adventurers should soon begin to tire of tranquillity and order, and to exercise their old trades of plunder and excess. [19] They overturned palaces, set fire to the public buildings, and stripped even the lead off the roofs of the churches, which they afterward sold to the Greeks from whom they had plundered it.

Horrified by these enormities, [20] the emperor soon found a pretext to hurry them across the Bosphorus, still giving them the humane caution, to wait the arrival of stronger forces, before they attempted to quit Bithynia. Here, however, their barbarous licentiousness soon exceeded all bounds, and Peter the Hermit himself, having lost command over his turbulent followers, returned to Constantinople in despair, upon the pretence of consulting with the emperor on the subject of provisions.[21]

After his departure, the Lombards and Germans separated themselves from the French and Normans, whose crimes and insolence disgusted even their barbarous fellows. *Gautier sans avoir* still continued in command of the French, who remained where Peter had left them; but the Italians [22] and Germans chose for their leader one Renault, or Rinaldo, and, marching on, made themselves masters of a fortress called Exorogorgon, or Xerigord. Here they were attacked by the *sultaun* Soliman, who cut to pieces a large body placed in ambuscade, and then invested the fort, which, being ill supplied with water, he was well aware must surrender before long.

For eight days the besieged underwent tortures too dreadful to be dwelt upon, from the most agonizing thirst. At the end of that time, Rinaldo and his principal companions went over to the Turks, abandoned their religion, and betrayed their brethren. The castle thus

---

19. Guibert.
20. Baldric.
21. Albert of Aix.
22. Guibert of Nogent, lib. ii.; Albert of Aix, lib. i.; Orderic Vital, lib. ix. Mills says it was the French and Normans who thus advanced into the country, but the great majority of writers is against him.

falling into the hands of the *infidels*, the Christians that remained were slaughtered without mercy.

The news of this disaster was soon brought to the French camp, and indignation spread among the crusaders.[23] Some say a desire of vengeance, some a false report of the fall of Nice, caused the French to insist upon hurrying forward towards the Turkish territory. Gautier wisely resisted for some time all the entreaties of his troops, but at length finding them preparing to march without his consent, he put himself at their head, and led them towards Nice. Before reaching that place, he was encountered by the Turkish forces. The battle was fierce, but unequal: Gautier and his knights fought with desperate courage,[24] but all their efforts were vain; the Christians were slaughtered in every direction; and Gautier himself, after having displayed to the last that intrepid valour for which he was renowned, fell under seven mortal wounds.

Not above three thousand Christians effected their escape to Civitot. Here again they were attacked by the Turks, who surrounded the fortress with vast piles of wood, in order to exterminate by fire the few of the crusaders that remained. The besieged, however, watched their moment, and while the wind blew towards the Turkish camp, set fire to the wood themselves, which thus was consumed without injury to them, while many of their enemies were destroyed by the flames.[25]

In the meantime one of the crusaders had made his way to Constantinople, and communicated the news of all these disasters to Peter the Hermit. The unhappy Peter, painfully disappointed, like all those who fix their enthusiasm on the virtues or the prudence of mankind, was driven almost to despair, by the folly and unworthiness of those in whom he had placed his hopes. He nevertheless cast himself at the feet of the emperor Alexius,[26] and besought him, with tears and supplications, to send some forces to deliver the few crusaders who had escaped from the scimitar of the Turks.

The monarch granted his request, and the little garrison of Civitot were brought in safety to Constantinople. After their arrival, however, Alexius ordered them to disperse and return to their own country; and with wise caution bought their arms before he dismissed them;[27]

---

23. Albert of Aix; William of Tyre.
24. Robert the Monk; William of Tyre; Guibert of Nogent; Albert of Aix.
25. Robert the Monk; Guibert of Nogent.
26. William of Tyre; Albert of Aix.
27. Robert the Monk; Guibert of Nogent.

thus at once supplying them with money for their journey, and depriving them of the means of plundering and ravaging his dominions as they went. Most of the historians[28] of that age accuse Alexius of leaguing with the Turks, even at this period, to destroy the crusaders, or, at least, of triumphing in the fall of those very men whom he had himself called to his succour.

The conduct of Alexius in this transaction is not very clear, but it is far from improbable that, fearful of the undisciplined multitude he had brought into his dominions, horrified by their crimes, and indignant at their pillage of his subjects, he beheld them fall by their own folly and the swords of the enemy, without any effort to defend them, or any very disagreeable feeling at their destruction. And indeed, when we remember the actions they did commit within the limits of the Greek Empire, we can hardly wonder at the monarch, if he rejoiced at their punishment, or blame him if he was indifferent to their fate.

Thus ended the great expedition of Peter the Hermit: but several others of a similar unruly character took place previous to the march of those troops, whose discipline, valour, and unity of purpose ensured a more favourable issue to their enterprise. I shall touch but briefly upon these mad and barbarous attempts, as a period of more interest follows.

The body of crusaders which seems to have succeeded immediately to that led by Peter the Hermit was composed almost entirely of Germans, collected together by a priest called Gottschalk.[29] They penetrated into Hungary; but there, giving way to all manner of excesses, they were followed by Carloman, the king of that country, with a powerful army, and having been induced to lay down their arms, that the criminals might be selected and punished, they were slaughtered indiscriminately by the Hungarians, who were not a little glad to take vengeance for the blood shed by the army of Peter at Semlin.

About the same period, immense bands of men and women came forth from almost every country of Europe, with the symbol of the crusade upon their shoulders, and the pretence of serving God upon their lips. They joined together wheresoever they met, and, excited by a foul spirit of fanatical cruelty, mingled with the most infamous moral depravity, proceeded towards the south of Germany. They gave themselves up, we are told,[30] to the pleasures of the table without

28. Robert the Monk; Guibert of Nogent
29. William of Tyre; Albert of Aix.
30. Albert. Aquensis; William of Tyre.

intermission: men and women, and even children, it is said, lived in a state of promiscuous debauchery; and, preceded by a goose and a goat,[31] which, in their mad fanaticism, they declared to be animated by the divine spirit, they marched onward, slaughtering the Jews as they went; and proclaiming that the first duty of Christians was to exterminate the nation which had rejected the Saviour himself. Several of the German bishops bravely opposed them, and endeavoured to protect the unhappy Hebrews; but still, vast multitudes were slain, and many even sought self-destruction rather than encounter the brutality of the fanatics, or abjure their religion.

Glutted with slaughter, the ungodly herd now turned towards Hungary; but at Mersburg they were encountered by a large Hungarian force, which disputed their passage over the Danube, absolutely refusing the road through that kingdom to any future band of crusaders. The fanatics forced their way across the river, attacked Mersburg itself with great fury and perseverance, and succeeded in making a breach in the walls, when suddenly an unaccountable terror seized them—none knew how or why—they abandoned the siege, dispersed in dismay, and fled like scattered deer over the country.

The Hungarians suffered not the opportunity to escape, and pursuing them on every side, smote them during many days with a merciless fury, that nothing but their own dreadful cruelties could palliate. The fields were strewed with dead bodies, the rivers flowed with blood, and the very waters of the Danube are said to have been hidden by the multitude of corpses.

Disaster and death had, sooner or later, overtaken each body of the crusaders that had hitherto, without union or command, set out towards the Holy Land; but each of these very bands had been composed of the refuse and dregs of the people. I do not mean by that word *dregs* the poor, but I mean the base—I do not mean those who were low in station, or even ignorant in mind; but I mean those who were infamous in crime, and brutal in desire. Doubtless, in these expeditions, some fell who were animated by noble motives or excellent zeal; but such were few compared with those whose objects were plunder, licentiousness, and vice.

The swords of the Hungarians and the Turks lopped these away; and I cannot find in my heart to look upon the purification which Europe thus underwent with anything like sorrow. The crusade itself was by this means freed from many a base and unworthy member;

31. Albert of Aix.

70

and chivalry, left to act more in its own spirit, though still participating deeply in the faults and vices of a barbarous age, brought about a nobler epoch and a brighter event.

CHAPTER 5

The Chivalry of Europe Takes the Field

While the undisciplined and barbarous multitudes who first set out were hurrying to destruction, various princes and leaders were engaged, as I have before said, in collecting the Chivalry of Europe under the banner of the Cross. Six distinguished chiefs—Godfrey of Bouillon, Duke of Loraine—Hugh the Great, Count of Vermandois, and brother of Philip, King of France—Robert, Duke of Normandy, brother of William Rufus—Robert, Count of Flanders—Boemond, Prince of Tarentum—and Raimond, Count of Toulouse—conducted six separate armies towards Constantinople: and I propose, in this chapter, to follow each of them till their junction in Bithynia.

It is indeed a pleasure to turn our eyes from scenes of horror and crime to the contemplation of those great and shining qualities—those noble and enthusiastic virtues, which entered into the composition of that rare quintessence, the spirit of chivalry.

Doubtless, in the war which I am about to paint there occurred many things that are to be deeply regretted, as furnishing abundantly that quantity of alloy which is ever, unhappily, mixed with virtue's purest gold: but, at the same time, I now come to speak of men, in many of whom splendid courage, and moral beauty, and religious zeal, and temperate wisdom, and generous magnanimity, combined to form the great and wonderful of this earth's children. Indeed, if ever there was a man who well merited the glorious name of a true knight, that man was Godfrey of Bouillon; and few have described him without becoming poets for that once.

I will not borrow from Tasso—who had the privilege of eulogium—but, in striving to paint the character of the great leader of the crusade, I shall take the words of one of the simplest of the writers of his age, [1] and give them as nearly as possible in their original tone: "He was beautiful in countenance," says Robert the Monk, "tall in stature, agreeable in his discourse, admirable in his morals, and at the same time so gentle, that he seemed better fitted for the monk than for the knight; but when his enemies appeared before him, and the combat approached, his soul became filled with mighty daring; like a lion, he feared not for his person—and what shield, what buckler, could resist the fall of his sword?"

Perhaps of all men of the age, Godfrey of Bouillon was the most distinguished. His mother Ida, daughter of Godfrey, Duke of Loraine, was celebrated for her love of letters, [2] and from her it is probable that Godfrey himself derived that taste for literature, so singular among the warriors of that day. He spoke several languages, excelled in every chivalrous exercise, was calm and deliberate in council, firm and decided in resolution; he was active, clear-sighted, and prudent, while he was cool, frank, and daring; in the battle he was fierce as the lion, but in victory he was moderate and humane.

Though still in his prime of years when the crusades were preached, he was already old in exploits: he had upheld Henry IV. on the imperial throne, had attacked and forced the walls of Rome, and had shone in a hundred fields, where his standard ever was raised upon the side of honour and of virtue.

Long ere the idea of such an enterprise as the crusade became general in Europe, Godfrey had often been heard to declare, when tales were brought him of the miseries of the Holy Land, that he longed to travel to Jerusalem, [3] not with staff and scrip, [4] but with spear and shield; and it may well be conceived that his was one of the first standards raised in the ranks of the Cross. A fever that had hung upon him for some time left him at the tidings, and he felt as if he had shaken off a load of years, and recovered all his youth. [5]

His fame as a leader soon collected an immense number of other barons and knights, who willingly ranged themselves under his banner; and we find that besides Baldwin, his brother[6]—and many other relations—the lords of St. Paul, of Hainault, of Gray, of Toul, of Hache,

1. Robertus Monachus, *lib.* i.
2. Guibert of Nogent.
3. Guibert of Nogent.
4. See Notes 8.
5. Will. Malmsbury.
6. Will. of Tyre; Albert of Aix.

of Conti, and of Montagne, with their knights and retainers, had joined him before the beginning of August,[7] and towards the middle of that month they began their march with all the splendour of chivalry.[8]

The progress of this new body of crusaders was directed, like that of Peter the Hermit, towards Hungary; but the conduct maintained by the followers of Godfrey was as remarkable for its strict discipline, moderation, and order, as that of his predecessors had been for turbulence and excess.[9] The first objects, however, that presented themselves on the Hungarian frontier were the unburied corpses of the fanatic crowd slain near Mersburg.

Here then Godfrey paused during three weeks,[10] investigating calmly the causes of the bloody spectacle before him; after which he wrote to Carloman, king of Hungary; and his letter on this occasion, mingling firmness with moderation, gives a fair picture of his noble and dignified character. Having mentioned the horrible sight which had arrested him in his progress, and the rumours he had heard, he proceeds:—

> However severe may have been the punishment inflicted on our brethren, whose remains lie round about us, if that punishment was merited, our anger shall expire; but if, on the contrary, you have calumniated the innocent, and given them up to death, we will not pass over in silence the murder of the servants of God, but will instantly show ourselves ready to avenge the blood of our brethren.[11]

It was easy for Carloman to prove that the aggression had been on the side of the crusaders; and after various acts of confidence between Godfrey[12] and the king, the army of the Cross was permitted to pass through Hungary, which they accomplished in safety and peace, maintaining the strictest discipline and regularity, and trading with the people of the country with good faith and courtesy. Hence, proceeding through Bulgaria and Thrace, Godfrey led his troops peacefully on to Philippopoli, where he was met by deputies from the emperor, charged with orders to see that the crusaders should be furnished with every kind of necessary provision.

---

7. Albert of Aix.
8. Guibert of Nogent.
9. Guibert; Will. Tyr.
10. Albert of Aix.
11. William of Tyre.
12. Albert of Aix.

In passing through Dacia and Bulgaria, the army of Godfrey had been not a little[13] straitened for food, and it is impossible to say what might have been the consequences, had the same dearth been suffered to continue. The prudent conduct of the emperor did away all cause of violence, and after the arrival of his deputies, the troops of the Cross celebrated his liberality with joy and gratitude.

News soon reached the army [14] of Godfrey, however, which changed their opinion of Alexius, and showed him as the subtle and treacherous being that he really was. To explain what this news consisted of, I must turn for a moment to another party of crusaders, who, while Godfrey pursued his peaceful course through Hungary, marched towards the general meeting-place at Constantinople, by the way of Italy.

Hugh, Count of Vermandois, had assembled an army even superior in number to that of Godfrey of Bouillon, and was himself in every respect calculated to shine at the head of such an armament. He was gallant,[15] brave, handsome, and talented; but the calm and dignified spirit of moderation, which so characterized Godfrey of Bouillon, was wanting in the brother of the French king. Joined to his expedition, though marching in separate bodies, and at distinct times,[16] were the troops of Robert, Duke of Normandy, and Stephen, Count of Blois; with those of Robert, Count of Flanders, in another division.[17]

The count of Vermandois, impetuous and proud, took his departure before his companions, traversed Italy, and embarking at Barri, landed with but a scanty train at Durazzo. His expectations were high, and his

---

13. Albert. Aquensis.
14. Will Tyr.; Albert. Aquens.
15. Guibert.
16. Fulcher; Guibert; Will. Tyr.; Albert.
17. I have taken perhaps more pains than was necessary to investigate this part of the crusaders' proceedings, which I found nearly as much confused in the writings of Mills as in those of the contemporary authors. Some assert that the whole mass of the western crusaders proceeded in one body through Italy; but finding that Fulcher, who accompanied Robert of Normandy and Stephen of Blois, never mentions Hugh of Vermandois; that Guibert speaks of that prince's departure first; that the Archbishop of Tyre marks the divisions distinctly, and that he certainly embarked at a different port in Italy from the rest, I have been led to conclude, that though probably looking up to Hugh as the brother of their sovereign, the three great leaders proceeded separately on their march. Robertus Monachus is evidently mistaken altogether, as he joins the Count of Toulouse with the army of Hugh, when we know from Raimond d'Agiles that that nobleman conducted his troops through Sclavonia.

75

language haughty, supposing he should find in the Greek emperor the same humbled supplicant who had craved, in abject terms, assistance against the infidels from his Christian brethren of the west. But the position of the emperor had now changed. The Turks, occupied with other interests, no longer menaced his frontier. The imperial city slept in peace and splendour; and if he had anything to fear, it was from his own restless and turbulent subjects rather than from his Saracen foes.

Nor, in fact, had he ever been desirous of anything like the expedition that was entering his dominions. He had prayed for aid and assistance to defend his country, but Urban had preached a crusade, and the princes were now in arms to reconquer the Christian territories in Asia, as well as to protect those of Europe. He had gladly heard of the crusade, and willingly consented to it, it is true, as he well knew it would afford a mighty diversion in his favour, but he then dreamed not of the armed millions that were now swarming towards his capital. His position, too, had changed, as I have said, and he immediately determined upon a line of policy well suited to the weak subtlety of his character.

Alexius was one of those men whose minds are not of sufficient scope to view life as a whole, and who therefore have not one great object in their deeds; who act for the petty interests of the moment, and whose cunning, compared with the talents of a really great mind, is like the skill of a fencing-master compared with the genius of a great general. He saw not, and felt not, the vast ultimate benefit which he might receive from maintaining a dignified friendship with the princes commanding the crusade. He did not perceive what an immense and powerful engine was placed, if he chose it, at his disposition.—In his narrow selfishness, he only beheld a temporary danger from the great forces that were approaching, and he strove to diminish them by every base and petty artifice. He did not endeavour to make himself great by their means, but he tried to bring them down to his own littleness. It is true, that on some occasions he showed feelings of liberality and humanity; but from his general conduct it is but fair to infer that these were the inconsistencies of selfishness; and that though he was sometimes prudent enough to be liberal, he was not wise enough to be uniformly generous.

On the arrival of Hugh at Durazzo, he was at first received with respect, and entertained with honour and profusion; and thus finding himself at ease, he was induced to remain for a time in confident security. Suddenly, however, without a pretence for such violence, he was arrested, together with his train, and sent to Constantinople, some authors say, *in chains.*[18]

Nevertheless, it is not probable that Alexius dared to carry his inhospitality so far; and one of the historians [19] of the day particularly marks, that the prisoner was treated with every testimony of respect. Guibert also ventures a supposition respecting the motives of Alexius, far superior to the general steril course of ancient chronicles. He imagines—and I wonder that the idea has not been adopted by any one—that the object of the Greek emperor, in confining Hugh, was to obtain from him, before the other princes should arrive, that act of homage which he intended to exact from all. The brother of the king of France himself having taken the oath, would be so strong a precedent, that it is more than probable, Alexius [20] fancied the rest of the crusaders would easily agree to do that which their superior in rank had done previous to their arrival.

At Philippopoli[21] the news of Hugh's imprisonment reached the army of Godfrey de Bouillon, and with the prompt but prudent firmness of that great leader's character, he instantly sent messengers to Alexius, demanding the immediate liberation of the Count of Vermandois and his companions, accompanying the message with a threat of hostilities, if the demand were not conceded.

Godfrey then marched on to Adrianople,[22] where he was met by his deputies, bringing the refusal of the emperor to comply with his request: in consequence of which the country was instantly given up to pillage; and so signal were the effects of this sort of vengeance, that Alexius speedily found himself forced to put his prisoners at liberty. The moment that a promise to this effect was received, Godfrey recalled his forces; and with wonderful discipline and subordination, they instantly abandoned the ravages they were before licensed to commit, and marched on peacefully towards Constantinople. Had the armies of the Cross continued to show such obedience and moderation, Palestine would now have been Christian.

In the neighbourhood of the imperial city Godfrey pitched his tents, and the innumerable[23] multitude of his steel-clad warriors struck

---

18. Albert of Aix; William of Tyre.
19. Guibert.
20. *Ibid. lib.* ii.
21. Will. Tyr. *lib.* ii.
22. Albert of Aix; William of Tyre.
23. Albert of Aix.

terror into the heart of the fearful monarch of the east.[24] To the Count of Vermandois, however, it was a sight of joy; and issuing forth from Constantinople with his friends and followers, he galloped forward to the immense camp of the crusaders, where, casting himself into the arms of Godfrey,[25] he gave himself up to such transports of delight and gratitude, that the bystanders were moved to tears.

The emperor now turned the whole force of his artful mind to wring from Godfrey an act of homage, and for several weeks he continued, by every sort of fluctuating baseness, to disturb his repose, and to irritate his followers. At one time, he was all professions of kindness and liberality; at another, he breathed nothing but warfare and opposition. Sometimes the markets were shut to the crusaders, sometimes the private stores of the emperor himself were opened.

At length, after having twice defeated the bands of plunderers sent by Alexius to attack him,[26] Godfrey gave way to his wrath, and for six days successively ravaged the country round Constantinople with fire and sword. Alexius on this again changed his conduct, and with every profession of regard demanded an interview with the chief of the crusaders, offering his son as a hostage for his good faith. With this safeguard Godfrey, followed by several other noble knights, entered Constantinople, and proceeded to the imperial palace, clothed in his robes of peace,[27] and bearing purple and ermine and gold, instead of the iron panoply of war.[28]

The great leader was received by the emperor with the highest

---

24. Guibert.
25. Albert of Aix; Robertus Monachus; Will. Tyr.
26. Will. Tyr.; Rob. Mon.; Guibert; Albert. Aquens.
27. Albert of Aix.
28. Mills, in speaking of this interview, does not distinguish between the coat-of-arms and the mantle or *pallium*. They were, however, very different, and never, that I know of, worn together. The coat-of-arms was usually extremely small; and the form may be gathered from the anecdote of an ancient baron, who, not readily finding his coat-of-arms, seized the cloth of a banner, made a slit in the centre with his sword, and passing his head through the aperture, thus went to battle. These customs however often changed, and we find many instances of the coat-of-arms being worn long. The mantle was the garb of peace, and was even more richly decorated than the coat-of-arms. Another peaceful habiliment was the common surcoat, which differed totally from the tunic worn over the armour, having large sleeves and cuffs, as we find from the notes upon Joinville. The size of this garment may be very nearly ascertained from the same account, which mentions 736 ermines having been used in one surcoat worn by the king of France. See Joinville by Ducange. For the use of the *pallium*, or mantle, see St. Palaye—notes on the Fourth Part.

distinction, was honoured with the kiss of peace, and underwent that curious ceremony of an adoption of honour (as it was then called) as son to the emperor. [29] He was clothed with imperial robes, [30] and the monarch, calling him his son, nominally placed his empire at Godfrey's disposal. In return for the distinctions he had received—and probably pressed by Hugh, Count of Vermandois, who loved not to stand alone, in having yielded homage to Alexius—Godfrey consented to give the emperor his hand, according to the feudal forms of France, and to declare himself his liegeman.

His fears dissipated by this concession, and his hopes of winning the princes who were to follow, by so illustrious an example, raised to the highest pitch, Alexius loaded Godfrey and his followers with magnificent presents, and suffered them to depart. Peace was now permitted to remain unbroken; and after having refreshed themselves for some days, the army of the crusaders passed the Hellespont, and encamped at Chalcedon, [31] to wait the arrival of their brethren.

It is more than probable that Godfrey was induced to quit the original place of rendezvous by the solicitations of Alexius, who took care, it has been since observed, to guard his capital from the presence of any two of the crusading hosts at one time.

Boemond, prince of Tarentum, and son of the famous Guiscard, had quitted Italy shortly after the departure of Godfrey from Loraine. Various tales are told of the manner in which he first declared his purpose of joining the crusade. Some have asserted, that on hearing of the expedition, while engaged in the siege of Amalfi, he dashed his armour to pieces with his battle-axe, [32] and caused it to be formed into small crosses, which he distributed among his soldiery. Others reduce

---

29. I have not chosen to represent this interview in the colours with which Mills has painted it. The princess Anna, from whom he took his view of the subject, can in no degree be depended upon. Her object was to represent her father as a dignified monarch, receiving with cold pomp a train of barbarous warriors; but the truth was, that Alexius was in no slight measure terrified at Godfrey and his host, and sought by every means to cajole him into compliance with his wishes. Almost every other historian declares that the crusaders were received with the utmost condescension and courtesy. Robert of Paris, one of Godfrey's noble followers, did indeed seat himself on the throne of Alexius, and replied to Baldwin's remonstrance by a braggart boast, for which the emperor only reproved him by a contemptuous sneer. This, however, would, if anything, prove that the pride and haughtiness was on the part of the crusaders rather than on that of the imperial court.
30. Albert of Aix; William of Tyre.
31. Albert of Aix.
32. Vertot.

the anecdote to a less chivalrous but perhaps more civilized degree of energy, and state, that he caused his mantle to be cut into crosses for his troops.[33]

As many relate the tale, it is likely to have had some foundation; and there is no doubt that Boemond abandoned all his vast possessions in Italy, with the reserve only of Tarentum, and devoted himself to the wars of the Cross. His presence might have proved more generally advantageous to the cause, had he not, by this enthusiastic renunciation, given himself other motives in the warfare before him, besides those of religion and humanity. He had naturally in his veins quite sufficient of the blood of Guiscard to require no additional stimulus to the desire of conquering for himself. He was nevertheless one of the best soldiers of the Cross, so far as military skill availed—bold, powerful, keen, and active; and possessing that sort of shrewd and even wily art, which, joined with his other qualities, formed an enterprising and successful leader, more perhaps than a distinguished knight.

With him, however, came the noblest of all the Christian Chivalry, Tancred—whose valour, generosity, enthusiasm, and courtesy have been the theme of so many a song—of whom Tasso, in seeking to describe him in the highest language of poetry, could say nothing more than truth,

> *Vien poi Tancredi, e non è alcun fra tanti*
> *Tranne Rinaldo—O feritor maggiore,*
> *O più bel di maniere e di sembianti*
> *O più eccelso ed entrepido di core.*[34]

Few characters can be conceived more opposed to each other than those of the relations,[35] Tancred and Boemond; and yet we find Tancred willingly serving in the army of the Prince of Tarentum, as second to that chief. The same unambitious modesty is to be discovered throughout the whole history of the young knight; and though we ever behold him opposed to meannesses, by whomsoever they may be adopted, we still see him willing to take upon himself the danger and labour of an inferior station.

Under the banners of these chiefs marched a host of Italian and

---

33. Robert the Monk.

34. *Gerusalemme, cant.* i.

35. What the relationship exactly was I have not been able to discover. Mills does not satisfy me that the mother of Tancred was the sister of Robert Guiscard. The expressions of Ralph of Caen on the subject appear to be obscure.

Norman nobles; the army, it is said, amounting to ten thousand horse,[36] and an immense multitude of foot, in which view of the forces we must remember that only men of noble birth were usually admitted to fight on horseback.[37] These troops were even increased as they marched to the seacoast of Apulia; and the great body of those Normans who, not a century before, had taken complete possession of the country, now left it for the Holy Land.

Mills,[38] following his particular theory, supposes Urban the pope to smile with triumphant self-gratulation on seeing the army of Boemond depart; but it seems strange, that the prelate should rejoice in the absence of the very men by whom he had been always protected, while his enemies remained, and were even in possession of the old church of St. Peter[39] at Rome, as we learn by a contemporary crusader.

The forces of Boemond and Tancred landed at Durazzo, and made their way, with much more regularity than could have been expected, through Epirus.[40] They were harassed, however, on their march by various skirmishes with the Greek troops, who did everything in their power to destroy the crusading army, although Alexius[41] had sent messengers to Boemond himself congratulating him on his arrival, and promising every kind of assistance. These attacks, nevertheless, only amounted to a petty degree of annoyance, till the host of the Cross came to the passage of the Axius. Here, a part of the forces having traversed the river with almost the whole of the cavalry, the rear of the army was suddenly attacked by an infinitely superior body of Greeks.[42]

Tancred, already on the other side, lost not a moment, but, spurring his horse into the water, followed by about two thousand knights, he charged the Greeks so vigorously as to drive them back with considerable loss in killed and prisoners. When brought before Boemond, the captives justified themselves by avouching the commands of the emperor, and Tancred would fain have pursued and exterminated the forces of the perfidious Greek. Boemond, however, more prudently forbore, and, without retaliation of any kind, advanced to Adrianople.

36. Albert of Aix.
37. St. Palaye.
38. Mills, chap. 3.
39. Fulcher.
40. Raoul de Caen.
41. William of Tyre.
42. Raoul de Caen; William of Tyre; Albert of Aix; Guibert.

I see no reason to qualify this moderation as subtilty, which Mills has not scrupled to do. Boemond was artful beyond all doubt, but this was not a fair instance of anything but wisdom and self-command. At Adrianople, well knowing the character of Alexius, to whom he had frequently been opposed, and foreseeing that his troops might be irritated by various acts of annoyance,[43] Boemond drew up his army, and, in a calm and temperate speech, represented to them that they had taken up arms in the cause of Christ, and therefore that it was their duty to refrain from all acts of hostility towards their fellow-Christians.

Shortly after this, the Prince of Tarentum was met by deputies from the emperor, inviting him to come on with all speed to Constantinople, leaving his army behind, under the command of Tancred. Boemond at first refused to trust himself in the power of his ancient enemy,[44] but Godfrey of Bouillon having visited him in person, and guarantied his security, the Italian chief agreed to the arrangement proposed, and accompanied the Duke of Loraine to the imperial palace. Gold and dominion were always motives of great force with the mind of Boemond, and Alexius did not spare such temptations, either present or to come, for the purpose of inducing the Prince of Tarentum to do homage to the eastern empire.

His promises were limitless, and the actual presents[45] which he heaped upon the Normo-Italian immense. He also granted him, it is said, a territory in Romania, consisting, in length, of as much ground as a horse could travel in fifteen days; and, in breadth,[46] of as much as could be traversed in eight; besides which, he loaded him with jewels and gold, and rich vestments, till Boemond, from one of his most inveterate enemies, became one of his firmest allies. This, indeed, proceeded from no confidence or friendship on either side. Boemond still felt how little Alexius could forgive the injuries he had in former days inflicted, and dared not trust himself to eat of the meat set before him at the emperor's table.

Alexius, with all the penetration of his race, evidently dived into the Norman's thoughts, and saw that he aspired even to the imperial crown itself.[47] No reliance, therefore, existed between them; but,

---

43. Orderic. *Vital. lib.* ix.

44. Boemond had inherited all his father's hatred to the Greek sovereigns, and had waged many a bloody and successful war against Alexius himself.

45. Will. Tyr.; Albert. *Aquens*

46. Raoul de Caen; Guibert.

47. Alexiad par Ducange.

on the one hand, Boemond, for considerations of interest, forgot his dignity, and did homage to the emperor, while Alexius, on his part, agreed that the homage should be void, if the promises he made were not exactly fulfilled.[48]

The news of his relation's humiliation soon reached Tancred, who was leading on their united forces towards Constantinople; and though unquestionably, the lamentation attributed to him by his biographer[49] is somewhat more poetical than real, little doubt can be entertained that the gallant prince was painfully struck by Boemond's disgraceful concessions. Hugh of Vermandois had done homage to obtain his liberty; Godfrey of Bouillon, to restore peace and unanimity between the Christian emperor and the crusaders; Boemond *sold* his homage, with no palliating circumstance.

The determination of Tancred seems to have been taken almost immediately on hearing this news, and marching upon Constantinople as if it were his intention to follow exactly the course of his relation, he suddenly crossed the Hellespont[50] without giving notice to any one, and joined the army of Godfrey at Chalcedon.[51]

This conduct greatly irritated Alexius, and he made several efforts to bring Tancred back without success; but the arrival of Raimond de St. Gilles, Count of Toulouse, with the immense army of the Languedocian crusaders, soon called the attention of the emperor in another direction. The Count of Toulouse has been very variously represented, and no doubt can exist that he was a bold and skilful leader, a courageous and resolute man. He was, it is said, intolerant and tenacious of reverence, fond of pomp and display, and withal revengeful, though his revenge was always of a bold and open character. Not so his avarice, which led him to commit as many pitiful meannesses as ever sprang from that basest of desires. He was proud, too, beyond all question; but where his covetousness did not overbalance the other great principle

---

48. Guibert, lib. iii.
49. Radulph. Cad. cap. 11.
50. Radulph. Cadom. cap. 12.
51. Albertus Aquensis says that Tancred took with him the whole army. William of Tyre follows the same opinion, as well as Guibert. Orderic Vital declares that when the troops were passing, Tancred dressed himself as a common soldier, and passed among the crowd; but Radulphus Cadomensis (or Raoul of Caen, as the French translate his name), who was his companion and friend in after-years, makes no mention of his having taken with him any part of the forces he commanded, merely stating, that in his eagerness to pass before he was discovered, he aided to row the boat himself.

of his nature, he maintained, in his general conduct, that line of moral firmness which dignifies pride, and raises it almost to a virtue.

Under the banners of the Count of Toulouse marched the gay chivalry of all the south of France—Gascons, and Provençals, and Auvergnats—people, in whose hearts the memory of Saracen invasions from Spain was still fresh; and whose quick and passionate dispositions had at once embraced with enthusiasm the holy war. A glorious train of lords and knights followed their noble chief, and the legate of the pope, as well as several other bishops, gave religious dignity to this body of the crusaders.

The count directed his course by Sclavonia towards Greece, notwithstanding that the season was unfavourable, as he set out in winter.[52] During the journey he displayed, in the highest degree, every quality of a great commander. Innumerable difficulties, on which we cannot pause, assailed him even during the first part of his march through the barren and inhospitable passes which lay between his own fair land and Greece. When he had reached the dominions of Alexius, whose call for aid he had not forgotten, the count imagined, to use the words of his chaplain, that he was in his native land, so much did he rely upon the welcome and protection of the Greek emperor. But he, like the chiefs who had preceded him, was deceived, and the same series of harassing persecutions awaited him on the way. An act of seasonable[53] but barbarous vengeance, however, in mutilating and disfiguring several of the prisoners, so much frightened the savage hordes which the emperor had cast upon his track, that the rest of the journey passed in comparative tranquillity. Like those who had gone before, the count was permitted to enter the imperial city with but few attendants.

Here the same proposal of rendering homage was made to Raimond which had been addressed to the other leaders of the crusade, but he rejected it at once with dignified indignation, and maintained his resolution with unalterable firmness.[54] The means which had been tried with Godfrey of Bouillon were now employed against the Count of Toulouse; and as no very strong body of crusaders was soon expected from Europe, the emperor seems confidently to have anticipated the destruction of the Languedocian force. The Bosphorus lay between it and the armies of Godfrey, of Hugh, of Boemond, and of

---

52. Raimond d'Agiles.

53. *Ibid.*

54. Raimond d'Agiles; Will. Tyr.; Guibert.

84

Robert of Flanders,[55] whose arrival we have not thought it necessary to dwell upon, as it was accompanied by no circumstance of interest. Alexius had taken especial care, that no vessels should remain on the other side of the Straits, which would facilitate the return of the crusaders even if they should wish it, [56] and Boemond was devoted to his cause from motives of interest.

Under these circumstances Alexius did not scruple to order a night attack to be made upon the camp of the French knights. At first it proved successful, and many fell under the treacherous sword of the Greeks. At length, however, the Languedocians recovered from their surprise, repulsed the enemy with great loss, and for some time gave full way to their indignation. Raimond even resolved to declare war against the emperor, but abandoned his intention on finding that the other princes would not succour him, and that Boemond threatened to join his arms to those of Alexius. Thus upheld, the emperor still continued to insist on the homage of the count; but Raimond declared that he would sooner lay down his head upon the block than yield to such an indignity.[57] He said:—[58]

> He had come to fight for one Lord, which was Christ, and for him he had abandoned country, and goods, and lands, but no other lord would he acknowledge; though, if the emperor would, in person, lead the host towards Constantinople, he would willingly put himself and his troops under his august command.

All that could ultimately be obtained from him, even at the intercession of his companions in arms, was a vow that he would neither directly nor indirectly do any act which could militate against the life or honour of the emperor.[59]

This concession, however, seemed to satisfy Alexius, upon whose weakness the ambitious spirit of Boemond was pressing somewhat too hard. The power of Raimond of Toulouse, the monarch saw, might be used as a good counterpoise to the authority which the Prince of Tarentum was inclined to assume; and in consequence, Alexius soon completely changed his conduct, and loaded the count with distinctions and courtesy. The pleasures of the imperial palace, the rivalry

55. Guibert; Albert of Aix.
56. Will. Tyr.
57. Guibert.
58. Raimond d'Agiles.
59. Guibert; Raimond; Will Tyr.

which the artful emperor contrived to raise up between him and Boemond, and the false but polished society of the Greek court, excited and pleased the Count of Toulouse, who remained sometime in the midst of pomp and enjoyment.

His character, also, though it had much of the steady firmness of the north, had, in common with that of his countrymen in general, a sparkling and vivacious urbanity, a splendid yet easy grace, which suited the taste of the Greeks much more than the simple manners of the northern crusaders. Indeed, to judge from the terms in which she speaks of him, his handsome person and elegant deportment seem to have made no small impression on the imagination of the princess Anna,[60] although Raimond had already passed the middle age.

Boemond, however, had by this time departed, and had marched from Chalcedon with Godfrey and the rest of the crusading host [61] towards Nice, the capital of the Turkish kingdom of Roum. [62] His honour demanded the presence of the Count of Toulouse, and abandoning the pleasures of Constantinople, he superintended the embarkation of his troops, and hastened to join the rest of his companions in arms.

Scarcely had the forces of the count quitted Constantinople, when another army appeared under the walls of that city. Its principal leader was Robert, Duke of Normandy—a man, debauched, weak, and unstable; endowed with sufficient talents to have dignified his illustrious station, had he possessed that rare quality of mind which may be called *conduct.* He was eloquent in speech, brave in the field, skilful in warlike dispositions, and personally humane, even to excess;[63] but at the same time he was versatile as the winds, and so easily persuaded, that the common expression, *he had no will of his own,* was, perhaps, more applicable to him than to any other man that ever existed.

On the first preaching of the crusade, he had caught the flame of enthusiasm with others, and perhaps not more than those around him; for we must not take the immediate sale of his dutchy of Normandy to William Rufus as a proof of his zeal. It was, in fact, but a proof of

---

60. Alexiad.
61. Raimond d'Agiles; Albert of Aix.
62. Raimond d'Agiles expressly states that the army of the Count of Toulouse, which he accompanied to the Holy Land, did not join the other crusaders till they were under the walls of Nice. Mills is therefore wrong in writing that the Provençals joined the other soldiers of the Cross before their arrival at Nice, and then let them march on again before them.
63. Guibert, lib. ii.

that wretched facility which ultimately brought about his ruin. The price he obtained,[64] was only ten thousand *marks* of silver, but with so petty a sum this modern Esau thought he could conquer worlds. With him was Stephen, Count of Blois, more famous in the council than the field,[65] while all the Norman and English crusaders of rank, together with Eustace, brother of Godfrey of Bouillon,[66] joined themselves to his forces.

Thus, followed by a numerous and well-equipped army, Robert took the way of Italy, and having encountered the pope at Lucca, proceeded to Apulia, where he remained to pass the winter. Here, however,[67] many deserted his army, and returned to their native land, and several were drowned, subsequently, in their passage to Durazzo; but, on the whole, the march of Robert of Normandy was more easy and less disastrous than that of any other chief of the crusaders.

We find no mention of any attack or annoyance on the part of Alexius; and, on the arrival of the Norman host at Constantinople, the oath of homage seems to have been presented and received, with a sort of quiet indifference well according with the indolent and careless character of the duke. [68] Alexius simply informed the leaders, that Godfrey, Boemond, Hugh, and the rest had undergone the ceremony proposed. "We are not greater than they,"[69] replied Robert, and the vows were taken without hesitation.

Loaded with presents, and supplied with money and provisions, of both which Robert stood in great want, the Norman crusaders now passed the Hellespont, and marched towards Nice to join their companions. The timid Alexius thus found himself delivered from the last body of these terrific allies; and, indeed, the description given of their arrival, in rapid succession, before Constantinople, is not at all unlike the end of Camaralzaman's history in the *Arabian Nights,* where no sooner is one army disposed of, than another is seen advancing towards the city from a different quarter of the globe.

---

64. Orderic Vital.
65. Guibert.
66. William of Tyre; Albert of Aix.
67. Fulcher.
68. Albert of Aix; Fulcher.
69. Will. Tyr.

CHAPTER 6

Germ of After-Misfortunes Already Springing Up in the Crusade

One of the most unfortunate events which occurred to the crusaders in their march was their stay at Constantinople, for it was the remote but certain cause of many other evils. The jealousies and differences raised up among them by the intriguing spirit of Alexius were never entirely done away; and besides this, the intervention of petty motives, long discussions, and schemes of individual aggrandizement chilled the fervour of zeal, and thus weighed down the most energetic spring of the enterprise.

Enthusiasm will conquer difficulties, confront danger and death, and change the very nature of the circumstances in which it is placed, to encouragement and hope; but it will not bear to be mingled with less elevated feelings and considerations. The common ambitions and passions of life, cold reasonings, and thoughtful debates, deaden it and put it out; and amid the intrigues of interest, or the speculations of selfishness, it is extinguished like a flame in the foul air of a vault. A great deal of the enthusiasm of the crusade died away amid the bickerings of Constantinople; and even the cowardly effeminacy of the Greeks proved in some degree contagious, for the army of the Count of Toulouse, we find, had at one time nearly disbanded itself. The luxury of the most luxurious court of Europe, too, was not without its effect upon the crusaders, and the memory of the delights of the imperial city was more likely to afford subjects of disadvantageous comparisons, when opposed to the hardships of Palestine, than the remembrance of the turbulent and governless realm from which they had first begun their march.

The greatest misfortune of all, however—the cause of many of their vices, and almost all their miseries,—was the want of one acknowl-edged leader, whom it would have been treason to disobey. Each chief was his own king, but he was not the king of even those who served under him. Many who had followed his banner to the field were nearly his equals in power, and it was only over his immediate vassals that he had any but conditional right of command. In respect to his vassals themselves, this right was much affected by circumstances; and over the chiefs around him, he had no control whatever. Thus, unity of design was never to be obtained; and discord, the fatal stumbling block of all great undertakings, was always ready in the way, whenever the folly, the passions, or the selfishness of any individual leader chose to dash upon it the hopes of himself and his companions.

Nevertheless, during the siege of Nice, which was the first under-taking of the crusaders, a considerable degree of harmony seems to have prevailed among the leaders. Each, it is true, conducted his part of the attack according to his own principles, but each seemed happy to assist the other, and we hear of no wrangling for idle punctilios. The morals, too, of the troops were hitherto pure, reaching a much higher point of virtue, indeed, than might have been anticipated from the great mixture of classes. I do not mean to say that they were free from vice, or were exempt from the follies of their nature or their age; but the noble and dignified manner in which the chiefs of the crusade, and the people in general, bore the conduct of Alexius (mentioned hereafter), would lead me to believe that they had preserved a consid-erable share of purity and singleness of heart.

The first body of the crusaders which reached the city of Nice was that led by Godfrey of Bouillon. He was not alone, however, being ac-companied by Hugh, Count of Vermandois; and very shortly after, the troops of Robert of Flanders and Boemond of Tarentum arrived, and took up their position on the northern side, while those of Godfrey had marked their camp towards the east. The Count of Toulouse and the Bishop of Puy followed, and sat down before the southern side,[1] leaving the west open for the Duke of Normandy, who was expected from day to day.[2]

---

1. Raimond d'Agiles; Guibert.
2. All authors, those who were present as well as those who wrote from the accounts of others, differ entirely among themselves concerning the dispositions of the siege. Fulcher, who accompanied the Duke of Normandy, says that that chief attacked the south; Raimond of Agiles, who was present also, says that the south was the post of the Count of Toulouse. I have, however, adopted the account of Raimond, who ap-pears to me to have paid more attention to the operations of the war than Fulcher.

This city, the capital of the kingdom of Roum, was occupied by the Seljukian Turks, and strongly defended by a solid wall, flanked by three hundred and fifty towers. It was situated in the midst of a fertile plain, and the waters of the lake Ascanius, to the west, gave it a facility of communication with a large extent of country. The army of the crusaders, after the arrival of the Count of Toulouse,[3] waited not the coming of Robert of Normandy, but began the siege in form. Their forces were already immense; and after the junction of Peter the Hermit with the ruins of his multitude, and the Duke of Normandy with his powerful army, the amount of the fighting men is said to have been six hundred thousand, without comprising those who did not carry arms.[4] The number of knights[5] is stated to have reached nearly two hundred thousand, which left a fair proportion of inferior soldiers.

The general disposition of the troops had been made before the arrival of the Count of Toulouse, and he marched his division towards the spot assigned him on the Sunday after Ascension-day.[6] His coming, however, was destined to be signalized by the first regular battle between the Turks and their Christian invaders.

Soliman, or Kilidge Aslan, the Sultaun of Roum, on the approach of the crusaders, had left his capital[7] defended by a strong garrison, and travelling through his dominions, hastened in every direction the levies of his subjects. He soon collected a considerable body of horse, [8] and leading them to the mountains which overlooked the plain of Nice, he sent down two messengers to the city to concert with the governor a double attack upon the camp of the Christians.

The messengers fell into the hands of the outposts of Godfrey. One was killed on the spot, and the other, under the fear of death, betrayed the secrets of the *sultaun*, giving at the same time an exaggerated account of his forces.[9] Information of Soliman's approach was instantly sent to Raimond of Toulouse, who was advancing from Nicomedia,[10]

3. Fulcher.

4. *Ibid.*

5. The word used is *loricati*; and Ducange, who seldom makes a positive assertion without the most perfect certainty, states, in the observations on Joinville, that we may always translate the word *loricatus*, a knight, "*et quand on voit dans les auteurs Latins le terme de loricati il se doit entendre des Chevaliers.*"—*Ducange, Observ. sur l'Hist. de St. Louis.*

6. Guibert.

7. Albert of Aix, lib. ii.

8. Albert.

9. *Ibid.*

10. Albert; Raimond d'Agiles; Guibert.

and by a night-march he succeeded in joining the army of the Cross in time. Scarcely had he taken up his position, when the Moslems began to descend from the mountains, clad like the Christians in steel,[11] and borne by horses fleet as the wind. Divided into two bodies,[12] the one attacked the wearied troops of the Count of Toulouse, seeking to force its way into the city, while the other fell upon the quarters of Godfrey of Bouillon.

Doubtless Soliman thought to meet, in the immense multitude before him, a wild and undisciplined crowd, like that of Peter the Hermit; but he soon found bitterly his mistake. The crusaders received him everywhere with chivalric valour, repulsed him on all points, became in turn the assailants, and the plain round Nice grew one general scene of conflict. The charging of the cavalry, the ringing of the lances and the swords upon shields and corslets, the battle-cries of the Christians, and the *techbir* of the Turks; the shouts, the screams, the groans, rose up, we are told, in a roar horrible to hear.[13]

At length, finding that the sally he had expected was not made, Soliman retreated to the mountains; but it was only to repeat the attempt the following day.[14] In this, although the besieged now comprehended his intention, and issued forth upon the Christians on the one side, while he attacked them on the other, he was not more fortunate than before. He was again repelled with great loss, owning his astonishment at the lion-like courage of the Christian leaders, who with a thousand lances would often charge and put to flight twenty times the number of Turkish horsemen.

According to a barbarous custom prevalent at that time, and which even descended to a much later period, the crusaders hewed off the heads of the fallen Moslems,[15] and cast many of them into the city. Others were sent to Constantinople in token of victory; and Alexius, as a sign of gratitude and rejoicing, instantly despatched large presents to the principal chiefs of the crusade, with great quantities of provisions for the army, which had long been straitened to a fearful degree.

After the defeat of Soliman,[16] the siege was pressed with renewed vigour; and battering-rams, catapults, and *mangonels* were plied inces-

---

11. Albert.
12. Raimond.
13. Albert.
14. Guibert.
15. Guibert; Albert of Aix.
16. Raimond d'Agiles; Fulcher; Albert of Aix; Robert. Mon.

santly against the walls, while moveable towers of wood, called *beffroys*, filled with armed men, were rolled close to the fortifications, for the purpose of carrying on the fight hand to hand with the enemy, and of endeavouring to effect a lodgement on the battlements.

In the meanwhile, the plains round Nice offered a spectacle of the most extraordinary brilliancy. The glittering arms of the knights, their painted shields, and fluttering pennons—the embroidered banners of the barons, their splendid coats-of-arms and magnificent mantles— the gorgeous robes of the Latin priests, who were present in immense numbers, and the animated multitude of bowmen and foot-soldiers, mingled with thousands of that most beautiful of beasts, the horse, all spread out in the unclouded brightness of an Asiatic sky, formed as shining and extraordinary a scene as the eye could look upon.

Not frightened, however, by the terrific splendour that surrounded them, the Turks continued to defend their battlements with persevering valour. Every attack of the Christians was met with dauntless intrepidity, and every laboured attempt to sap the wall, or its towers, was frustrated with unwearied assiduity. Those who approached near were either slain by poisoned arrows,[17] or crushed under immense stones; and the moment any one was killed at the foot of the wall, [18] "it was horrible to see the Turks," says an eyewitness, "seize upon the body with iron hooks let down from above, and lifting it up through the air strip it completely, and then cast it out from the city." Innumerable artifices were resorted to by the assailants to force their way into the town; and none of the chiefs seem to have been more active and ingenious than the Count of Toulouse,[19] who once succeeded in undermining a tower, and casting it to the ground. Before this work was concluded, however, night had fallen over the army, and ere the next morning the laborious activity of the Turks had repaired the damage which their wall had suffered.

Two of the principal[20] German barons, also, contrived a machine of wood, to which they gave the name of *the fox*. It was capable of containing twenty knights, and was secured by its immense solidity from all the efforts of the enemy. When this was completed, a vast multitude began to push it towards the part of the curtain which they intended to sap, but the inequality of the ground and the great weight

---

17. Robert. Mon.
18. Fulcher.
19. Guibert; Raimond d'Agiles.
20. Albert of Aix.

of the machine itself caused some of the joints to give way, when the whole fabric fell to pieces, crushing under its ruins the unhappy knights within.

The arrival[21] of Robert of Normandy brought a vast accession of strength to the besiegers; notwithstanding which, during the remainder of the siege of Nice, the immense numbers of the crusaders did not produce that scarcity of provision which ultimately fell upon them; for Alexius, interested more than anyone in the capture of the city, took care, after the first few days, that the supplies should be ample and unremitted.

Nevertheless the courage of the garrison did not at all decrease, and for five weeks they still continued to return the assailants combat for combat, the whole day being consumed in a storm of arrows from the bows and arbalists, and of stones from the catapults and *mangonels*.[22]

Numerous instances of extraordinary personal courage, shown on both sides, are of course recorded, and each different historian has his own hero, whose deeds are lauded to the sky. One Turk in particular signalized himself by an immense slaughter of the crusaders, showing himself exposed upon the battlements, and plying his terrible bow, which winged death in every direction. The Christians became so fearful of him, that that most imaginative passion, terror, began to invest him with some supernatural defence.[23] The best-aimed arrows proved totally ineffectual, and reports spread rapidly that he might be seen, still sending destruction around from his hand, while twenty shafts—each carrying the fate of a common mortal—were sticking unheeded in his flesh. Godfrey of Bouillon, to end the panic that this man occasioned, at length took a crossbow himself, though that machine [24] was considered but a fit weapon for a yeoman, and directing the quarry with a steadier hand than those which had before aimed at the Turkish archer, he sent the missile directly to his heart.[25]

A multitude of the noblest crusaders had now fallen before the bows of the enemy, and many more had yielded to the effects of a climate totally different from their own. "Thus," says one of the followers of the Cross, "nothing was to be seen on the highways, in the woods, and the fields, but a crowd of tombs, [26] where our brethren had been buried."

---

21. Fulcher.
22. Idun; Albert of Aix.
23. Albert of Aix.
24. The Philippide.
25. Albert of Aix.
26. Fulcher.

At last, the leaders perceived the existence of a circumstance, their neglect of which, in the very first instance, showed how much the art of warfare was then in its infancy. One evening, after a fierce assault, the soldiers stationed near the water, who, in common with the rest of the host, usually rested from the labours of the siege during the night, suddenly perceived boats upon the lake Ascanius, and it immediately became evident that the Turks received every kind of supply by this easy means of communication. As soon as this was discovered, various vessels were brought from Constantinople, and being drawn to the lake over a narrow neck of land which separated it from the sea, were filled with imperial archers;[27] and the blockade of the town was thus rendered absolute. This was executed during the night, and all hope abandoned the Turks from the next morning, when they beheld that which had proved their great resource suddenly cut off.

The crusaders now hoped to force the city to surrender at discretion; and their expectations of such an event were much raised by the fact of the *sultauness*, the wife of Soliman, who had hitherto courageously undergone all the miseries and dangers of a siege, being taken in endeavouring to make her escape by the lake.[28]

By this time the besieged had determined to surrender; but Alexius had taken care to send with the army of the Cross an officer on whose art and fidelity he could depend, to secure for the imperial crown a city which he would probably have rather seen still under the dominion of the Turks, than in the hands of the Latins.

This man's name was Taticius, or, according to the crusaders' corruption, Tatin.[29] His face was dreadfully mutilated, and his mind seems to have been as horrible as his countenance. What communication he kept up within the town it is difficult to discover; and how this communication was concealed from the Latins is hardly known, but probably it took place, as Mills conjectures, by means of the lake and the Greek vessels which now covered it. Certain it is, that the Turks entered into a private treaty with the emissary of Alexius, who granted them the most advantageous terms, securing to them not only life,[30] but immunity and protection.

It had been covenanted beforehand, between the emperor and the crusaders, that on the fall of the city it should be resigned to Alexius,

27. Raimond d'Agiles; Albert of Aix; Guibert.
28. Will. Tyr.
29. Albert of Aix.
30. Guibert; Albert.

who promised to give up to the troops all the riches it contained,[31] and to found there a monastery, and an hospital for pilgrims, under the superintendence of the Latins.[32] Not contented with this, or doubting the faith of his allies, he took the means I have stated to secure possession. Suddenly the imperial ensigns appeared upon the walls of Nice, when the host of the crusade was just rushing to the attack in the full confidence of victory. It was now found that the people of the city had surrendered privately to Alexius, and had admitted his troops within the walls; but it required the greatest efforts of the leaders of the crusade, although disgusted with this treachery themselves, to quiet their forces, and reconcile them to the perfidy of their base ally.[33]

On the part of the Christians, the wife and children of Kilidge Aslan, who had fallen into their hands, were delivered to the Turks; and, at the same time, all those prisoners which had been taken by Soliman, on the defeat of *Gautier sans avoir*, were restored to liberty. So little, however, did Alexius keep his treaty with the crusaders, that, instead of yielding to them the whole plunder of Nice, he contented himself with distributing some rich presents to the chiefs,[34] and some money to the poor of the army; and suffered them, thus dissatisfied and injured, to raise their camp and march on towards Jerusalem, without permitting them to set foot within the city they had conquered.[35]

The army of the Cross waited no time under the walls of Nice, but as soon as the principal leaders had returned from Pelicanum, whither they had gone once more to confer with Alexius, it began its march.[36] At the end of the second day the forces of the different chiefs [37] were accidentally separated, [38] Boemond and the Duke of Normandy tak-

---

31. William of Tyre; Raimond.
32. Raimond de Agiles.
33. William of Tyre; Raimond de Agiles; Guibert de Nogent.
34. Fulcher, cap. 4; William of Tyre.
35. Ten at a time were admitted within the walls, but not more.
36. June 29, *A. D.* 1097.
37. Fulcher, cap. 5; Raimond d'Agiles; Orderic Vital; Raoul de Caen.
38. Mills avers that the chiefs separated by mutual consent. I have found nothing to confirm this opinion. Radulphus says that there was a rumour to that effect, but shows that it could not be just, as the baggage of the troops of Boemond and his party had, by the error that separated them, been left with the other division. William of Tyre leaves the question undecided. Fulcher says, absolutely, that the separation originated in a mistake. Orderic Vital follows the same opinion. Raimond d'Agiles is not precise, but he says that it was done inconsiderately; and Guibert decidedly affirms that it was accidental, and through the obscurity of the morning in which they began their march.

ing a path considerably to the left of that followed by Godfrey and the rest of the host. They proceeded on their way, notwithstanding, knowing that they could not be very far from the principal body, and towards night pitched their camp in the valley of Gorgon, in the midst of some rich meadows, and near a running stream.[39]

Their situation was, nevertheless, not near so desirable as they imagined, for Soliman, who during the siege of Nice had made the most immense efforts for the purpose of relieving that city, now that it had fallen, hung with the whole of his force,[40] to the amount of nearly two hundred thousand men,[41] upon the left flank of the army of the crusaders, concealing his own evolutions by his perfect knowledge of the country, and watching those of his enemies with the keen anxiety of a falcon hovering over her prey. No sooner had the separation we have mentioned taken place in the host of the Cross, than the *sultaun* hastened his march to overtake the army of Boemond, which was infinitely the weaker of the two divisions.

Accustomed to every sort of rapid movement, Soliman soon came up with the forces of the Prince of Tarentum and the Duke of Normandy.

The crusaders had been from time to time warned, during the preceding day, that an enemy was in the neighbourhood, by the sight of scattered parties of Arabs hovering round their army.[42] They nevertheless encamped by the side of a beautiful stream, that, flowing on through the rich valley in which they were advancing, proceeded to join itself to the waters of the Sangarius. Here they passed the night in repose, taking merely the precaution of throwing out sentinels to the banks of the stream. Early the next morning, Boemond and Robert again commenced their march, and had advanced some way,[43] when the immense army of Soliman began to appear upon the hills.

Boemond instantly sent off messengers to Godfrey of Bouillon, and the rest of his noble companions, of whose proximity he had now become aware, and gave orders for drawing up his forces, for pitching the tents, and for making a rampart of the wagons [44] and baggage for the defence of the sick and the weak from the arrows of the Turks. In

39. William of Tyre.
40. Fulcher; Raimond d'Agiles; Albert.
41. Fulcher makes it amount to nearly three hundred and sixty thousand combatants; and Raimond reduces the number to one hundred and fifty thousand.
42. Fulcher.
43. *Ibid*; Guibert.
44. William of Tyre; Guibert; Fulcher, cap. 5.

the meanwhile, turning to his knights and men at arms, he addressed them with the brief eloquence of courage. "Remember the duties of your calling!" he exclaimed. "Behold the peril in which you are placed—charge boldly to meet the infidels—defend your honour and your lives!"

While he spoke, the Turks rushed down to the battle with terrific cries,[45] which, mingling with the tramp of two hundred thousand horse, and the ringing of their armour, together with the trumpets of the Christian host, and the shouts of the chiefs and the heralds, raised so fearful a din, that no one could hear another speak among the followers of the Cross.

The army of Boemond, hastily drawn up, presented a mingled front of horse and foot soldiers, and pilgrims,[46] some but half-armed, some not armed at all; while the Turks came down in one torrent of cavalry. The immense numbers which it contained all blazing with glittering arms, and provided with bows of horn and scimitars, dazzled and dismayed the troops of the Christians. As the *infidels* approached, the European Chivalry dropped the points of their long lances, and prepared to hurl back their foes, as was their wont, by the heavy and decided charge which proved always so effective; but suddenly, each Moslem raised his bow even as he galloped forward, [47] a thick cloud seemed to come over the sun, and then, two hundred thousand arrows dropping at once among the crusaders, a multitude [48] of men and horses were instantly stretched upon the plain.

Before the Christians could rally from the surprise, a second flight of arrows followed the first, doing dreadful execution among the foot-soldiers and the steeds of the knights.[49] But now Tancred and Boemond led on their troops to the charge, and spurred their horses into the midst of the enemy. The Turks, as was their habit, yielded ground on every side, avoiding, by the swiftness of their chargers, the lances and the swords of the Christians, and, like the Parthians of old, continuing their fearful archery even as they fled.

Vain were all the efforts of the European Chivalry, though, throwing away their useless spears, they endeavoured to reach the Turks with their swords;[50] but now, in turn, the swarming multitudes of their foes,

45. Guibert; Will. of Tyr.
46. Fulcher; Radulph. Cad. cap. 21.
47. William of Tyre; Guibert; Fulcher.
48. Fulcher, cap. 5; William of Tyre.
49. William of Tyre.
50. Raoul of Caen.

pouring down fresh from the mountains on every side, no longer re-treated, but pressed closer and closer upon them; and as each adversary fell beneath the vigorous blows of the knights, new foes started up to meet them.

In the meanwhile, thick and fast was mown the flower of the Christian army. The brother of Tancred, famed alike for his beauty and his courage, was slain before the eyes of his relation.[51] Tancred himself, surrounded by a thousand enemies, fought as if Fate had put the weapon in his hands, but fought in vain. Boemond, with all his efforts, could scarcely extricate his gallant cousin from the torrent of adversaries in the midst of which he struggled, and even then it was with the loss of the banner of Otranto.[52]

Borne back by the growing multitude that pressed upon them, the knights gave way before the Saracens, and were driven struggling upon the very pikes[53] of the foot-soldiers that were advancing to their sup-port. At the same time Soliman, whose numbers gave him the means of surrounding the army of the crusaders, directed several large bodies of his cavalry through some marshes to the rear of the Christians, and in a moment the camp[54] of Boemond was invaded and deluged with the blood of the old, the women, and the helpless![55]

Robert of Normandy, however, who had commanded the reserve, now beholding the flight of his allies, roused all the courage of his heart; and uncovering his head in the midst of the fray, shouted forth his battle-cry[56] of "Normandy! Normandy! Whither fly you Boe-mond?" he exclaimed; "Your Apulia is afar! Where go you Tancred? Otranto is not near you! Turn! turn upon the enemy! God wills it! God wills it!" And seizing his banner, he spurred on with his follow-ers against the Turks, drove them back, rallied the cavalry, and restored

51. Albert; Raoul of Caen; William of Tyre.
52. Albert.
53. Raoul of Caen.
54. Fulcher; Albert; Raoul of Caen.
55. Albert of Aix informs us, that the ladies of Boemond's camp, seeing the merciless fury with which the Turks were dealing death to all ages and sexes, clothed them-selves in their most becoming garments, and strove to display their charms to the best advantage, for the purpose of obtaining the durance of the harem rather than the grave. Albert was not present, and did not even visit the Holy Land; and I find his account in this respect confirmed by no other historian. The good canon, in-deed, was somewhat fond of little tales of scandal, so that I feel inclined to doubt his authority, where such matters are under discussion. He has an anecdote in a similar style appended to his history of the taking of Nice.
56. Radulphus, cap. 22.

order and regularity to the defence.

Boemond, in the meanwhile, had turned his arms towards the camp; and the Turks had retreated from that quarter of the field, bearing with them all that was valuable, and a considerable number of prisoners. The army of the crusade was now concentrated on one spot, while that of the Turks, surrounding it on all sides, gave it not a moment's repose. Soldier fell beside soldier, knight beside knight.[57] Fatigue and thirst rendered those that remained little capable of defence; and the dust and the hot sun made many of the wounds mortal, which otherwise would have been slight in comparison. In this conjuncture,[58] the women that remained proved infinitely serviceable, bringing to the troops water from the river, and by prayers and exhortations encouraging them to the fight.

Thus lasted the battle for many hours, when first a cloud of dust, rising from behind the hills, announced that some new combatants were hurrying to the field. Then rose above the slope banner, and pennon, and lance, and glittering arms, while the red cross fluttering on the wind brought hope and joy to the sinking hearts of the crusaders, and terror and dismay to the victorious Turks.[59] In scattered bands, spurring on their horses as for life, came the chivalry of the west to the aid of their brother Christians. None waited for the others; but each hastened to the fight as the fleetness of his charger would permit, and rank after rank, troop after troop, banner followed by banner, and spear glittering after spear, came rushing over the mountains to the valley of the battle. "God wills it! God wills it!" echoed from hill to hill.[60]

Robert of Normandy shouted his war-cry, Boemond, with renewed hope, couched his lance, and Tancred rushed upon the slayers of his brother.

At the same time[61] Godfrey of Bouillon arrayed his army as they came up, and, with levelled lances, drove down upon the Turks. Hugh of Vermandois attacked them on the flank, and Raimond of Toulouse, with the warlike bishop of Puy, soon increased the forces of the Cross.

The Turks[62] still made great and valorous efforts to maintain the superiority they had gained, but the charge of the Latin Chivalry was

57. William of Tyre.
58. Orderic Vital; Guibert
59. Albert of Aix; Fulcher, cap. 5; William of Tyre.
60. Radulph. Cadom. cap. 26.
61. Fulcher; Albert of Aix.
62. Albert; Radulphus Cadomachus, cap. 27, 28, *et seq.*; William of Tyre.

irresistible. The *infidels* were driven back, compelled to fly in disorder, and pursued over the mountains by the victorious crusaders.[63] In the hills the Christians, who followed hard upon their course, discovered the camp of the Saracens, where immense booty, both in gold and provisions,[64] became the recompense of their exertions. Here, also, they found all the prisoners who had been taken in the first part of the battle, and a great number of beasts of burthen, of which they were themselves in great need. Among the rest was a multitude of camels, an animal which few of the Franks had ever seen before. These were all brought to the Christian encampment, and rejoicing succeeded the fatigues and horrors of the day.

The loss of the crusaders, after so long and severe a battle, if we can depend upon the account generally given, was very much less than might have been anticipated. Only four thousand men[65] are supposed to have fallen on the part of the Christians; these were principally, also, of the inferior classes, who, unprotected by the armour which defended the persons of the knights, were fully exposed to the arrows of the Turks.

Three men of great note, among the champions of the Cross, were added to this list of killed[66]—William, the brother of Tancred; Geoffrey of Mount Scabius; and Robert of Paris, whose conduct at the court of Alexius we have before mentioned. The loss on the part of the Turks was infinitely more considerable, and thus, at the close of the Battle of Dorylœum, the Christian leaders found that they had marked their progress towards the Holy Land by a great and decisive victory.

The crusading armies now paused for several days,[67] enjoying the repose and comfort which the spot afforded, and which their exhausted troops so much required. The wounds of the soldiers who had suffered in the late battle were thus in some degree healed; and the abundance of provisions the enemy had left behind served to renovate the strength and raise up the hopes and enthusiasm of the Chris-

---

63. Many of the Christians attributed their victory to the miraculous interposition of two canonised martyrs, who, in glittering armour, led on the army of Godfrey and the count of Toulouse, and scared the Turks more than all the lancers of the crusaders. Though the supposed interposition of such personages certainly robbed the leaders of no small share of glory, yet it gave vast confidence and enthusiasm to the inferior classes.

64. Albert of Aix; Fulcher; Guibert.

65. William of Tyre.

66. Guibert; William of Tyre; Albert of Aix.

67. Albert of Aix.

tians. In the meanwhile, the Turks, who had survived their defeat at Dorylœum, spread themselves in large bands over the country, and, pretending to have totally overcome the Latins, forced themselves into the cities, destroying and wasting everything in their way.[68]

The Christians thus, in their march through Phrygia, had to cross a large tract which had been completely ravaged by the enemy. With their usual improvidence, they had exhausted the provisions they had found in their adversary's camp; and ignorant of the country, they had provided themselves with no water, so that they had to encounter all the heat of the solstitial days of a Phrygian climate, without a drop of liquid to allay their burning thirst. Men and horses fell by thousands in the way;[69] and the women, parched with drought, and dying with fatigue, forgot delicacy, feeling, and even the ties of human nature—rolled prostrate on the ground with the agony of thirst—offered their naked bosoms to the swords of the soldiers, and prayed for death—or threw down their new-born children in the track of the army, and abandoned them to a slow and miserable fate!

The most terrible mortality prevailed among the beasts of burden, so that the animals accustomed to bear the baggage of the host having nearly all died by the way, dogs and oxen, and even hogs,[70] are said to have been loaded with the lighter articles of necessity, while an immense quantity of luggage was cast away on the road. Many falcons and dogs—a part of knightly equipage never forgotten—had been brought from Europe to Asia; but the dogs, spreading their nostrils in vain to the hot wind for the least breath of moisture, left the long-accustomed hand that they were wont to love, and straying through the desolate land, died among the mountains; while the clear eye of the noble falcon withered under the fiery sky, which nothing but a vulture could endure; and, after long privation, he dropped from the glove that held him.[71]

At length water was discovered, and the whole army rushed forward to the river. Their intemperate eagerness[72] rendered the means of relief nearly as destructive as the thirst which they had endured, and many were added to the victims of that horrible march by their own imprudent indulgence in the cool blessing that they had found

---

68. Guibert, lib. iii.
69. Albert of Aix, lib. iii.; William of Tyre.
70. Fulcher; Guibert.
71. Albert.
72. *Ibid.*

at last. The country now had changed its aspect, and nothing presented itself but splendid fertility till the host of the crusade reached the city of Antiochetta, where, surrounded by rivulets, and forests, and rich pastures, they pitched their tents, determined to enjoy the earthly paradise that spread around them.

Some of the warriors, however, whose energetic spirit no fatigues could daunt [73] or subdue, soon tired of the idle sweets of Antiochetta[74] and voluntarily separated themselves from the army, seeking either renown or profit, by detached enterprises. Tancred on the one hand, with the Prince of Salernum, and several other nobles, five hundred knights, and a party of foot-soldiers, set out from the army of Boemond, to explore the country, and ascertain the strength of the enemies by which they were surrounded. Detaching himself, at the same time, from the division of Godfrey of Bouillon, Baldwin, the brother of that leader, joined Tancred with a somewhat superior force, actuated probably more by the hope of his own individual aggrandizement, than by any purpose of serving the general cause of the crusade.

After wandering for some time through the districts round Iconium and Heraclea,[75] which the Turks had taken care to desolate beforehand, the two chieftains again separated, and Tancred, pursuing his way by Cilicia, came suddenly before Tarsus. The Turks, by whom that city was garrisoned, knowing that the greater part of the populace was opposed to them, surrendered almost immediately on the approach of the Christian leader, and while he encamped with his forces under the walls, waiting, according to stipulation, for the arrival of Boemond, his banner was hoisted upon the towers of the town.[76] Scarcely had this been done when Baldwin also appeared, and at first, the two armies, each conceiving the other to be an enemy, prepared to give one an-

<hr>

73. Radulph. Cadom. cap. 33; Guibert. lib. iii.; Will. Tyr.

74. All the authors of the day that I have been able to meet with declare this expedition of Baldwin and Tancred to have been voluntary. Mills only, as far as I can discover, attributes their conduct to an order received from others. I mark the circumstance more particularly, because, under my view of the case, the fact of Tancred and his companions having separated themselves from the rest of the host, after such immense fatigues, abandoning repose and comfort, and seeking new dangers and fresh privations, is one of the most extraordinary instances on record of the effect of the chivalrous spirit of the age. Under this point of view, all the historians of that time saw the enterprise which they have recorded; but Mills, writing in the least chivalrous of all epochs, has reduced the whole to a corporal-like obedience of orders.

75. Albert of Aix, lib. iii.; Radulph. cap. 37.

76. Albert of Aix, lib. iii.; Guibert; Will. Tyr.

other battle.

The mistake was soon discovered, and Tancred welcomed his comrade in arms to Tarsus. The feelings of Baldwin, however, were less chivalric than those of the noble chief of Otranto, and the banner of Tancred flying on the walls of Tarsus was an object that he could not long endure. After passing a day or two in apparent amity, he suddenly demanded possession of the city, declaring, that as he led the superior force, he was entitled to command. Tancred scoffed at the absurd pretence, and both parties had nearly betaken themselves to arms.[77] The noble moderation of the Italian leader brought about a temporary reconciliation. He agreed that the people of the city themselves should be referred to, and choose the chief to whom they would submit. This was accordingly done, and the inhabitants instantly fixed upon the knight to whom they had first surrendered.[78]

But Baldwin was yet unsatisfied; and after having made a proposal to sack and pillage the town, which was rejected with scorn and abhorrence by his more generous fellow-soldier, he caballed with the citizens and the Turks, till he won them to throw down Tancred's banner, and yield themselves to him. Mortified, indignant, even enraged, the steady purpose of right within the bosom of the chief of Otranto maintained him still in that undeviating course of rectitude which he had always pursued; and, resolved not to imbrue a sword drawn for honour and religion in the blood of his fellow-Christians,[79] he withdrew his forces from before Tarsus, and turned his arms against Mamistra. The Turks here, more bold than those of the former city, beheld his approach unawed, and held out the town for several days, till at length it fell by storm, and the victorious chief planted his banner on those walls with far more honourable glory than that which surrounded the standard of Baldwin at Tarsus.

In the meanwhile, another body of crusaders, detached from the troops of Boemond, arrived before the city in which Baldwin had established himself, and demanded entrance, or at least assistance and provisions. Baldwin[80] cruelly caused the gates to be shut upon them; and had it not been for the charitable care of some of the Christian inhabitants, who let them down wine and food from the walls, they would have been left to expire of want. A fate hardly better awaited them. The

77. Radulphus, cap. 38.
78. Albert of Aix; Guibert, lib. iii.
79. Radulphus; Albert of Aix; Guibert of Nogent.
80. Albert. lib. iii.

Turks had still, by their capitulation, maintained possession of several of the towers of Tarsus, but fearful of the superior force of Baldwin, they sought but a fair opportunity to escape without pursuit.

The very night that the detachment of which I have spoken above arrived, the Turks carried their intentions into effect,[81] and finding a small body of Christians sleeping under the walls without defence, they made the massacre of the whole the first step in their flight. The soldiers of Baldwin and the citizens of Tarsus, who had together witnessed, with indignation, the barbarous conduct of the French chieftain, now rose in absolute revolt. [82] Baldwin, however, having remained in concealment for a few days, contrived to pacify his followers, and to overawe the city. After this he joined himself to a band of piratical adventurers, who about that time arrived accidentally at Tarsus, and who, mingling their lust of prey with some dark and superstitious notions of religion, had turned their course towards the Holy Land, in the pleasant hope of serving both God and Mammon with the sword.[83] With these Baldwin continued to ravage Cilicia, and at length approaching Mamistra, in which Tancred had established himself, he pitched his tents upon the immediate territory of that city.

Tancred now gave way to his indignation, and issuing forth, though accompanied by very inferior forces, he attacked Baldwin sword in hand, when a fierce engagement ensued between the two Christian armies. The struggle was severe but short: the superior numbers of the French prevailed, and Tancred was forced to retreat into the city. On one side, the Prince of Salernum was made prisoner by Baldwin,[84] and on the other, Gilbert of Montclar was taken; but the next day, shame for their unchristian dissensions took possession of each chief. Peace was agreed upon; they embraced in sight of the two hosts; the captives were exchanged, and, as usual, Satan got the credit of the dispute. Baldwin proceeded, after this, to join the main army, and left his piratical associates to aid Tancred in laying waste the country.

During these events the great body of the crusade had remained for some time at Antiochetta, where the people continued to acquire new health and strength, in the enjoyment of that tranquillity and abundance which had been so long withheld from them. Not so the chiefs, two of whom[85]—and those of the most distinguished—had

---

81. Albert.
82. *Ibid.*
83. Albert; Raoul de Caen. See also Fulcher, who was chaplain to Baldwin.
84. Albert of Aix; Raoul of Caen.

nearly, in this period of repose and peace, found that death which they had so often dared in the midst of battle and hardship.

Godfrey of Bouillon, in delivering a pilgrim from the attack of a huge[86] bear in the woods of Antiochetta, had almost fallen a victim to his chivalrous courage: he received so many wounds, that even after having slain his ferocious adversary, he could not drag himself from the forest to the camp; and remained long and dangerously ill in consequence. At the same time, the Count of Toulouse was seized with a violent fever, which brought him to the brink of the grave. He was taken from his bed and laid upon the ground—as was customary among the pilgrims at the hour of death, that they might expire with all humility—and the Bishop of Orange administered the last sacraments of the church:[87] but a certain Count of Saxe, who accompanied the army, came to visit the leader of the Provençals, and told him that St. Giles (the patron saint of the Counts of Toulouse) had twice appeared to him in a dream, assuring him that so valuable a life should be spared to the crusaders.

Whether from the effect of that most excellent medicine, hope, or from a natural turn in his disease, the count suddenly began to recover, and before long was sufficiently well to accompany the army in a litter. The chiefs of the crusade now directed their march towards Antioch, suffering not a little from the desolate state of the country, which, devastated on every side by the Turks, afforded no means of supplying the immense multitude that followed the standard of the Cross. After passing Iconium and Heraclea, their fatigues were destined to increase rather than diminish. Their road now lay through uninhabited wilds, which Robert the Monk describes in language at once picturesque and terrific.[88] Says he:—

> They travelled with deplorable suffering through mountains where no path was to be found except the paths of reptiles and savage beasts, and where the passages afforded no more space than just sufficient to place one foot before the other, in tracks shut in between rocks and thorny bushes. The depths of the precipices seemed to sink down to the centre of the earth, while the summits of the mountains appeared to rise up to the firmament. The knights and men-at-arms walked forward with

85. Albert of Aix; William of Tyre; Raimond d'Agiles.
86. Albert of Aix; William of Tyre.
87. Raimond d'Agiles.
88. Robert. Mon. lib. iii. Albert of Aix; Guibert.

uncertain steps, the armour being slung over their shoulders, and each of them acting as a foot-soldier, for none dared mount his horse. Many would willingly have sold their helmets, their breastplates, or their shields, had they found any one to buy, and some, wearied out, cast down their arms, to walk more lightly. No loaded horses could pass, and the men were obliged to carry the whole burdens. None could stop or sit down: none could aid his companion, except where the one who came behind might sometimes help the person before him, though those that preceded could hardly turn the head towards those that followed. Nevertheless, having traversed these horrible paths, or rather these pathless wildernesses, they arrived at length at the city named Marasia, the inhabitants of which received them with joy and respect.

At Marasch the host was rejoined by Baldwin, whose wife died a few days before his arrival. His brother Godfrey, [89] too, was still suffering from the effects of his combat with the wild beast, and all the chiefs of the crusade, indignant at his conduct at Tarsus, gave him but a chilling and gloomy reception. [90] The spirit of individual aggrandizement was still the strongest passion in the breast of Baldwin, and the coldness of his companions in arms yielded him no great encouragement to stay and employ his efforts for the general object of the expedition, rather than for the purposes of his own selfish ambition. He very soon abandoned the rest of the chiefs, contriving to seduce two hundred knights, and a large party of foot-soldiers, to join him; and as his course was thenceforth separate from the rest of the crusaders, I shall follow the example of Guibert, and briefly trace it out, till it falls again into the general stream of events.

Accompanied by Pancrates,[91] an Armenian, who painted in glowing colours the wealth of the provinces on the other side of the Euphrates,[92] and the facility with which they might be conquered, he set out with the vague hope of plundering something and overcoming someone, he knew not well what or whom. However, his skill as a commander was certain to find matter on which to exercise itself, in a country possessed by an active enemy, while his rapacious propensities were very likely to be gratified in a rich and plentiful land, where the

89. Albert of Aix.
90. William of Tyre.
91. Albert of Aix.
92. The population of these countries was in general Christian.

many were oppressed by the few. Turbessel[93] and Ravendel fell immediately into his hands, and were at first placed under the command of his companion, Pancrates; but beginning to suspect that personage, he forced him to deliver up the cities, by imprisonment, torture, and a threat of having him torn limb from limb.[94]

He then passed onward, crossed the Euphrates, and at the invitation of Thoros, sovereign of Edessa, entered that city, to free it from the power of the Turks. Thoros, a weak and childless old man, was driven by the inhabitants—who were terrified at their *infidel* neighbours, and had no confidence in their feeble monarch—to adopt the brother of Godfrey, with all the curious ceremonies then practised on such occasions. He passed his own shirt over Baldwin's shoulders,[95] pressed him to his naked breast, and publicly declared him his son.[96]

The transactions that followed are very obscure, and as I have not been able to satisfy myself in regard to the share which Baldwin had in the tumults that succeeded, and the death of Thoros, I will but state the facts, without attempting to trace them to secret causes, which are now hidden in the dark tabernacle of the past. Something we know— Baldwin was ambitious, unscrupulous, intriguing, cruel—and shortly after his arrival, the people of Edessa rose against their unhappy prince, slew him, and elected Baldwin in his place. It does not absolutely appear that Baldwin was the instigator of these riots, or the prompter of the death of Thoros; but it does appear that he did not exert himself as he might have done to put them down. That it was in his power to suppress them is evinced by the rapidity with which he reduced the Edessians[97] to the most submissive obedience, immediately that the rank for which he had to contend was his own. He afterward proceeded to aggrandize his dominions, by attacking various of the neighbouring cities, and thus, in continual struggles, he passed his days, till some time after his companions in arms had completed their conquest of the Holy Land.

In the meanwhile, Tancred took possession of the whole country as far as the town of Alexandretta, in the Gulf of Ajasse; and the great army of the crusade continued its march, throwing forward Robert of Flanders to seize on Artesia.[98] The Mahommedan soldiery prepared to resist; but

---

93. Fulcher; Albert.
94. Albert; Guibert, lib. iii.
95. Guibert.
96. Albert.
97. Guibert, lib. iii.; where see the manner in which Baldwin contrived to subjugate the inhabitants.

the Armenian inhabitants opened the gates to their Christian deliverers, and the *infidels* were massacred without mercy. On the news of this event, Baghasian, the commander of the Turkish garrison of Antioch, apparently not knowing the immediate proximity of the whole Christian force, endeavoured to cut off, by stratagem, the small army of the Count of Flanders, who was accompanied by only one thousand knights.

For this purpose the Turk advanced from Antioch,[99] followed by nearly twenty thousand horsemen, whom he placed in ambush in a plain near the city, while he himself, at the head of a petty detachment, armed alone with bows of horn,[100] advanced as if to reconnoitre the Christian troops. Robert of Flanders and his knights suffered themselves to be deceived, and charged the enemy, who fled before them, but in a moment they were surrounded by immensely superior numbers, who, with terrific cries, rushed on, to what appeared a certain victory. The gallantry [101]and courage of the Christian warriors served to deliver them from the danger into which the excess of that very courage had brought them, and charging the Turks with vigour in one decided direction, they succeeded in cutting their way through, and effecting their retreat to the city.

Here, however, they were besieged by the enemy; but the arrival of Tancred, on his return from his victorious expedition, together with reinforcements from the main army, relieved them from the presence of the Turks, who retreated upon Antioch.

---

98. Albert of Aix.
99. Guibert.
100. Albert.
101. Mills declares, that the Christians were rescued from this ambuscade by the arrival of Tancred. I find the account of Albert of Aix totally opposed to such a statement; while the passage in Raoul of Caen relating to this event is so full of errors in other respects, that no reliance could be placed upon it, even if it justified the assertion of Mills, which, however, it does not do. He states, that Tancred arrived long before the ambuscade, and that he found Baldwin at Artesia. By this he might mean Baldwin de Bourg, who, after the other Baldwin became King of Jerusalem, was also created Count of Edessa; but this interpretation cannot be admitted here, as he mentions the former disputes between the soldiers of Tancred and of the Baldwin to whom he refers, and who could therefore be none other than the brother of Godfrey, who was, we know, in Edessa at the time. We may therefore conclude, that as a principal part of this account is notoriously false, Raoul of Caen cannot be considered as any authority, so far as this event is concerned. Finding the statement of Tancred's assistance here not confirmed by any other good authority, I have abided by the account of Albert.

CHAPTER 7

The Host of the Crusade Invests Antioch

The army now began to approach towards Antioch; and it was evident, that the task which the champions of the Cross had undertaken was becoming more and more difficult, as it drew near its consummation. The host was proceeding further and further from all resources; its enemies were gathering strength and falling back upon fresh supplies; multitudes of the invaders had died, and others were each day joining the dead: little hope of fresh reinforcements could be entertained, and the flame of enthusiasm was waxing dim, while fatigue, privation, and continual anxiety were gradually bringing disgust to the enterprise.

The council of leaders,[1] well aware of the increasing dangers, now issued orders that in future no party whatever should absent itself from the main body; and all considerable detachments having rejoined it, they marched on to the valley of the Orontes. Over that river a stone bridge of nine arches was the only passage: this was strongly fortified, and closed with doors plated with iron, from which circumstance it had received the name of the iron-bridge. The Turks defended this formidable position with great valour against Robert, Duke of Normandy, who commanded the advance guard of the crusading army; but on the arrival of Godfrey and the other forces, the bridge was carried, the river passed, and Antioch invested.

In the vast plain situated at the foot of the mountains,[2] the Orontes wanders on towards the sea, skirting, during a part of its course, the steep boundary which closes in the plain of Antioch from the south. On one of the bendings of the river was situated the town of

1. Albert of Aix.
2. Raimond d'Agiles.

Antioch, which, climbing up the hills, took within the embrace of its massy walls three high peaks of the mountain, one of which standing towards the north is separated from the others by a steep precipice, and was then crowned by a high and almost impregnable citadel.[3] The town itself, which extended in length two miles, was so strongly fortified by art and nature, that none of the active means then known seemed likely to take it by assault.

The walls of the city were not absolutely washed by the Orontes; for between them and that river was a space of level ground, the breadth of which Raimond d'Agiles estimates at an arrow's flight; but, as the river turned in its course, it approached nearer to the town, and an antique bridge,[4] which the crusaders at first neglected to secure, gave infinite facility to the Turks, both in annoying their adversaries, and in procuring supplies. On the other side, spreading from the river to the foot of the mountains, was a marsh supplied constantly by some fresh springs. Over this also was thrown a bridge, which equally remained in the hands of the *infidels*.

The encampment of the crusaders was conducted without any degree of military science.[5] Various points were left open and unguarded; each chief seemed to choose his own situation, and form his own plan of attack; and the most scandalous waste and profusion from the very first laid the foundation of after want and misery.

Such were the obstacles which impeded the progress of the forces of the Cross, and which might, ultimately have rendered all their efforts abortive, had not other circumstances arisen to bring about an event that their own skill and conduct would never have accomplished. It is not necessary here to describe the position of the several leaders: suffice it, that Tatin, as he is called by the writers of that day, the commander of the troops of Alexius, took up his station in a spot detached from the rest. Three hundred thousand men capable of bearing arms,[6] sat down under the walls of Antioch; and such a profusion of provisions was found, even for this immense multitude, that the greater part of each animal slaughtered was wasted, the crusaders in the wantonness of luxury refusing to eat any but particular parts of the beast.[7]

---

3. Will. Tyr., Raimond.
4. Albert of Aix.
5. Raimond; Guibert of Nogent.
6. Raimond; Albert says six hundred thousand; Guibert of Nogent.
7. Raimond.

Such was the formidable appearance of the city, however, that a council was held to consider whether it would be advisable to attack it at once, or, remaining beneath the walls, to wait and see if famine would spare the work of the sword, or spring bring fresh resources to the besiegers. This opinion was soon negatived, and the attack began; but the walls of Antioch resisted all efforts. Every means then known was employed by the crusaders to batter the heavy masonry of those mighty bulwarks, but in vain. Moveable towers, and catapults, and mangonels, and battering-rams, were all used ineffectually; while the besieged, in a variety of sallies, harassed night and day the Christian camp, and destroyed many of the assailants.

The consequences [8] of their first improvidence were soon bitterly visited on the heads of the crusaders. Famine began to spread in the camp; and pestilential diseases, engendered by unwholesome food and the neighbourhood of a large tract of marshy land, in the autumn and winter seasons, raged through the hosts of the Cross, and slew more fearfully even than the arrows of the enemy. Death in every shape grew familiar to their eyes, and the thought of passing to another world lost all the salutary horror which is so great a check on vice. Crimes of various descriptions were common;[9] and the sharp urgency of famine, joined with that horrible contempt of all human ties, which the extreme of mortal need alone can bring, induced many of the crusaders, deprived of other aliments, to feed upon the dead bodies of the slain. [10]

At the same time, the Turks suffered not their miseries to pass without aggravation, but kept the unsparing sword constantly at their throats; [11] while, by a number of spies, dressed in the garb of Greeks and Armenians, the garrison became aware of all the movements and necessities of their besiegers.[12] To correct the crimes of the camp, a court was instituted, with full power to try and punish; while, to prevent the immorality which was growing too glaring for endurance, the women were separated from the general host, and provided for and protected apart.

At the same time, Boemond employed a somewhat savage mode of freeing the army from the spies by which it was infested. Having de-

---

8. Raimond d'Agiles; Albert d'Aix; Guibert de Nogent, lib. iv.; Robert.
9. Raimond d'Agiles; Albert of Aix; Guibert de Nogent.
10. Malmsbury.
11. Albert; Raimond d'Agiles.
12. Guibert de Nogent; Robertus Monachus, lib. iv.

tected some Turks in disguise, he caused them to be slain and roasted in his presence; declaring, that famine knew no delicacies, and that in future he should feed upon such fare. Still, however, the mortality and the dearth increased; and though an excursion made by Boemond[13] and Robert of Flanders brought a temporary supply to the camp, yet that was soon improvidently wasted like the rest, and the scarcity became more rigorous than ever.

Desertion of course followed.[14] Among such a multitude, there were many whose hearts were not of that firm and all-enduring mould which could alone carry on an enterprise surrounded by such horrors and distresses. Taticius,[15] the Greek, upon pretence of searching for assistance at Constantinople, retreated with the few troops he commanded; and his example was fatal to the resolution of many others. Various bodies of crusaders abandoned the army, and found refuge in the different Christian states that still subsisted in the neighbouring countries: many tried to tread their way back to Europe; and the Count de Melun,[16] a celebrated warrior, but a notorious plunderer, attempted to quit the host of the Cross, and seek some other adventure, where personal danger was not accompanied by famine and privation.

Even Peter the Hermit himself,[17] no longer looked upon as a great leader or an inspired preacher, seeing misery, death, and horror pursuing the object of all his enthusiasm, and feeling himself, perhaps, less valued than his zeal merited, was abandoned by that ardour which had been his great support. Whereas, had he been still regarded as a prophet, or followed as a mighty chief, he would probably have borne the extremity of suffering without a murmur; now, told to endure want and wretchedness as a private individual, he yielded, like the weakest of those that surrounded him, and tried to flee from the pangs which he had no stimulus to endure. Both of these fugitives [18] were brought back by Tancred; and after undergoing a severe reprimand, were forced to vow that they would never abandon the enterprise till the army had reached Jerusalem.

In the meanwhile,[19] the camp of the crusaders received embassies from two different and unexpected quarters. Which arrived first, or at

13. Guibert; Albert; Robert. Mon.
14. Raimond d'Agiles.
15. *Ibid*; Guibert; Robertus Monachus
16. Guibert says he was a boasting coward; but this is contradicted by others.
17. Guibert de Nogent; Robert.
18. Guibert; Robertus Monachus, lib. iv.
19. Robert. Monac.

what period of the siege either arrived, is of little consequence, and impossible exactly to determine; for on this subject, as well as every other collateral circumstance, each of the contemporary authors differs from his fellows; and the historian may think himself fortunate when he finds them agreeing even on the principal facts. The news of the progress of the Christian host had spread even to Cairo;[20] and the *calif* of Egypt, from whose hands Syria had been wrested by the Turks, sent deputies to the leaders of the crusade, probably more with the intent of ascertaining their real condition, and the likelihood of their ultimate success, than for the purpose of binding himself to them by any formal treaty. His messengers, however, were charged to congratulate the Latins on their progress, and to offer the most advantageous terms of union, if they would consent to act in concert with the Egyptian power. They [21] detailed the mild and liberal measures which the *calif* had employed towards the Christians of their country, and they engaged the leaders to send back ambassadors to the court of their sovereign.[22]

After the siege had continued some time, a most welcome aid, both in men and stores, arrived at the little port of St. Simeon, situated at the mouth of the Orontes. This town had already, for many years, served as a seaport to Antioch, which, in its high prosperity,[23] had carried on considerable trade with the Italian cities of the Mediterranean; and to it the states of Genoa and Pisa now sent a large reinforcement of soldiers,[24] and several ship-loads of provisions.

The famished crusaders proceeded towards the spot in straggling crowds, and Boemond,[25] with the Count of Toulouse, at the head

---

20. Albert of Aix.
21. Raimond d'Agiles; Vertot; Guibert; William of Tyre.
22. This is one of the points on which the authorities of the day are in direct opposition to each other. Mills has chosen the opinion of Robertus Monachus, who states that the message of the *calif* was haughty and insolent. I have followed another version of the story, because I find it supported by a greater weight of evidence, and because I do not think the *calif* would have taken the trouble of sending all the way from Egypt to insult a party of men whose persevering conduct showed that they were not likely to be turned back by words. Guibert says, that the *calif* promised even to embrace the Christian faith, in case the crusaders overcame the Turks, and restored to him his Syrian dominions. Albert of Aix also vouches the same proposal, which, however improbable might have been made for the purpose of deceiving the crusaders.
23. Robertson's *Historical Disquisition on India*.
24. Robert, lib. iv.
25. Albert of Aix.

of some regular troops, marched down to escort their newly arrived brethren, and the supplies they were conveying, to the general camp of the crusaders. The Turks of Antioch, however, let no opportunity of vengeance and annoyance pass unemployed. Boemond, embarrassed with a multitude of rabble, and encumbered with baggage, was encountered, as he returned through the mountains, by a large body of Moslems, who, taking him unprepared, slew a great number of the people, and put the leaders and their knights to flight. Boemond arrived breathless at the camp, but the rumour of the battle had preceded him. Godfrey of Bouillon[26] was already in the saddle; and now, joined by Raimond and Boemond, together with Hugh of Vermandois, the Duke of Normandy, and Robert of Flanders, he advanced to the top of the hills, behind which the victorious Turks were winding onward, on their return to the city.

A skirmish took place for the position on the mountains, but the Christians obtained it with little difficulty; and thus cut off the enemy from the town.[27] The Turks were forced to fight once more; but they were opposed no longer by an undisciplined crowd; and the chivalry of Europe never displayed that almost superhuman valour[28] which distinguished them, with greater effect. Allowing even for the exaggeration of eulogy, the efforts of the knights must have been extraordinary. Godfrey is reported to have mown the heads of the Turks as a mower strikes down the thistles; and all the authorities of that day repeat the tale of his having at one blow severed an armed *infidel* in twain, though protected by his *cuirass*.[29] Every chief rivalled the other; and, beyond all doubt, several of the *infidels* must have fallen by the hand of each knight. While thus the sword raged among the Turkish host, many made their way to the bridge, and rushed across it in such crowds, that hundreds were thrust over into the water.

On the other side, too, Boemond, with a large body of pikemen on foot, opposed their passage,[30] and hurled them at the point of the lance into the river, the banks of which were lined with the crusaders, who repelled even those that swam to land.[31] Thus lasted the fight till the sun going down put a stop to the carnage; and the Christians, with songs of victory and loaded with spoil, returned to their camp for the

26. Albert; Robert. Mon.
27. Albert of Aix, lib. iii.
28. Robertus, lib. iv.
29. Robert.; Albert of Aix, lib. iii.
30. Guibert; Albert of Aix, lib. iii.
31. Robertus; Albert.

night. More than two thousand men, several of whom were of high rank, were left by the Turks on the field of battle: a multitude found death in the Orontes; but the number of the fallen was never correctly ascertained,[32] although the Christians, with the characteristic barbarity of the time, dug up many of the dead bodies that the Turks had buried during the night.[33]

Various efforts both from within and without were made to raise the siege, but in vain. On one occasion an immense body of Saracens, Arabs, and Turks was defeated by seven hundred Christian knights, to which small number[34] the disposable cavalry of the army was reduced. Famine, however, disease, and tempests did more to alarm and destroy the crusading force than all the efforts of the *infidels*. The winds[35] became so high that the tents even of the chiefs were blown down, and for some time they were forced to sleep in the open air. An earthquake[36] was felt towards the beginning of the year, and was of course considered as an omen. A comet,[37] too, blazed through the sky; but as the superstitious fancied they beheld in it the form of the Cross, this rather increased than abated their hope. In the midst of these circumstances Stephen,[38] Count of Blois, never very famous for his valour, pretended illness, and retired from the army of the crusade, accompanied by four thousand men, whom he led to Alexandretta.

A more serious desertion, also, was threatened, though no design ever existed of its execution: Boemond[39] himself began to murmur at the length of the siege. He was poor, he declared: he had given up everything in his native country for the Cross, and he could not waste his blood and treasure, and see all his soldiers fall in a siege which was to be productive of no advantage to himself. Such murmurs had their object, and might perhaps spring, in some degree, from a weak quarrel with Godfrey of Bouillon, on the subject of a tent, which had been sent to the duke by the Prince of Armenia, but which had been waylaid by Pancrates, the Armenian I have had occasion to mention

---

32. Five thousand perished on the bridge and in the water, according to Robert the Monk.
33. Robertus Monachus.
34. Guibert mentions previously that the number of horses was reduced to a thousand; lib. iv.
35. Robertus; Guibert.
36. Raimond d'Agiles.
37. Guibert, lib. v.; Fulcher, cap. 7.
38. Will. Tyr.; Albert; Fulcher, cap. 8.
39. Raimond d'Agiles.

in speaking of Baldwin; and had by him been given to Boemond. The Prince of Tarentum had been obliged to yield it by the decision of all the leaders; but though this was a subject of irritation, he had more ambitious projects in view.

Boemond for some time, through a proselyte Turk to whom he had given his name at baptism, had kept up a communication with the commander of one of the chief towers, on that part of the city wall which looked towards the gorges of the mountains. This man,[40] by birth an Armenian, had embraced Mahometanism, and raised himself high in the opinion of the prince of Antioch. He had in consequence received the command of the important[41] station I have mentioned, while his two brothers occupied the neighbouring towers.[42] The origin of his communication with Boemond is variously stated, but the event is the same. He was won over by magnificent promises to engage that he would admit that chief and his followers into the town when called upon.

Boemond, however, did not intend at all that the intelligence which he had thus practised within the walls should be lost to himself, and benefit others alone:[43] but knowing[44] the jealous nature of his companions, he waited patiently till circumstances compelled them to concede to him the sovereignty of Antioch, in the event of its being taken by his means. At first the proposal was rejected by the other leaders; but soon, increasing reports that an immense army, commanded by the warlike Sultaun of Persia, was advancing to the relief of the besieged, induced the Christian chiefs, under the distress and despondency which affected the army generally, to concur in the views of the ambitious Prince of Tarentum. Boemond then intrusted his secret to Godfrey and the other great leaders, but it was under the most solemn promises of silence[45] on the subject; for, notwithstand-

40. William of Tyre says he was a noble Armenian, chief of the tribe of *Benizerra*, or the sons of the armour-forgers, and calls him Emir Feir. Abouharagi, however, says he was a Persian, and calls him Ruzebach.
41. Guibert; Will. Tyr.; Albert.
42. Guibert.
43. William of Tyre, lib. v.; Robert, lib. v.; Guibert, lib. v.
44. This transaction is reported variously. Albert of Aix says, that the proposal of Boemond was at once received with joy. Raoul of Caen gives a different account, and states that the bishop of Puy, on the suggestion of Boemond, suggested that the town should be given to him who could first obtain it. Guibert and Robert relate it as I have done above. The archbishop of Tyre declares that no one opposed the proposal of Boemond but the Count of Toulouse.
45. Will. Tyr.; Albert of Aix; Guibert, lib. v.

ing all the precautions that could be taken, it was well known that the Turkish spies infested the Christian camp.

With the utmost caution all the measures were concerted for carrying the project into effect, and through the whole army the rumour was spread that the preparations made by the chiefs were for the purpose of laying an ambush for the Persian forces, that were approaching. Phirouz, the Armenian traitor, was warned that Boemond was about to take advantage of his offer; and as soon as night had completely set in, the Prince of Tarentum, with a body of chosen knights, proceeded into the mountains,[46] as if with the design of surprising the host of the Persians. Only seven hundred men, however, were selected for this perilous expedition; and marching in the dead of the night, they crossed the valleys and precipices of the rocky chain on which the city rested, and halted in a deep dell at some distance from the walls.

The wind was blowing in sharp gusts, and its howlings among the gorges of the mountains prevented the tramp of the armed men from reaching the watchers on the walls. Having assembled their forces in the valley, Godfrey and Boemond explained to their followers the real nature of the enterprise they meditated. A single interpreter was sent forward, to confer with their traitorous coadjutor, and to ascertain that all was prepared. Phirouz assured him that he was ready, and asked eagerly where were the knights; being told that they were near,[47] he pressed them to advance, lest anything should excite the suspicion of the other commanders, especially as, from time to time, men with lighted torches patrolled the wall during the night, and it was necessary that they should take advantage of the interval. Godfrey, Robert of Flanders, and Boemond instantly led the troops to the foot of the fortifications; a rope was let down, and a ladder of hides raised. At first,[48] no one could be found to mount.

Unaccustomed to carry on any warlike operations during the night, a thousand unwonted fears took possession of the bosoms of the crusaders. At length, urged by the chiefs, and encouraged by Phirouz from above, one knight—which of the body is not certain[49]—began

---

46. Albert of Aix; Robertus, lib. v.
47. Robertus, lib. v., 2d June, *A. D.* 1098.
48. Guibert, lib. v.; Raimond d'Agiles; Albert.
49. There is some reason to believe that Boemond was the first who entered, as stated by William of Tyre; but as Albert of Aix makes no mention of the fact, and as Guibert de Nogent declares positively that Boemond, who is certainly his favourite hero, did not mount till sixty others had preceded him, as Raimond d'Agiles gives the honour of the feat to Fulcher de Chartres, and as (continued next page)

117

to ascend the ladder, and was followed by several others. Silence then succeeded, and temporary hesitation once more took possession of the force below: but the voices of their companions who had ascended, whispering assurances of safety and fidelity, soon renewed their courage, and many attempting to climb the ladder at once,[50] it gave way under their weight, precipitating them upon the lance-heads that were buried in the fosse.

The clang of their armour as they fell was a new cause of alarm, lest the sound should reach the other towers: so loud, however, was the roaring of the wind, and the hollow rushing sound of the Orontes, that the noise was not heard by any but those immediately around. The ladder was easily repaired, and more than sixty knights had reached the top of the battlements when the torch of the patrol began to gleam along the walls in its approach towards them. Hid[51] in the shadows of the tower, the crusaders waited the officer's approach, and before he could spread the alarm death had fixed the seal of silence on his lips forever. The knights now descended through the staircase in the masonry, and finding the soldiers of the guard asleep, they speedily rendered their slumbers eternal. A postern gate was then forced open,[52] and the seven hundred champions rushed into the city sounding their horns in every direction, as had been agreed between the chiefs, in order that on this signal the town might be at the same time attacked from without.

It would be painful to dwell upon the scene of slaughter that ensued. The Turks were soon awakened by the shrieks of their falling comrades, and by the trumpets of their victorious foe: they ran to

Robert the Monk confirms that assertion, I have left the matter in doubt, as I found it. In regard to the story of Phirouz murdering his brother in his sleep, because he would not aid in his design, I believe fully that it was but one of those ornamental falsehoods with which men are ever fond of decorating great and extraordinary events. I doubt not that the tale was current in the time of William of Tyre, who reports it; and the act was, beyond question, looked upon as a noble and devoted one on the part of Phirouz; but as I find nothing to confirm it in any book I possess, except the simple fact of that Armenian having been a traitorous rascal, please God, till further evidence I will look upon it all as a lie. Robert the Monk represents, in very glowing terms, the grief of Phirouz for the death of his two brothers, who were killed in the *melée*. Phirouz became a Christian, at least in name; and to cover the baseness of his perfidy, he declared that the Saviour himself had appeared to him in a vision, commanding him to deliver up the town.

50. Albert of Aix; Guibert, lib. v.; Raimond d'Agiles.
51. Albert of Aix, lib. iv.
52. Guibert; Albert; Raimond d'Agiles.

arms,[53] and for many hours manfully opposed their conquerors hand to hand, though all hope of victory was now over. The Greeks and Armenians hastened to force open the gates and give entrance to the rest of the army of the Cross: but, in the darkness that prevailed, many of the Christians as well as the Turks were slaughtered by the victors, who butchered all ages, sexes, and conditions, with indiscriminate rage and haste,[54] in which fear and agitation had probably as much to do as cruelty and fanaticism.

During the whole of the night the crusaders continued the massacre of their enemies; and Albert of Aix[55] declares, that the following morning they found they had slain many of their own countrymen by mistake. Such a fact is not difficult to conceive of a body of men wandering without guide through a hostile town, with the paths of which they were unacquainted. As ever follows the violent capture of a large city, the soldiery first satisfied themselves with bloodshed, and perhaps added some extra cruelties to gratify their fanaticism, and then betook themselves to plunder and debauchery; nevertheless, they committed not greater excesses than we have seen perpetrated in days not very distant from our own, by the troops of civilized nations, without the fiery stimulus of religious zeal for a palliation.

I mean not to defend the cruelties of the crusaders, but I mean to say, that they were not extraordinary in that age, or in any age that has yet passed: God only knows what may be to come. The crusaders treated the *infidels* as the *infidels* had often treated the Christians; and as Christians, unhappily, have too often treated Christians like themselves. Their plunder was not at all of a more atrocious kind than that which attends every storm; and as to the hypocrisy[56] with which Mills charges them, that writer quite loses sight of the spirit of the age on which he writes, and metes men's actions by a standard that they never knew. The crusaders were *not* hypocrites, they were merely fanatics; and in the relentless fury with which they pillaged, injured, and massacred the Turks, they thought they did God as good and pleasing service as in singing praises to him for the victory they had obtained. They were fearfully wrong in their principle, it is true, but still they acted upon principle, and therefore in this they were not hypocrites.

Baghasian, the Turkish prince of Antioch,[57] fled with a part of his

53. Raimond; Robertus Monachus, lib. vi.; Albert.
54. Guibert, lib. v.
55. Albert of Aix, lib. iv.
56. See Mills's *History of the Crusades.*
57. Robertus Monachus, lib. vi.; Guibert; Fulcher; Albert.

troops to the citadel, but finding that security could not long be found within the walls of the town, he escaped alone to the mountains, where he was waylaid by some Syrian Christians and slain. His head, with all the venerable marks of extreme age, was struck off by his slayers, and carried, with his rich sword-belt, into Antioch, where it proved an acceptable present to the rude victors.

Though much spoil[58] of various kinds was found in Antioch, little that could satisfy the cravings of hunger had been left by the Turks. They, themselves closely blockaded, had been driven nearly to want; and the Christians soon began to suffer from the very precautions they had formerly taken against their enemies. In the first joy of their conquest, too, the little discipline that ever existed in a chivalrous host was completely relaxed, and before it could be sufficiently restored for necessary measures to be taken in order to procure supplies, famine was in the city, and the hosts of the Persian *sultaun* [59] encamped beneath the walls.

The invasion of the Christians, the fall of Nice, and the siege of Antioch had spread consternation through the empires of the Crescent; and the monarch of Persia had roused himself from the contemptuous sloth in which he had first heard of the crusades, and raised an immense army, to sweep away, as the Moslem expressed it, the band of locusts that had fallen upon the land.

Kerboga, or Corbohan, as he was named by the Christians, the Emir of Mosul, and favourite of the *calif*, took the command of the army; and being joined by Kilidge Asian, the Sultaun of Roum, with a considerable force, proceeded at the head of about three hundred thousand men towards Antioch. He would, in all probability have reached that city in time to prevent its fall, had he not turned from the direct road to ravage the principality of Edessa, and dispossess Baldwin.[60] From thence, however, he was called, before he could accomplish his object, by the news of the Christians' success, and in a few days Antioch was once more invested. The first attempt of the Moslems was to throw supplies into the citadel, which the Latins had hitherto neglected to attack. In this they in some degree succeeded; and the crusaders, being roused to watchfulness, took what measures they could against further reinforcements reaching the castle.

In the meanwhile the Christians, who had suffered what ap-

---

58. Guibert, lib. v.; Robertus; Albert.
59. Guibert; Albert of Aix.
60. William of Tyre; Albert of Aix.

peared the extreme of privation while assailing the very walls they now defended, were reduced to a state of famine which beggars all description.[61] The most noisome animals, the most unsavoury herbs, became dainties at the tables of the great. The horses that remained were slaughtered without consideration, and all virtue and order gave way under the pressure of necessity.

All sorts of vice became rife, and debauchery grew the more horrid from being the debauchery of despair. The Persians, encamped closely round them, had burnt the vessels, destroyed the port of St. Simeon, and cut off all communication with the neighbouring country. Nevertheless their guard was not so strict but that many of the crusaders escaped over the walls,[62] and fled to the Count of Blois at Alexandretta, excusing their pusillanimity by tales of the horrors they had undergone. Stephen of Blois, now rejoicing in his timely evasion, abandoned his comrades altogether, and with the stragglers who had joined him from Antioch, among whom were many knights and nobles of distinction, he retreated towards Constantinople.[63] By the way he encountered a large force commanded by Alexius, who was marching, not to succour the crusaders, whose condition he did not yet know, but to take advantage of their conquests.

The cowardly monarch, in deep sympathy with the cowardly fugitives, turned his back upon Antioch the moment he heard of its danger, and pursued his journey towards his capital, forcing along with him a considerable body of French and Italian crusaders, who, under the command of Guy,[64] the brother of Boemond, had been advancing to the aid of their brethren. The news of Alexius's approach had filled the hearts of the besieged with joy, and the tidings of his retreat of course cast them into still deeper despair. The soldiers forgot their honour and abandoned their posts, hiding in the houses and avoiding every thing that called them into activity.

As a last resource to drive them to their duty, Boemond[65] set fire to parts of the town where they were supposed principally to linger; but hope seemed extinguished in every breast, and though the inferior troops returned to some degree of energy, yet the leaders knew full well that without succour—and no succour was near—nothing short of a miracle could save them from their distress. Within the

61. Robertus, lib. vi.; Albert of Aix, lib. iv.; William of Tyre.
62. Robertus Monachus, lib. vi.; Guibert, lib. v.
63. Albert of Aix.
64. Robertus, vi.; Albert of Aix.
65. Guibert.

walls they starved,[66] and died, and wasted; and they could hardly be expected to issue forth upon the enemy, when Godfrey himself, their noblest leader, and tacitly their chief, was destitute of even a horse to carry him to the battle. At the same time, from the walls of the city, the luxuries of the Turkish camp might be beheld in tantalizing splendour.[67] Gold and jewels, and rich silks, and beautiful horses, and gay *seraglios*, seemed rather indications of some joyous company than of a fierce besieging army. Troops of cattle, too, of all kinds, were seen feeding round about, while the acute tooth of famine was gnawing the entrails of those who stood and looked upon all the magnificence and profusion before them.

Many even of the leaders of the crusade[68] were reduced to absolute beggary, and several became completely dependent on the bounty of Godfrey for mere food, till he himself had no more to give. The people, accustomed to privation, still in some degree bore up, but the knights themselves gave way, and had it not been for the noble firmness of Adhemar, Bishop of Puy, Godfrey, Raimond, Boemond, and Tancred, the whole of the barons would have fled, and left the people to their fate.[69]

The chiefs I have named, however, never ceased their exertions. They bound themselves by the most solemn vows not to abandon each other or the cause they had undertaken; and Tancred, always the first where chivalrous enthusiasm was concerned, pledged himself by oath not to turn back from the road to Jerusalem so long as forty knights would follow his banner. At length superstition came to animate the courage of the soldiery. Visions were seen promising victory to those who endured to the last. The apostles, the saints, and even the Saviour appeared to many of the priests, who took care that their miraculous visitations should be noised abroad.[70]

Whether originating in the policy of the leaders, or in the cunning of the lower order of priests, these supernatural consolations had a prodigious effect upon people who, their reliance on every earthly means being gone, were fain to turn to heaven. Enthusiasm, supported by superstition, proved a most excellent nurse to hope. Activity, energy, resolution, returned; and the wan and ghastly herds demanded loudly to be led against the enemy. One more pious fraud[71] was destined to

66. Guibert; Fulcher; Albert, lib. iv.
67. Guibert, lib. v.
68. Albert of Aix, lib. iv.
69. Albert.
70. Guibert; Fulcher; Albert.
71. Raimond d'Agiles; Fulcher; William of Tyre; Albert; Guibert.

be committed before the troops were brought to the last resource of an almost hopeless battle. A clerk of Provence, serving under Raimond of Toulouse, sought out the chiefs of the armament, and declared that St. Andrew the Apostle had manifested himself in a vision, and had revealed to him that the lance with which our Saviour's side was pierced, at the crucifixion, might be found in a certain spot in the church of St. Peter of Antioch. Accompanied by this holy relic the army was directed by the saint to issue forth upon the Saracens with assurances of victory.

The Bishop of Puy,[72] whose religious feelings were of too pure a kind to practise, or even countenance, such cheats, declared that the tale must be false, and several chiefs agreed with him in opinion:[73] but Raimond of Toulouse and others strongly supported the story; and the whole of the leaders soon became convinced that good policy required the lance should be found, a battle seeming the only resource. As no support could be given to the bodies of the emaciated troops, it was as well, also, to stimulate their minds as far as possible.

The lance was therefore sought for in form, and though at first it could not be discovered, because it was not there, it very naturally happened that no sooner did the clerk who had been favoured with the vision descend into the pit,[74] than the iron head was perceived, and brought up to the wonder and edification of the people. The matter being now decided, the hearts of the multitude were all enthusiasm, a great many more almost sacrilegious visions were seen, fasting and prayer, and the ceremonies of the church were used to excite and increase the popular ardour; and, in the end, Peter the Hermit was sent out to the camp of Kerboga,[75] not to offer terms of capitulation, but rather to threaten vengeance, and to bid the Turks depart. The reply of the *emir* was as contemptuous as might have been expected, and Peter returned with a message that would have somewhat quelled the daring of the crusaders if it had been repeated. This, however, was prevented by Godfrey, and every preparation made for a battle.

The citadel,[76] I have before said, had remained in the hands of the Turks, who had fled thither on the taking of Antioch. Its commanding situation enabled the garrison to see whatever passed in the town; and the governor being strictly enjoined to give due notice to the army of Kerboga of all the Christian movements, on the morning of the

72. Fulcher; Raimond.
73. Radulph. Cadom.
74. Raimond d'Agiles.
75. Fulcher; Raimond; Albert; Guibert of Nogent.
76. Albert of Aix; Raimond d'Agiles; Will. Tyr.

28th of June, *A. D.* 1098, a black flag,[77] hoisted on the highest tower of that fortress, announced to the besiegers that the Latins were about to march out and attack them.

The army of the Cross presented but a miserable sight; the ghastly hand of famine had wrought horribly on the wan countenances of the soldiery. Of all the fair Chivalry of Europe, whose heavy horses and steel-clad limbs had crushed like the fall of a mountain everything that opposed them, but two hundred knights appeared mounted as was their wont.[78] Those who could get them were glad to go forth upon mules and asses; some having sold or lost their arms, were furnished with the small shields and scimitars taken from the Turks; and Godfrey of Bouillon himself rode the borrowed horse of the Count of Toulouse, who was left to guard the town. In this state of wretchedness, the crusading army marched out against a splendid force, which, at the beginning of the siege amounted to more than three hundred thousand fighting men, and had every day been increasing.[79]

Nevertheless, all was enthusiasm in the Christian ranks. The priests in their pontifical robes,[80] bearing crosses and holy banners, mingled with the soldiers, and, singing hymns of joy, already taught them to anticipate victory. The number of knights going to the fight on foot encouraged the common men by their presence and their example; and, in fact, though destitute of many of the physical means which had given them superiority in former battles, the valour and the self-confidence,[81] which are the soul of victory, were never more present among the Christian warriors.

Kerboga committed the great fault that has lost a thousand battles. He despised his enemy. When first the news was brought to him that the Christians were advancing, he was playing at chess,[82] and hardly rose from his game. It was only the complete route of two thousand men, whom he had stationed to defend the bridge, that convinced him the attack was serious. He thus lost the opportunity of annoying the crusaders as they defiled, and now he found his error and began to tremble for the consequences.

Hugh of Vermandois,[83] Robert of Flanders, and the Duke of Nor-

---

77. Albert of Aix.
78. Albert of Aix; Guibert, lib. iii.
79. Albert of Aix.
80. Guibert; Albert; Raimond.
81. Raimond d'Agiles; Fulcher.
82. Raimond; Raoul de Caen.
83. Raimond.

mandy, each advanced steadily at the head of his followers towards the mountains, where the Turkish cavalry were likely to find more difficulty in manœuvring. Godfrey of Bouillon followed; and then Adhemar, Bishop of Puy, clothed in armour,[84] and bearing the sacred lance, led on the troops of Provence. Boemond and Tancred brought up the rear, and thus the whole wound on towards their position.

Kerboga now used every effort to remedy his first neglect, and made several skilful movements for the purpose of surrounding the crusaders. They, on their part, with little attention to the arts of warfare, continued to march on, their courage increasing rather than diminishing, and persuading themselves that even the morning dew of a fine summer's day, which refreshed both themselves and their horses, was a special sign of favour from Heaven.[85] It is said, that Kerboga, at this moment seized with a sudden and unaccountable fear, sent messengers to declare that he would accept the terms formerly offered, and commit the decision of the quarrel to a combat of five or ten champions to be chosen on each side.[86]

This proposal (if really made) was instantly refused, and Kerboga, drawn up before his camp, waited the attack of the Christians; while Soliman or Kilidge Aslan, taking a wide circuit with an immense force of cavalry, prepared to fall upon the rear of the army commanded by Boemond. To conceal this evolution the vizier caused the dry grass and weeds with which great part of the ground was covered to be set on fire, and by the smoke thus raised[87] succeeded in obscuring the movements of his cavalry. During this manœuvre he extended his line, and endeavoured to turn the flanks of the crusading army. The banner-bearers,[88] in front of the host, were now within bow-shot of the enemy, and the arrows began to fall like hail on either side. The columns of the Christians came up one after another to the attack, and fighting hand to hand forced back the Turkish centre upon their camp, so that in that part of the field victory seemed leaning towards the champions of the Cross.

At the same time, however, Soliman had fallen upon the rear of Boemond,[89] who, enveloped by infinitely superior forces, was pressed hard and separated from the rest of the army. The dense cloud occa-

---

84. Raimond d'Agiles.
85. Histor. Hieros; Jacob.Vit.
86. Raimond d'Agiles; Fulcher.
87. Guibert.
88. Will.Tyr. lib. vi.
89. Raoul of Caen.

sioned by the burning weeds embarrassed the Lombards and Italians, and the sword of the Persians was reaping a terrible harvest in the ranks of the crusaders. Tancred flew to the rescue of Boemond, and Hugh of Vermandois as well as Godfrey of Bouillon abandoning the attack[90] they were making on the centre of the infidel army, turned to the rear, and succeeded in repelling the troops of Soliman.

Still, the battle raged undecided;[91] while Kerboga used every effort to secure the victory, and hurrying up the columns from his wings, caused them to charge the rear of Godfrey as he advanced to the succour of the Prince of Tarentum. All was now confusion in that part of the field, the fight became hand to hand, blade crossed with blade, and man struggled against man. Meanwhile the Bishop of Puy, still bearing the sacred lance,[92] pressed forward upon a corps at the head of which Kerboga had placed himself; and with the Provençals urged the battle manfully against the *infidels*. The Persians fought bravely, and their numbers, as well as their great superiority in cavalry, gave them vast advantages over the Latins. Returning again and again to the charge with unequalled rapidity, fighting as well when their columns were broken as when their ranks were entire, and unrivalled in the use of the bow, they gave the crusaders not a moment to pause, without some enemy to attack, and some blow to repel.

At length a report was raised through the Christian host that the saints were fighting on their side; and either by accident, by the force of imagination, or by some preconcerted artifice, the crusaders saw— or thought they saw—some figures clothed in white raiment, and mounted on white horses, coming over the mountains to their aid.[93] All fear, all suspense was at an end. The enthusiasm was prodigious, extraordinary, overpowering. The redoubted battle-cry "God wills it! God wills it!" once more rang over the field, and the weapons of the Christians seemed swayed by the force of giants. At the same time, among the Moslems spread the sickening news that the Latins had forced their way into the camp. The hopes of the *infidels* fell, and terror took possession of them, while the courage of the people of the Cross, raised into ecstasy by the belief of visible aid from on high, bore down all that opposed it, and soon converted feeble resistance into flight.

In vain Kerboga tried to rally his troops, the panic was general, the

---

90. Albert.
91. Albert.
92. Raimond d'Agiles.
93. Will. Malmsbury; Guibert de Nogent; Raimond d'Agiles.

pursuers fierce and resolute; and the mighty army of the Persians was scattered to the four winds of heaven. Tancred,[94] leaving to others the plunder of the camp, followed the fugitives over the hills, and prevented them from reassembling, while the rest of the chiefs entered the tents of the Persians, and added to their slaughtered enemies the blood of the helpless and unoffending.[95] A number of women and children were either slain by the sword or borne down in the flight, and an immense booty in gold, arms, horses, cattle, and rich vestments made the host of the crusade richer than even when it took its departure from Europe. The pavilion of Kerboga himself, though not the most valuable, was perhaps the most curious part of the spoil, being formed like a town, with walls, towers, and battlements,[96] and comprising streets, squares, and avenues within itself. It fell to the share of Boemond, and was capable, they say, of containing two thousand men.

Sixty-nine thousand Turks[97] died in the battle of Antioch, while the loss of the crusaders is not estimated at more than ten thousand; but it must be remembered that this is the account of the Christians themselves. One of the immediate consequences[98] of this great victory was the surrender of the citadel of Antioch, which was now given up in despair. A considerable number of the soldiers forming its garrison embraced Christianity, and remained in the town; while the rest, who firmly adhered to their ancient faith, were honourably conducted beyond the conquered territory. The whole army, loaded with wealth, and rejoicing in abundance, entered once more the walls of the city, and offered up to Heaven manifold thanksgivings for the victory they had obtained.

The only occurrence that for the time troubled the public joy[99] was, that the Count of Toulouse, who had remained behind to guard the town, looked upon the citadel, which had surrendered previous to the return of the host, as his own conquest, and had raised his banner on the walls.[100] The council of leaders determined that their agreement with Boemond embraced the castle as well as the town, and Raimond was, in consequence, forced to resign the authority he had usurped to the Prince of Tarentum. The count, notwithstanding, still

---

94. Albert; Raoul of Caen; Guibert.
95. Fulcher; Albert.
96. Guibert; Albert.
97. Mills.
98. Guibert; Fulcher.
99. Raimond d'Agiles; William of Tyre.
100. See Notes 9.

retained possession of one of the city-gates,[101] with its adjoining towers, which he maintained for some months, but was obliged at last, by force of arms, to yield the whole.

The first occupation of the crusaders after quieting this dispute was to restore the temples, which the Moslems had converted into mosques, to the service of the Christian religion. The priests were re-established, the ceremonies of the church recalled; and though they adhered to the forms of the Latin ritual, with wise and Christian moderation they abstained from interfering with the Greek patriarch, notwithstanding that they considered his dogmas heretical. The next question more related to their further advance into the country; and the people, proud in their victory, and forgetful of privations in the fullness of sudden satiety, clamoured loudly to be led on to Jerusalem.

The chiefs,[102] however, saw how greatly repose was required; their army was lamentably diminished; most of the soldiers were suffering from wounds or weariness, and few, though refreshed by their lately acquired stores, were capable of bearing more fatigue and fresh necessities. At the same time, the fiery months of August and September, with the exposed plains of Syria, lay before them; and it was known that water, scanty on the road to Jerusalem even in the best times, was now hardly to be procured.

On these considerations, the chiefs determined to postpone their advance till October, and in the meanwhile despatched Hugh[103] the Great, Count of Vermandois, with Baldwin of Mons, Count of Hainault, to the court of Constantinople. These ambassadors were instructed to urge the base Alexius to fulfil the many promises which he had made and neglected; and to threaten him, in case of his refusal, with the anger both of God and man.

Baldwin of Mons was betrayed into a Turkish ambuscade, and his fate was never clearly ascertained;[104] but Hugh of Vermandois made his way safely through Asia Minor, and arrived at Constantinople. Admitted to the presence of Alexius, he detailed the sufferings of the Christians, and their diminished forces, and showed the necessity which they felt of supplies and reinforcements. He announced also their victory over the Turks, and the signal humiliation which had been

---

101. Albert of Aix; Will. Tyr.; Raimond d'Agiles.
102. Guibert.
103. Guibert; Albert; Will. Tyr.
104. Guibert; Albert.

inflicted on the proud Moslems. This news in both respects gratified Alexius: but, equally well content that the Turks should be made weak, and that the Latins should not grow strong, he found the affairs of the east progressing exactly as he could have desired, and determined to leave them in the course which they had themselves taken.

The wrath of Heaven for his broken engagements, and the vengeance of the crusaders on the same score, were far too remote evils for the narrow-minded despot to yield them any consideration. Hugh of Vermandois—now near home[105] and the comforts which he had so long abandoned, anticipating little pleasure and no small danger on the journey back, and having neither satisfactory news nor necessary reinforcements to take to the crusaders—determined upon pursuing his journey into France, and leaving his companions to their fate. Knowing, however, that it would be difficult to justify himself in their eyes, he did not even take the trouble to write for that purpose; others on his part have done so for posterity, and have failed.

---

105. Guibert.

CHAPTER 8

Pestilence in Antioch

The crusaders[1] in Antioch had reason to regret they had not at once marched onward. A pestilence began to spread in the city, and multitudes were buried every day. Among the first was the venerable Bishop of Puy,[2] whose high qualities of mind and excellent character as a priest had given much dignity and strength to the enterprise. Many celebrated knights also fell victims to this plague; and all the dissensions[3] and crimes that indolence acting on semi-barbarians can produce, begin to spring up within the walls of Antioch. To effect some change, the chiefs agreed to separate, and to canton their men in the countries round about. Boemond proceeded to reduce all Cilicia to obedience, and carried on a desultory but successful warfare against the Turks. Godfrey[4] led his men to the assistance of the *emir* of Hezas, who solicited his aid against the Sultaun of Aleppo.

Being joined by Baldwin, and by some auxiliary forces from Antioch, Godfrey succeeded in delivering the *emir*, who was besieged in his fortress by the *sultaun*. Hezas was then placed by the prince under the protection of his new allies, whom he found somewhat exacting in their friendship. The plague still raging in Antioch, Godfrey turned his steps towards Edessa, the principality of his brother Baldwin, to whom he was now fully reconciled. After a short repose at Turbessel,[5] he engaged in the wars which his brother was carrying on against the Turks, whose dominions surrounded Edessa, and also punished Pancrates for the rapine which he had for some time exercised with im-

---

1. Albert of Aix.
2. Guibert; Raimond d'Agiles; Albert.
3. Raimond d'Agiles.
4. Albert of Aix.
5. William of Tyre.

punity against all parties. The other princes in various bodies carried on the same separate hostilities against the Saracens, and many towns were added to the Christian dominions.

The time fixed for the march of the general army at length arrived; but, whether from a taste for the desultory sort of warfare to which they had now habituated themselves, or from the hope of still receiving some aid from Europe, the crusaders tarried on their way, and laid siege to Marrah.[6] The Moslems made a brave resistance, and the Latins having, with their wonted improvidence, begun the siege without any supplies whatever, were soon again reduced to famine and the most horrible cannibalism.[7] At length Marrah was taken by storm on the arrival of Boemond and his forces.

The slaughter was terrible, and a repetition of all the scenes on the taking of Antioch was here enacted with many circumstances of aggravation. New disputes now arose between Boemond and the Count of Toulouse, upon the possession of Marrah; the Prince of Tarentum refusing to give up the portion of the city he had conquered, till Raimond should yield the towers which he still held in Antioch.[8] Days and weeks passed in these unworthy contests, other chiefs attempting in vain to reconcile the two ambitious princes. At length the people, indignant at the conduct of their leaders, broke out into revolt, and destroyed the fortifications of Marrah, in spite of all that could be done to prevent them,[9] vowing that it, at least, should not be a new cause of delay. They declared also that they would choose a chief for themselves, who should conduct them to Jerusalem.

This, of course, compelled the leaders of the army to begin their march, but it in no degree produced a reconciliation, and Raimond of Toulouse,[10] with Robert of Normandy and Tancred, proceeded on their way to Jerusalem, leaving the rest of the princes to follow as they might. Town after town submitted to Raimond; but Archas proved a stumbling block to his glory, and resisted the efforts of all the force he could bring against it. The Saracen *emirs* of the neighbouring country, however, whether from fear of the Christians, or from misunderstandings among themselves, no longer pursued the firm and destructive plan formerly adopted of desolating the land before the steps of the

6. Albert; Guibert.
7. Fulcher; Albert of Aix; Guibert; Raoul of Caen.
8. Raimond d'Agiles; Guibert de Nogent.
9. Raimond d'Agiles.
10. Raoul of Caen; Raimond.

invaders. The army of the Cross found provisions in plenty, and many of the towns which it approached bought immunity from attack, at the price of large presents to the crusaders.[11]

Soon after the departure of Raimond, Godfrey of Bouillon, Robert of Flanders, Boemond, and the other leaders marched out of Antioch, and directed their course towards Laodicea, where Boemond[12] again quitted them, and returned to his new principality, leaving a great part of his troops to aid his brethren. As some compensation for this desertion, the host of the crusade was joined by a considerable body of English who had sailed round Spain; and, entering the Mediterranean by Gibraltar, had touched first at St. Simeon, and then proceeded to Laodicea—a wonderful undertaking, indeed, as Raimond d'Agiles observes, considering the state of the art of navigation in that day.

From Laodicea, Godfrey, marching along the coast, turned his arms against Ghibel, or Gabala, whither he was accompanied by the ships of the band of pirates whom we have seen serving under Baldwin; and who, having fallen into the hands of the Greeks of Laodicea, had been kept in strict imprisonment till the arrival of the crusaders. The *emir* of Ghibel attempted, by the offer of large bribes, to divert the forces of the Cross from the attack of his city, but his proposals were met with contempt by Godfrey and the chiefs who accompanied him; and the *infidel* commander, in consequence, sent messengers to Raimond of Toulouse[13] (then besieging Archas), whose disinterestedness was reported to be of a different quality. Raimond, always fond of gold, caught at the bait held out, and immediately agreed to draw his fellow-crusaders from Ghibel by artifice.

He lost no time, therefore, in sending word to Godfrey, that an immense body of Saracens was marching down against his Provençals under the walls of Archas. This tale of course caused Godfrey[14] to raise the siege of Ghibel, and hasten to the assistance of his comrade. On his arrival, however, Tancred, and the other knights of Raimond's army, undeceived the duke of Loraine, who, indignant at the treachery of the Count of Toulouse, renounced all communication[15] with him, and withdrew his men to the distance of two miles, resolving to give him no aid in the siege of Archas. Tancred, at the same time, disgusted

11. Guibert.
12. Guibert, lib. vi.; Albert of Aix, lib. v.; William of Tyre.
13. Albert of Aix.
14. Fulcher; Guibert.
15. Albert of Aix.

with the avarice of the count, who withheld from him the recompense he had promised for his services, retired with the forty[16] lances that accompanied him, and joined himself to Godfrey.

New disputes of every kind arose among the leaders, and as Raimond of Toulouse affected a sort of spiritual superiority, as guardian of the holy lance that had been discovered at Antioch, its virtues and authenticity were manfully denied. Peter Barthelmy, who had found it, had vision after vision, till his commerce with heaven drew so heavily on belief, that men, even the most superstitious, yielded him no further credit. The business was investigated, and Barthelmy brought before a sort of council of inquiry, where he maintained his position, supported by the Count of Toulouse and his chaplain, our worthy chronicler, Raimond d'Agiles, who, fully convinced of the truth of the miracle, unhappily proposed that his *protégé* should prove his virtue by the fiery ordeal.[17]

This was agreed to; fasts and prayers succeeded: Peter walked through the fire with the lance in his hand, got frightened, stopped in the middle, and was burned to death.[18] Some still believed; and, declaring that their martyr had been pressed to death by the crowd,[19] held to their credulity the more eagerly, because it was unsupported by anything like reason.

The fame of the Count of Toulouse suffered as much by the affair of the lance as by his deceit in respect to Ghibel; and the crusaders, wearied with the delay before Archas, determined to raise the siege and proceed to Jerusalem. In the meanwhile, the *emir*[20] of Tripoli,[21] finding that the Christians were about to traverse his country, sent messengers to the leaders, begging them to spare his towns and fields, and offering abundant supplies, together with several rich presents. These proffers were so favourably received that the *emir* even visited the camp of Godfrey himself, and concluded a treaty which was inviolably adhered to on both sides.

At the same time[22] the deputies who had been despatched to the *calif* of Egypt returned, with very unfavourable accounts of their en-

---

16. Raimond d'Agiles; Albert of Aix.
17. Raimond d'Agiles.
18. Fulcher; Raoul of Caen.
19. Guibert; Raimond.
20. Albert of Aix; Guibert; Robert. Mon. lib. viii.
21. Mills follows Raimond d'Agiles. I have chosen the account of Albert of Aix, because I find it better supported by evidence.
22. William of Tyre.

tertainment. The Saracen monarch still offered to join his arms to those of the Christians, for the purpose of subduing Palestine; but it was evident that he proposed to enjoy the fruits of victory without participation. His envoys, and the presents which they bore, were sent back with scorn,[23] the crusaders declaring that they would conquer Jerusalem with the sword of Christ, and keep it with the same. Ambassadors from Alexius were received also under the walls of Archas; and by their lips the perfidious emperor dared to remonstrate against the cession of Antioch to Boemond, who by this time had expelled the troops of Raimond of Toulouse, [24] and was in full possession of the town.

The reply given to these messengers was not less haughty than that which had been sent to the *calif*.[25] The emperor, the crusaders said, had broken his most sacred oaths; he had neglected to succour them when succour was needful; he had betrayed the cause of Christ, and violated his covenant with them. They could not, therefore, be bound by an engagement which he had not found binding on him; and they would neither stay for his coming, as he desired, nor would they yield him what they had conquered with their own hands.

These measures of decision having been taken, Godfrey and his companions set fire to their camp, and quitted the siege of Archas: many of the Provençals abandoned Raimond, and hastened after the rest; and the count himself, [26] though unwillingly, was obliged to follow. The noble sincerity and moderation of the crusaders in their conduct to the Emir of Tripoli has not been dwelt upon sufficiently by those authors who have lost no opportunity of pointing out their cruelties and excesses. They entered a rich and beautiful country, where spoil of every kind lay around them. The inhabitants were *infidels*, and had been enemies: but the host of the crusade passed through the whole without the slightest violation of their treaty.[27]

To prevent even casual injury, they encamped at a distance from the towns, waited for the supplies that had been promised them, and followed, with confidence and regularity, the guide who was appointed to conduct them through the land.[28] When at war, the crusaders

---

23. Raimond d'Agiles.
24. Fulcher. Raimond d'Agiles.
25. William of Tyre, lib. vii.
26. Robert. Mon.
27. Albert.
28. William of Tyre; Albert of Aix.

waged it with all the barbarity of the age—the slaughter of the *infidel* adversary was a virtue praised by historians, and sung by poets, and mercy would have been held a weakness: but with those to whom they had bound themselves in peace, we seldom find that, *as a body,* they violated the most chivalric adherence to their promises.

In the neighbourhood of Tripoli, the Europeans first beheld the sugar-cane,[29] and learned the method of preparing the valuable juice which has since been such an article of commerce in Europe.

So great was the reliance between the people of Tripoli and the crusaders, that they mutually frequented the camp [30] and the city during the stay of the army. The *emir* also delivered from the chains in which they had long remained, three hundred Christian pilgrims; and, according to some authorities, promised to embrace the faith of his new allies,[31] in case they were ultimately successful. At the end of three days, the host of the Cross was once more in motion; and passing by Sidon, Acre, Ramula, and Emmaus, approached the city of Jerusalem.[32] At Emmaus, deputies arrived from the Christians of Bethlehem, praying for immediate aid against their *infidel* oppressors. Tancred was[33] in consequence sent forward with a hundred lances; but the tidings of a deputation from Bethlehem spread new and strange sensations through the bosoms of the crusaders.

That word Bethlehem, repeated through the camp, called up so many ideas connected with that sweet religion, which, however perverted, was still the thrilling faith of every heart around. The thoughts of their proximity to the Saviour's [34] birthplace, banished sleep from every eyelid; and before midnight was well past, the whole host was on foot towards Jerusalem. It was a lovely morning, we are told, in the summer time; and after they had wandered on for some time in the darkness, the sun rushed into the sky with the glorious suddenness of eastern dawn, and Jerusalem lay before their eyes.

The remembrance[35] of all that that mighty city had beheld; the enthusiasm of faith; the memory of dangers, and ills, and fatigues, and privations, endured and conquered; the fulfilment of hope; the gratification of long desire; the end of fear and doubt; combined in every

29. Albert.
30. Robert; Guibert.
31. *Ibid.*
32. Albert.
33. Raoul of Caen; Albert; Fulcher.
34. Albert of Aix, lib. v.
35. Guibert.

bosom to call up the sublime of joy. The name was echoed by a thousand tongues—Jerusalem! Jerusalem! Some shouted to the sky;[36] some knelt and prayed; some wept in silence; and some cast themselves down and kissed the blessed earth. "All had much ado," says Fuller, with his emphatic plainness, "to manage so great a gladness."[37]

To rejoicing, at the sight of the Holy City, succeeded wrath, at seeing it in the hands of the *infidels*. The army marched forward in haste, drove in some parties of Saracens, who had vauntingly come forth from the gates; and Jerusalem was invested on all sides. Some of the people, indeed, approached barefoot, in deep humiliation, and in remembrance[38] of the sufferings of Him who had purchased salvation to a world by agony and death; but the greater part of the soldiers advanced with purposes of wrath, and took up their various warlike positions round about the town. The attack was begun almost immediately after the first preparations; and Godfrey of Bouillon, Tancred, the Duke of Normandy, and Robert of Flanders, by a vigorous effort, carried the barbicans, and reached the wall.[39] A portion of this, also, was thrown down with axes and picks; and several knights, mounting by ladders[40] to the top of the battlements, under a hail of arrows and Greek fire, fought for some time hand to hand with the Turks.

At length, after many had fallen on both sides, it became evident to the leaders that nothing could be effected without the usual machines, and the assault was suspended.

All the energies of the host were now employed in constructing implements of war. Timber was procured from Sichon:[41] some Genoese seamen, having arrived at Jaffa, were pressed by the crusaders into the service of the Cross, and by their mechanical skill greatly facilitated the construction of the engines required.

Catapults, *mangonels*,[42] and large moveable towers were prepared, as in the siege of Nice; and to these was added a machine called the sow, formed of wood, and covered with raw hides to protect it from fire, under cover of which soldiers were employed in undermining the walls.[43] During the fabrication of these implements, a dread-

36. Guibert, lib. vii.; Robert.
37. Holy War.
38. Raimond.
39. Robert; Albert; Guibert, lib. vii.
40. Fulcher mentions several ladders, but says they were too few.
41. Albert of Aix; Guibert.
42. Raimond; Albert.
43. Albert of Aix.

ful drought pervaded the army; and all the wells in the circumjacent country having been filled up by the Turks, the only water that reached the camp was brought from far, and paid for as if each drop had been gold. The soldiers, unable to procure it, wandered away in the search, or watched[44] the morning dew, and licked the very stones for moisture. Vice and immorality again grew prevalent, and superstition was obliged to be called, in aid of virtue.

From forty to sixty thousand men were all that remained of multitudes; and it became obvious to the leaders that dissensions could no longer exist without hazarding their destruction. Tancred,[45] the first in every noble act, set the example of conciliation, and embraced his foe Raimond of Toulouse, in the sight of the whole army. An expiatory[46] procession was made by the chiefs, the soldiers, and the clergy, round the city of Jerusalem; and prayers were offered up on each holy place in the neighbourhood for success in this last field. The Turks, on their part, forgetting the desperate valour which the crusaders had displayed on every occasion, beheld these ceremonies with contempt; and raising up the image of the Cross upon the walls, mocked the procession of the Christians, and threw dirt at the symbol of their faith. The wrath of the crusaders was raised to the uttermost, and the sacrilegious insult[47] was remembered to be atoned in blood.

The engines were at last completed, and the attack once more begun. The towers [48] were rolled on to the walls, the battering-rams were plied incessantly, the sow was pushed on to the foundations; and while the Saracens poured forth fire [49] and arrows upon the besiegers, the crusaders waged the warfare with equal courage from their machines. Thus passed the whole day in one of the most tremendous fights that the host of the Cross had ever sustained. Night fell, and the city was not taken. The walls of the town were much injured, as well as the engines used by the assailants; but by the next morning both had been repaired, and the assault recommenced, and was received with equal ardour.[50] The leaders of the Christian army occupied the higher stages

---

44. Guibert; Albert.
45. Albert of Aix.
46. Raimond d'Agiles; Guibert.
47. Albert of Aix.
48. Raimond d'Agiles; Albert of Aix.
49. Albert describes perfectly the effect of the Greek fire, and says it could only be extinguished by the means of vinegar, which, on the second day, the crusaders provided in great quantity.
50. Raimond.

of their moveable towers, and Godfrey of Bouillon himself,[51] armed with a bow, was seen directing his shafts against all who appeared upon the walls.

Such soldiers as the machines could not contain were ranged opposite the walls, urging the battering-rams, plying the mangonels, and, by flights of arrows, covering the attack from the towers. The enthusiasm was great and general; the old, the sick, and the feeble lent what weak aid they could, in bringing forward the missiles and other implements of war, while the women encouraged the warriors to daring, both by words and their example; and hurried through the ranks, bearing water to assuage the thirst of toil and excitement. Still the Saracens resisted with desperate valour. For their homes and for their hearths they fought; and so courageously, that when more than half the day was spent, the host of the crusade was still repulsed in all quarters. At that moment a soldier was suddenly seen on Mount Olivet, waving on the crusaders to follow.[52] How he had penetrated does not appear, or whether he was not the mere creature of fancy. The idea, at all events, instantly raised the fainting hopes of the Christians.

Immense and almost supernatural efforts were made in every quarter; the tower of Godfrey of Bouillon was rolled up till it touched the wall; the moveable bridge was let down, and a knight called Lutold[53] sprang upon the battlements—his brother followed—another and another came to his support.—Godfrey, Baldwin de Bourg, and Eustace de Bouillon rushed in; and the banner of the Cross announced to the anxious eyes of the army that[55] forced his way into another part of the city by escalade. The Turks fought[56] for a time in the streets, but then fled to the mosques, and were in every direction massacred by thousands. It is dreadful to read of the blood which on that awful day washed the pavements of Jerusalem. The courts of the mosque of Omar floated in gore, and scarcely the most remote and obscure corners of the city gave shelter to an infidel head. The soldiers[57] remembered the impious mockeries with which the Turks had insulted the Cross, and the leaders believed that they were doing God good service in exterminating the blasphemous strangers who had polluted

---

51. Guibert; Albert of Aix.
52. Raimond d'Agiles; William of Tyre.
53. Robert; Guibert. lib. vii.; Albert.
54. 15th July. *A. D.* 1099.
55. Guibert; Raimond.
56. Albert; Robert.
57. *Ibid*; Guibert.

the holy places of Jerusalem, persecuted and butchered the unhappy Christians of Judea, and desecrated the altars of God. To have spared them or their accursed race would have been considered impious: and Godfrey himself not only encouraged the slaughter, but aided with his own hand.

An immense number of Saracens had betaken themselves to the temple of Soliman, as it was called,[58] and there had prepared to defend themselves to the last; but the pursuers were too strong to be resisted, and nearly ten thousand men are said to have fallen in that building. Those even who had climbed to the roof were sought out the next day,[59] and several, to avoid the sword, cast themselves down and were dashed to pieces.

Some authors mention a second massacre,[60] and greatly exaggerate the butchery that was perpetrated. In regard to this second massacre, there is much historical evidence to show that no such event took place; and I would fain believe that it was not the case. It cannot, however, be denied, that the most humane of the Christian leaders in that age were taught to look upon all mercy to the *infidels* as an injury to religion; and it is beyond doubt, that after the general slaughter committed on the capture of Jerusalem, Godfrey de Bouillon,[61] with the other leaders and soldiers, washed away the marks of gore, cast off

---

58. Guibert; Raimond d'Agiles; Robert.

59. Tancred and Gaston of Bearn had promised quarter to these unhappy wretches, and had given them a banner as a certain protection. It was early the next morning, before those chiefs were awake, that this massacre was committed by some of the more bloodthirsty of the crusaders. Tancred was with great difficulty prevented from taking signal vengeance on the perpetrators of this crime.—Guibert; Albert.

60. The story of the second massacre rests upon the authority of Albert of Aix, from whose writings it has been copied by all who have repeated it. Albert of Aix never visited the Holy Land. None of those who were present at the fall of Jerusalem (that I can discover) make the slightest mention of such an occurrence; and we have the strongest proof that part of Albert's story is false; for he declares that all the Saracens were slaughtered in this second massacre, even those who had previously been promised protection; and we know that many were sent to Ascalon.—See *Guibert*, lib. vii. Robert, who was present speaks of many who were spared.—*Robertus*, lib. ix. Fulcher, who was in the country, if not present, does not allude to a second massacre. Raimond d'Agiles, who was a witness to the whole, passes it over in silence; though each of these persons always speaks of the slaughter of the Saracens as the most praiseworthy of actions. The Archbishop of Tyre also, who copied Albert wherever he could be proved correct, has stamped doubt upon this anecdote by omitting it entirely. I have thought fit to notice this particularly, because Mills lays no small stress upon the tale.

61. Guibert; Albert; William of Tyre.

their armour, assumed the robe of penitents, and, going to the holy sepulchre, offered up their prayers to the mild Teacher of our beautiful religion, convinced that they had accomplished a great and glorious work, and consummated an acceptable sacrifice in the blood of the *infidels*.

Such was the doctrine which, in that day, men were taught from their cradles: such the strange interpretation put upon the Gospel of Peace.

CHAPTER 9

Election of a King

The great end of the crusade was now accomplished. Jerusalem was delivered from the hands of the *infidels*; but much remained to be done. To conquer the Holy City had been a work of prodigious difficulty; to keep it was perhaps more so; and it became evident that its defence must be intrusted to one powerful chief. For this purpose the several leaders who had formed the general council of the crusade met to elect a King of Jerusalem. The nomination to that high office was so extraordinary an honour, that the writers of each nation whose forces contributed to the crusade have declared their own particular prince to have been chosen;[1] and, as it was known that none of these did actually reign, they have furnished each with a suitable excuse for declining the distinguished task. It is probable, however, that the choice of the assembly really fixed at once upon the only person fitted for the office; and (to combine the words of Fulcher and Robert the Monk) that:—

Considering the excellence of his nobility,[2] his valour as a knight, his gentleness and patient modesty, as well as the purity of his morals, Godfrey of Bouillon was elected king by the whole people composing the army of God, with the unanimous wish, the general consent, and the judgment of all.

Various clerical cabals followed for the dignity of patriarch, of which it is not necessary to speak here.

Scarcely was the new monarch[3] seated on his throne, when the

1. See Raimond d'Agiles; Guibert; Albert; Brompton; William of Malmsbury.
2. Fulcher, cap. 18; Robert. Mon. lib. ix.
3. Godfrey appears never to have taken the title of king, from a feeling of religious humility.

gathering forces of the Moslems called him again into the field. With the wise policy of activity, Godfrey did not wait to be besieged in Jerusalem, but marching out with all the troops he could muster, he advanced towards Ascalon, where a large *infidel* army had assembled, attacked and routed it completely, and thus secured the conquest he had gained.[4] But the virtues of Godfrey were not long destined to bless, or his talents to protect, the new kingdom of Jerusalem.[5] In the month of July, 1100, he was seized with a severe illness, on his return from a distant expedition, and in a few days the throne of the Holy Land was vacant.

Such an unexpected event of course spread dissension and consternation among the crusaders. Tancred, who was at Jerusalem, and from his great military name enjoyed no small power, offered the crown to Boemond, and beyond all doubt would have succeeded in causing his election, had Boemond been able to accept immediately the sceptre thus held out to him.[6] But the Prince of Antioch[7] was at the moment a prisoner in the hands of some Armenian Turks.[8] The Patriarch, on his part, endeavoured to raise Jerusalem into a simple hierarchy,[9] and to unite the crown with the mitre. The partisans of the Count of Toulouse also struggled in his behalf for the supreme power; but in the end, Baldwin, Prince of Edessa, the brother of Godfrey, was elected, and after some intriguing on the part of the Patriarch, was anointed King of Jerusalem.

It does not enter into the plan of this book to give a history of Jerusalem under its Latin kings: I shall, however, briefly notice each, that the occasion and object of the after-crusades may be properly understood.

Baldwin, on his election,[10] displayed virtues that had slumbered,

---

4. Robert.

5. Albert; Will. Tyr.

6. Albert.

7. He was taken, after having suffered a complete defeat from the emir Damisman, as he was hastening to the succour of Gabriel of Armenia.

8. Will. Tyren.; Radulph.; Cadom.

9. Arnould, one of the most corrupt priests in the army, had been elected patriarch, but was deposed almost immediately; and Daimbert, who arrived from Rome as legate, was chosen in his stead. This Daimbert it is of whom I speak above. He seems to have conceived, from the first, the idea of making Jerusalem an eastern Rome, and wrung many concessions from Godfrey, which were little respected by that chief's successors.

10. William of Tyre.

and lost vices that had been displayed on other occasions. He extended the boundaries of his kingdom, humbled its Saracen enemies, instituted wise and salutary laws, and showed firmness, moderation, and activity in his new station, as well as the great military skill and enterprising spirit he had formerly evinced. He took Assur,[11] Cesarea, and Acre; and added Beritus, Sidon, and several other places to the kingdom of Jerusalem. At length, in the execution of a bold expedition into Egypt, Baldwin died, and his body, after being embalmed, by his own particular direction, was carried back to the Holy City.

Baldwin de Bourg, who, on the elevation of Baldwin I. to the throne of Jerusalem, had received the principality of Edessa, was now called to the vacant throne, and proved himself one of the wisest and most valiant of the Latin sovereigns of Judea. He also greatly extended the limits of his dominions; but in passing between Turbessel and Edessa, accompanied by a few soldiers only,[12] and unsuspicious of any ambuscade, he was suddenly surrounded, and carried a prisoner to Khortopret, where he remained in close confinement for several years.

During his imprisonment Tyre was added to the territories of Jerusalem,[13] and various successful battles were fought against the Moslems. After his liberation he offered the hand of his daughter to Foulk of Anjou, who had some time before visited Jerusalem upon an armed pilgrimage. The Count of Anjou gladly accepted the proposal, and returning to the Holy Land, espoused Melesinda, soon after which he ascended the throne of Jerusalem, on the death of Baldwin. Foulk combined many virtues;[14] was kind, affable, and humane, as well as skilful and courageous in the field. After a reign of thirteen years he left the kingdom to his son, entire, indeed, but neither more extended in territory, nor more consolidated in power, than when he received it.

Baldwin III. succeeded; at the time of his accession being but a boy. Dissensions and animosities raged among all the feudal dependants of the crown of Jerusalem.[15] The Moslems scattered through the country, and girding it on every side, took advantage of each new dispute to harass their Latin invaders with desultory warfare. The emperors of the east strove continually to wrest something of their old possessions from the descendants of the crusaders, and thus divided the forces, and

---

11. Hist. Hieros.; Jacob. lib. i.; William of Tyre; Fulcher; Albert.
12. Will. of Tyre; Fulcher of Chartres.
13. Fulcher.
14. William of Tyre.
15. Hist. Hieros.; Jacob. Vit.; Will. of Tyre.

paralyzed all the efforts made by the Christians to establish and secure their yet infirm dominion.

At length Zenghi, *emir* of Aleppo, and Mosul marched against Edessa, the government of which principality had been transferred, on the accession of Baldwin de Bourg to the throne of Jerusalem, to Joscelyn de Courtenay, and from him had descended to his son. The son had not inherited the virtues or the valour of his father; and while Zenghi attacked, stormed, and took Edessa, he was rioting in debaucheries at Turbessel. So severe a reverse spread consternation through Palestine. Others, though of a less important nature, followed; and the news of these misfortunes soon reached Europe, where it gave matter to the eloquence of St. Bernard, and occasion for a new crusade.

Long before this period, all the chiefs who had at first led the armies of the Cross to Jerusalem had tasted of the cup reserved for all men, and few words will end the history of each. Godfrey, Baldwin, and Baldwin de Bourg we have already conducted to the tomb. Boemond,[16] as I have said, fell into the hands of the Moslems; and after a captivity of two years, was permitted to pay a ransom, and return to his principality. On arriving, he found that his noble relative, Tancred,[17] had not only preserved, but increased his territories during his absence; and after several years continual warfare with Alexius on the one hand, and the Moslems on the other, mingled with opposition to the King of Jerusalem, Boemond sailed for Europe. There the fame he had acquired obtained for him the hand of Constantia,[18] daughter of the King of France. Her younger sister, Cecilia, was bestowed upon Tancred, who had remained in the government of Antioch.

By the aid of France, Boemond raised large forces and landing in Greece, ravaged the dominions of Alexius, who was at length fain to conclude a peace with the powerful and enterprising Italian. The Prince of Antioch then sent forward the greater part of his troops to the Holy Land, while he himself returned to Italy to prepare for the same journey. Death, however, staid his progress;[19] for, after a short illness, he ended his career in Apulia, in 1109.[20] Tancred still survived,

---

16. Fulcher; Albert.

17. Raoul of Caen; Will. Tyr.; Fulcher.

18. Guibert; lib. vii.

19. Will. of Tyr.; Guibert.

20. Guibert says that Boemond died from the effects of poison. Other authors declare that grief for having been obliged to enter into a less advantageous treaty with Alexius than he had anticipated occasioned his death; but, from his whole history, I should not look upon Boemond as a man likely to die of grief.

and defended constantly the territories of his cousin against every attack for three years after the decease of Boemond. At last the consequences of a wound he had received some time before proved fatal, and the noblest and most chivalrous of all the Christian warriors died in the prime of his days.

On his death-bed he called to him his wife, and Pontius, the son of the Prince of Tripoli,[21] and, aware of the necessity of union among the Christians, he recommended strongly their marriage, after death should have dissolved the ties between himself and Cecilia. The government of Antioch he bequeathed to his cousin Roger;[22] but, with the same noble integrity which he had displayed through life, he made the new regent promise, that in case the son of Boemond should ever come to claim those territories, they should be resigned to him without dispute. Thus died Tancred; who, from all that we read of the crusaders, was, with the exception of Godfrey, the noblest of the followers of the Cross—a gallant leader, a disinterested man, a generous friend, a true knight.

Previous to his death, however, he had been engaged in all the great events in Palestine. After the election of Godfrey, and the Battle of Ascalon, the other chiefs of the crusade had either returned to Europe or spread themselves over the country, in pursuit of their own schemes of private ambition, leaving the new kingdom of Jerusalem to be supported by its king and Tancred, with an army of less than three thousand men. This penury of forces however, did not long continue, or the Holy Land must soon have resumed the yoke it had thrown off. The spirit of pilgrimage was still active in Europe; and combined with this spirit was the hope of gain, springing from vague and exaggerated accounts of the wealth and the principalities which the leaders of the first expedition had acquired.

Pilgrimages now differed from those that had preceded the conquest of Jerusalem, in being armed; and many bodies, of several thousand men each, arrived both by sea and land, and proved exceedingly serviceable in peopling the devastated lands of Palestine. Various larger enterprises, more deserving the name of crusades, were planned and attempted, which it would be endless to name, and tedious to recount. Nearly five hundred thousand people set out from Europe for Syria,[23]

---

21. He was the grandson of that Raimond, Count of Toulouse, of whose conduct I have so often had occasion to speak already, and whose perseverance against Tripoli will be mentioned hereafter.
22. Will. Tyr.
23. Fulcher; Albert of Aix; William of Tyre.

and to these several of those crusaders who had gone back to Europe joined themselves, urged either by shame for their former desertion, or by the hope of obtaining easier conquests, and less dangerous honours.

Of these, then, I will speak first, before noticing more particularly the armed pilgrimages, in order that I may trace to the end all those leaders of the first crusade who died in the Holy Land. The first great expedition set out not many years after the taking of Jerusalem, and consisted of several smaller ones from various countries, which united into larger bodies as they proceeded, and endeavoured to force their way through Asia Minor. At the head of these armies were Count Albert,[24] of Lombardy; Conrad, Constable of the Western Empire; Stephen, Count of Blois, whom we have seen flying from the land to which shame now drove him back; Stephen, Duke of Burgundy; the Bishops of Laon and of Milan; the Duke of Parma; Hugh, Count of Vermandois,[25] who now again turned towards Jerusalem; and the Count of Nevers: as well as William, Count of Poitiers; Guelf, Duke of Bavaria; and Ida, Marchioness of Austria.

At Constantinople the first division met with Raimond of Toulouse,[26] who had returned to that city from the Holy Land, in search of aid to pursue the schemes of a grasping and ambitious spirit. The new crusaders put themselves, in some degree, under his command and guidance; but their first step was to disobey his orders, and to take the way of Paphlagonia, instead of following the track of the former crusade. They were for many days harassed in their march by the Turks, then exposed to famine and drought, and finally attacked and cut to pieces by Kilidge Aslan, who revenged, by the death of more than a hundred thousand Christians,[27] all the losses they had caused him to undergo. The principal leaders made good their escape, first to Constantinople, and then to Antioch; except Hugh of Vermandois, who died of his wound at Tarsus.

The Count of Nevers,[28] who commanded the second body, met the same fate as the rest, and followed them to Antioch, after the destruction of his whole force. William of Poitiers, with the Duke of Bavaria and the Marchioness Ida, were also encountered by the victo-

---

24. Albert of Aix; William of Tyre.
25. Fulcher.
26. Albert of Aix.
27. Fulcher; Albert.
28. Albert.

rious Saracens, and their defeat added another to the triumphs of the infidels and to the Christian disasters. The Duke of Bavaria, stripping himself of his arms, fled to the mountains, and made his escape. The precise fate of Ida of Austria remained unknown; but it appears certain she was either suffered to die in captivity, or was crushed to death under the horses' feet.[29] The Count of Poitiers, completely destitute of all resources, and separated from his companions, wandered on foot till he arrived at Antioch,[30] where he was kindly received by Tancred, still alive, and met the other chiefs who had encountered disasters like his own.[31]

The principal leaders proceeded straight to Jerusalem, with the exception of Raimond of Toulouse, who had long fixed his heart upon the conquest of the rich tract of Tripoli, which he attempted for some time in vain. Death staid him in his progress,[32] and Baldwin succeeded in accomplishing what he had designed; after which the king erected the territory acquired into a feudal county, which was bestowed upon the son of the deceased Raimond.

In the meanwhile Stephen, Count of Blois, reached Jerusalem; and having, by a second completed pilgrimage, wiped out, as he thought, the disgrace of having quitted the first crusade, he embarked, with William of Poitiers, to return to Europe. A contrary wind, however, drove back the vessel into Jaffa,[33] and here Stephen found himself called upon to join Baldwin in an attack upon the Turks. The king advanced with only seven hundred knights,[34] deceived by reports of the enemy's weakness; but in the plains of Ramula he found himself suddenly opposed to the whole Turkish army. The spirit of chivalry forbade his avoiding the encounter, and in a short time the greater part of his force was cut to pieces. He himself, with his principal knights, made their way to the castle of Ramula, from which he contrived to escape alone. The rest were taken, fighting bravely for their lives; and though some were spared, Stephen of Blois[35] was one of several who were only reserved for slaughter.

Thus died the leaders of the first crusade who met their fate in Palestine, and thus ended the greater and more general expeditions which

29. Albert of Aix.
30. Fulcher.
31. Albert.
32. Fulcher, cap. 35, *A. D.* 1105
33. Fulcher, cap. 27.
34. Albert, lib. ix.; Fulcher.
35. Albert; Fulcher.

had been sanctioned by the council of Clermont, and excited by the preaching of Peter the Hermit. The ultimate fate of that extraordinary individual himself remains in darkness. On the capture of Jerusalem, when the triumphant Europeans spread themselves through the city, the Christian inhabitants flocked forth to acknowledge and gratulate their deliverers.[36] Then it was that all the toils and dangers which the Hermit had endured, were a thousand fold repaid, and that all his enthusiasm met with its reward.

The Christians of Jerusalem instantly recognised the poor pilgrim who had first spoken to them words of hope, and had promised them, in their misery under the Turkish oppression, that aid and deliverance which had at length so gloriously reached them.[37] In the fervour of their gratitude they attributed all to him; and, casting themselves at his feet, called the blessing of Heaven on the head of their benefactor. After that period Peter is mentioned several times by the historians of Jerusalem;[38] and we find that he certainly did act a very principal part in the clerical government of the city.[39] Whether he returned to Europe or not I confess I do not know. He is said to have founded the abbey of Montier, in France, and to have died there; but this rests upon no authority worthy of confidence.

In the meanwhile, many of the Christians who had escaped the active swords of the Saracens in Asia Minor made their way to Jerusalem, and served to people and protect the land. Various armaments, also, arrived at the different seaports, bearing each of them immense numbers of military pilgrims, who, after having visited the holy places, never failed to offer their services to the king of Jerusalem, for the purpose of executing any single object that might be desirable at the time.

Three only of these bodies are worthy of particular notice, that of the English, Danes,[40] and Flemings, who assisted Baldwin at the unsuccessful siege of Sidon—the Norwegian expedition which succeeded in taking that city—and that of the Venetians, who afterward aided in the capture of Tyre. The Genoese[41] and the Pisans, also, from

36. James of Vitry; Hist. Hieros. ab.

37. Hist. Hieros. abrev.

38. Mills says that the last historical mention of Peter is that which relates to his recognition by the Christians of Jerusalem; but such is not the case. We find him mentioned as a very influential person on the occasion of the battle of Ascalon.—See *Raimond d'Agiles*; *Guibert*, lib. vii.

39. Guibert, lib. vii.

40. Albert of Aix, lib. x.; William of Tyre.

41. Fulcher; William of Tyre.

time to time sent out vessels to the coast of Palestine; but these voyages, which combined in a strange manner the purposes of traffic, superstition, and warfare, tended rather to the general prosperity of the country by commerce, and to its protection, by bringing continual recruits, than to any individual enterprise or conquest.

Many anecdotes are told of the first crusaders by their contemporary historians, which—though resting on evidence so far doubtful as to forbid their introduction as absolute facts—I shall mention in exemplification of the manners and customs of the time.

The number of women and children who followed the first crusaders to the Holy Land is known to have been immense; but it is not a little extraordinary, that in spite of all the hardships and dangers of the way, a great multitude of both arrived safe at Jerusalem. The women we find, on almost all occasions, exercising the most heroic firmness in the midst of battles and destruction; and Guibert gives a curious account of the military spirit which seized upon the children during the siege of Antioch.

The boys of the Saracens and the young crusaders, armed with sticks for lances, and stones instead of arrows, would issue from the town and the camp, and under leaders chosen from among themselves,[42] who assumed the names of the principal chiefs, would advance in regular squadrons, and fight in the sight of the two hosts, with a degree of rancour which showed to what a pitch the mutual hatred of the nations was carried. Even after the crusaders had fallen in battle or had died of the pestilence, their children still pursued their way, and getting speedily accustomed to fatigue and privation, evinced powers of endurance equal to those of the most hardy warriors.

With the army of the Cross also was a multitude of men—the same author declares—who made it a profession to be without money; they walked barefoot, carried no arms, and even preceded the beasts of burden in the march, living upon roots and herbs, and presenting a spectacle both disgusting and pitiable. A Norman,[43] who, according to all accounts, was of noble birth, but who, having lost his horse, continued to follow as a foot-soldier, took the strange resolution of putting himself at the head of this race of vagabonds, who willingly received him for their king.

Among the Saracens these men became well known, under the name of *Thafurs* (which Guibert translates *Trudentes*), and were held

42. Guibert, lib. vii.
43. *Ibid.*.

149

in great horror from the general persuasion that they fed on the dead bodies of their enemies: a report which was occasionally justified, and which the king of the Thafurs took care to encourage. This respectable monarch was frequently in the habit of stopping his followers one by one, in any narrow defile, and of causing them to be searched carefully, lest the possession of the least sum of money should render them unworthy of the name of his subjects.[44] If even two *sous* were found upon anyone, he was instantly expelled from the society of his tribe, the king bidding him, contemptuously, buy arms and fight.

This troop, so far from being cumbersome to the army, was infinitely serviceable, carrying burdens, bringing in forage, provisions, and tribute, working the machines in the sieges, and, above all, spreading consternation among the Turks, who feared death from the lances of the knights less than that further consummation, they heard of, under the teeth of the Thafurs.

Mercy towards the Turks was considered, by the contemporary clergy, to whom we owe all accounts of the crusades, as so great a weakness, that perhaps fewer instances of it are on record than really took place; for we seldom find any mention of clemency to an *infidel*, without blame being attached to it. Thus the promise of Tancred to save the Turks on the roof of the temple is highly censured, as well as the act of the Count of Toulouse, in granting their lives to some five hundred wretches, who had taken refuge in the Tower of David.

One deed of this kind is told of Baldwin I., more as in its consequences it saved the king's person, than as anything praiseworthy in itself. Passing along one day on horseback, after his troops had been employed in wasting the country, Baldwin is said to have met with an Arabian woman, who had been taken in labour by the way.[45] He covered her with his own cloak, ordered her to be protected by his attendants, and having left her with two skins of water, and two female camels, he pursued his march. The chances of the desultory warfare of those times soon brought back her husband to the spot, and his gratitude was the more ardent as the benefit he had received was unusual and unexpected.

After the fatal day of Ramula, while Baldwin, with but fifty companions, besieged in the ill-fortified castle of that place, was dreaming of nothing but how to sell his life dearly, a single Arab approached the gates in the dead of the night, and demanded to speak with the king.

44. Guibert, lib. vii.
45. William of Tyre..

He was in consequence brought to Baldwin's presence,[46] where he recalled to his mind the kindness once shown to the Arab woman, his wife; and then offered to lead him safely through the lines of the enemy. The fate of Palestine at that moment hung upon Baldwin's life, and, trusting himself in the hands of the Arab, he was faithfully conducted to his own camp,[47] where he appeared, says William of Tyre, like the morning star breaking through the clouds.

Superstition, which in that age was at its height in Europe, was, of course, not unknown in Palestine, and all sorts of visions were seen. Battles, according to the monkish accounts, were won by relics and prayers more than by swords and lances. A part of the Holy Cross was said to be found in Jerusalem, a thousand more martyrs were dug up than ever were buried, and we find one of the bishops *ferens in pyxide lac sanctæ Mariæ Virginis*. Ghosts[48] of saints, too, were seen on every occasion, and the Devil himself, in more than one instance, appeared to the crusaders, tempting them with consummate art to all kinds of crimes. The evil spirit, however, often—indeed generally—found himself cheated by his victims in the end, who, by repentance, gifts to the church, and fanatical observances, easily found means to "swear the seal from off their bond."

The appearance of an army in the times of the first crusade was highly gorgeous and magnificent.[49] The number of banners of purple and gold, and rich colours—each feudal baron having the right to bear his banner to the field—rendered the Christian host in full array as bright a spectacle as the sun could shine upon. The armour of the knights also gave a glittering and splendid effect to the scene; nor was this armour as has been represented, entirely of that kind called chain mail, which formed the original hauberk. It varied according to various nations, and it is evident from the continual mention of the corslet or breastplate, by all the authors I have had occasion to cite in this work, that that piece of plate armour was used during the first crusade.[50]

It is probable, however, that the armour generally worn was prin-

46. Albert of Aix and Fulcher give a different account of Baldwin's escape.

47. Will. Tyr. lib. x.

48. Albert; Raimond d'Agiles; Fulcher; William of Tyre; Guibert.

49. Albert of Aix; Raimond d'Agiles; Guibert.

50. Mills is wrong in supposing that plate armour was not at all known before the beginning of the thirteenth century. As far back as the time of Louis the Debonair, the Monk of St. Gall gives a full description of a man in plate armour, and also mentions the barb, or iron covering of the horse.

cipally linked mail, which, in the case of the knights, enveloped the whole body, being composed of a shirt of rings, with hose, shoes, and gauntlets, of the same materials. The helmet might also be covered with a chain hood, which completed the dress. In addition to this, it is not unlikely that a *cuirass* was frequently worn with the shirt, as we find, from the poem of William the Breton on Philip Augustus, that it was even then a common practice to wear a double plastron or *cuirass*, though plate armour had returned into common use. The shield, charged with some design, but certainly not with regular armorial bearings, together with the lance, sword, and mace, completed the arms, offensive and defensive, of a knight of that day.[51]

I cannot find that either the battle-axe or the armour for the horse is mentioned during the crusade; yet we know that both had been made use of long before. The foot-soldiers were in some cases allowed to wear a shirt of mail, but not a complete hauberk, and were armed with pikes, bows, and crossbows; though it would seem that they gained their knowledge of the latter instrument from the Saracens, there being several lamentations, in all the accounts of their first entrance into Asia Minor, over their unskilfulness in the use of the *arbalist*. The luxury with which the Christians marched to the crusade may be conceived from the narrative given by Albert of Aix, of the rout of the troops of Conrad and his companions, who followed to the Holy Land, immediately after the capture of Jerusalem. Among the spoils taken by the Turks, he mentions ermines,[52] sables, and all kinds of rich furs, purple and gold embroidery, and an incalculable quantity of silver. The roads, he says, were so strewed with riches, that the pursuers trod upon nothing but *besants* and other pieces of money, precious stones, vases of gold and silver, and every sort of silk and fine stuff.

The Turks proceeded to battle with even greater magnificence; and, after the victories of Antioch and Ascalon, we read continually of invaluable booty, jewels,[53] golden helmets and armour standards of silver, and scimitars of unknown worth. The arms of the Turks were lighter, in all probability, than those of the Christians, and in general consisted of the sword and the bow, in the use of which they were exceedingly skilful.[54] We find, however, that the various nations of

---

51. See, for these particulars, the Monk of St. Gall; Albert of Aix; Raimond d'Agiles; Fulcher; Guibert; William of Brittany; Menestrier St. Palaye; Ducange.
52. Albert of Aix, lib. viii.
53. Fulcher; Guibert.
54. Albert of Aix; Fulcher; Robertus Monachus.

which the Mahommedan armies were composed used very different weapons; though all were remarkable for the manner in which they eluded their enemies, by their skill in horsemanship, and the fleetness of their chargers. One nation, mentioned by Albert of Aix under the title of Azoparts, are called *the invincible*, and were furnished with heavy maces, with which they aimed at the heads of the horses, and seldom failed to bring them down.

After the conquest of Palestine by the Christians,[55] the surrounding tribes continued to wage an unceasing war against their invaders; but nevertheless many of the Mussulman towns within the limits of the kingdom of Jerusalem submitted to the conquerors, and were admitted to pay tribute. A free communication also took place between the followers of the two religions, and a greater degree of connexion began to exist than was very well consistent with the fanaticism of either people. A mixed race even sprang up from the European[56] and Asiatic population, the children of parents from different continents being called Pullani. At the same time the country was governed by European laws,[57] which, not coming within the absolute scope of this book, I must avoid treating of, from the very limited space to which I am obliged to confine myself.

Suffice it to say, that Godfrey of Bouillon, among the first cares of government, appointed a commission to inquire into the laws and customs of the various nations which formed the population of the country he was called to rule. From the investigation thus entered into was drawn up an admirable code of feudal law, under the title of *Assizes de Jerusalem*. Two institutions of a strictly chivalrous nature, which were founded, properly speaking, between the first and second crusades,[58] I must mention here, as all the after-history of knighthood is more or less connected with their progress. I mean the two military orders of the Hospital and the Temple.

The spirit of religious devotion and military fervour had been so intimately united during the whole of the crusade, that the combination of the austere rules of the monk, with the warlike activity of the soldier, seems to have been a necessary consequence of the wars of the Cross.

Long previous to the crusade, some of the citizens of Amalfi hav-

---

55. Fulcher; William of Tyre; Albert.
56. Ducange.
57. Assizes par Thaumassiere.
58. William of Tyre, lib. xviii.

ing been led to Jerusalem,[59] partly from feelings of devotion, partly in the pursuit of commerce, had witnessed the misery to which pilgrims were exposed on their road to the Holy Land, and determined to found an hospital in which pious travellers might be protected and solaced after their arrival at the end of their journey. The influence which the Italian merchants possessed through their commercial relations at the court of the *calif*, easily obtained permission to establish the institution proposed. A piece of ground near the supposed site of the holy sepulchre was assigned to them, and the chapel and hospital were accordingly built, at different times, and placed under the patronage, the one of St. Mary, and the other of St. John the Almoner.

A religious house was also constructed for those charitable persons, of both sexes, who chose to dedicate themselves to the service of the pilgrims, and who, on their admission, subjected themselves to the rule of St. Benedict. All travellers, whether Greeks or Latins, were received into the hospital; and the monks even extended their charitable care to the sick or poor Mussulmans who surrounded them.

During the siege of Jerusalem by the crusaders, all the principal Christians of the town were thrown into prison; among others, the abbot (as he is called by James of Vitry)[60] of the monastery of St. John. He was a Frenchman by birth, named Gerard; and, after the taking of the city, was liberated, with other Christian prisoners, and returned to the duties of his office, in attending the sick and wounded crusaders who were brought into the Hospital. After the Battle of Ascalon, Godfrey visited the establishment, where he still found many of the followers of the crusade, who, struck with admiration at the institution, and filled with gratitude for the services they had received, determined to embrace the order, and dedicate their lives also to acts of charity.

Godfrey, as a reward for the benefits which these holy men had conferred on his fellow-Christians, endowed the Hospital (now in a degree separated from the abbey of St. Mary) with a large estate, in his hereditary dominions in Brabant. Various other gifts were added by the different crusaders of rank; and the Poor Brothers of the Hospital of St. John began to find themselves a rich and flourishing community. It was at this period that they first took the black habit and the white cross of eight points, and subjected themselves, by peculiar vows, to the continual attendance on pilgrims and sick persons.[61]

---

59. Vertot.
60. Hist. Hierosol., Jacob. Vitri.
61. Vertot Preuves.

Pascal II. soon after bestowed upon the order several valuable privileges, among which were, exemption from all tithes, the right of electing their own superior, and absolute immunity from all secular or clerical interference. The constant resort of pilgrims to the Holy Land not only increased the wealth of the Hospitallers, but spread their fame to other countries. Princes and kings conferred lands and benefices upon them, and the order began to throw out ramifications into Europe, where hospitals, under the same rule, were erected, and may be considered as the first *commanderies* of the institution.

At the death of Gerard, which took place almost immediately after that of Baldwin I., Raimond Dupuy, one of the crusaders who had attached himself to the Hospital on having been cured of his wounds received at the siege of Jerusalem, was elected master, and soon conceived the idea of rendering the wealth and number of the Hospitallers serviceable to the state in other ways than those which they had hitherto pursued. His original profession of course led him to the thought of combining war with devotion, and he proposed to his brethren to reassume the sword, binding themselves, however, by a vow, to draw it only against the enemies of Christ. In what precise year the Hospitallers first appeared in arms is not very clearly ascertained; but it is a matter of no moment, and it is certain that they became a military body during the reign of Baldwin du Bourg.[62]

The order of St. John was then divided into three classes, knights, clergy, and serving brothers. Each of these classes still, when absent from the field, dedicated themselves to the service of the sick; but the knights were chosen from the noble or military rank of the Hospitallers, and commanded in battle and in the hospital. The clergy, besides the ordinary duties of their calling, followed the armies as almoners and chaplains; and the serving brothers fought under the knights in battle, or obeyed their directions in their attendance on the sick. At first, the garments and food of these grades were the same. The vows also were alike to all, and implied chastity, obedience to their superior and to the council, together with individual poverty.

The objects now proposed were war against the *infidels*, and protection and comfort to the Christian pilgrims. The knights were bound by strict and severe rules; they were enjoined to avoid all luxury, to travel two or three together, seeking only such lodging in the various towns as was provided for them by their community, and burning a light during the night, that they might be always prepared against

---

62. Vertot.

the enemy. Their faults[63] were heavily punished by fasts, by imprison-
ments, and even by expulsion from the order; and they were taught to
look for no reward but from on high. Nevertheless, before the good
Bishop of Acre composed his curious work on the Holy Land, probably about the year 1228, the Hospitallers, he tells us, were buying
for themselves castles and towns, and submitting territories to their
authority like the princes of the earth.

The origin of the order of Red-cross Knights, or Templars, was
very different, though its military object was nearly the same. The
Christian power in Palestine was probably as firmly established at the
time of Baldwin du Bourg, as during any other period of its existence;
yet the mixture of the population, the proximity of a thousand in-
imical tribes, the roving habits of the Turks, who—generally worsted
by the Christians in the defence of cities and in arrayed fields—now
harassed their enemies with a constant, but flying warfare; all rendered
the plains of the Holy Land a scene of unremitting strife, where the
pilgrim and the traveller were continually exposed to danger, plunder,
and death. Some French knights, who had followed the first crusade,[64]
animated beyond their fellows with the religious and military fury
which inspired that enterprise, entered into a solemn compact to aid
each other in freeing the highways of the Holy Land, protecting pilgrims and travellers, and fighting against the enemies of the Cross.

They embraced the rule of St. Augustin; renounced all worldly
goods, and bound themselves by oath to obey the commands of their
grand master; to defend the Christian faith; to cross the seas in aid of
their brethren; to fight unceasingly against the *infidel*, and never to turn
back from less than four adversaries.[65] The founders of this order were
Hugh de Paganis and Geoffrey de St. Aldemar—or, according to some,
de St. Omer—who had both signalized themselves in the religious
wars. Having no fixed dwelling, the Templars were assigned a lodging
in a palace in the immediate vicinity of the Temple, from whence they
derived the name by which they have since been known.

The number of these knights was at first but nine, and during
the nine years which followed their institution, they were marked by
no particular garb,[66] wearing the secular habit of the day, which was
furnished to them by charity alone. The clergy of the temple itself

---

63. Jacob Vitriaci in Hist. Hierosol.
64. William of Tyre.
65. Jac. Vitriaci; Hist. Hierosol.
66. Will. Tyrensis, lib. xxii.; Jacob. Vit.

conferred on their body a space of ground between that building and the palace,[67] for the purpose of military exercises, and various other benefices speedily followed. At the council[68] of Troyes, their situation was considered, and a white garment was appointed for their dress. Their vows became very similar to those of the knights of St. John; the numbers of the body rapidly augmented; possessions and riches flowed in upon them apace, as their services became extended and general. They added a red cross to their robe, and raised a banner of their own, on which they bestowed the name of *Beauséant*.

The order, as it increased, was soon divided into the various classes of servants of arms, esquires, and knights; and, in addition to their great standard, which was white with the red cross—symbolical, like their dress, of purity of life, and courage, even to death—they bore to battle a banner composed of white and black stripes, intended to typify their tenderness to their friends and implacability towards their enemies.— Their valour became so noted, that, like that of the famous tenth legion,[69] it was a support to itself; and, according to James of Vitry, any Templar, on hearing the cry to arms, would have been ashamed to have asked the number of the enemy. The only question was, "Where are they?"

On entering the order, the Grand Master cautioned the aspirant that he was, in a manner, called upon to resign his individuality. Not only his property and his body, but his very thoughts, belonged, from the moment of his admission, to the institution of which he became a part. He was bound in everything to obey the commands of his superior, and poverty of course formed a part of his vow. His inclinations, his feelings, his passions, were all to be rendered subservient to the cause he embraced; and he was exhorted to remember, before he engaged himself to the performance of so severe an undertaking, that he would often be obliged to watch when he desired to sleep, to suffer

---

67. William of Tyre.

68. William of Tyre marks precisely, that the particular rules to which they were subjected, and the dress to which they were restricted, were regularly fixed by the church at the council of Troyes, in the course of the ninth year after their first institution. Now the council of Troyes took place in 1128, and Baldwin du Bourg ascended the throne of Jerusalem on the 2nd or April, 1118, ten years previously. Their first institution, therefore, could not be in the reign of Baldwin I., as Mills has stated it, without a gross error on the part of the Archbishop of Tyre, who wrote in the year 1184, and therefore was not likely to be mistaken on a subject so near his own days.

69. *Hist. Hierosol;* Jacob. Vitriaci.

toil when his limbs required rest, and to undergo the pangs of thirst and the cravings of hunger when food would be most delightful.

After these and similar warnings of the painful and self-denying nature of the task which he was about to impose upon himself, he was asked three times if he still desired to enter into the order, and on giving an answer in the affirmative, he was invested with the robe, and admitted to the vows, after previous proof that he was qualified in other respects, according to the rules of the institution.

No possible means has ever been devised of keeping any body of men poor; and the Templars, whose first device was two knights riding on one horse, to signify their poverty and humility, were soon one of the richest, and beyond comparison the proudest, of the European orders. Their preceptories were to be found in every country, and as their vows did not embrace[70] the charitable avocations which, with the knights of St. John, filled up the hours unemployed in military duties, the Templars soon added to their pride all that host of vices which so readily step in to occupy the void of idleness. While the knights of St. John, spreading benefit and comfort around them, notwithstanding many occasional faults and errors, remained esteemed and beloved, on the whole, both by sovereigns and people; the knights of the Temple were only suffered for some centuries, feared, hated, avoided; and at last were crushed, at a moment when it is probable that a reform was about to work itself in their order.[71]

---

70. The Templars founded many charitable institutions, but attendance on the sick was not a part of their profession.

71. For a more particular and correct account of the armour of the crusades, I must refer to the invaluable work of Dr. Meyrick, which I regret much not to have had by me while writing this book. My sources of information have been alone the historians of the day, in consulting whom the ambiguity of language is very often likely to induce error in matters which, like armour, are difficult to describe.

CHAPTER 10

Consequences of the Loss of Edessa

The loss of Edessa shook the kingdom of Jerusalem; not so much from the importance of the city or its territory, as from the exposed state in which it left the frontier of the newly established monarchy. The activity, the perseverance, the power of the Moslems had been too often felt not to be dreaded; and there is every reason to believe, that the clergy spoke but the wishes of the whole people, when in their letters to Europe they pressed their Christian brethren to come once more to the succour of Jerusalem. Shame and ambition led the young Count of Edessa to attempt the recovery of his capital as soon as the death of Zenghi, who had taken it, reached his ears. He in consequence collected a large body of troops, and on presenting himself before the walls during the night, was admitted, by his friends, into the town.

There he turned his whole efforts to force the Turkish garrison in the citadel to surrender, before Nourhaddin, the son of Zenghi, could arrive to its aid. But the Saracens held out; and, while the Latin soldiers besieged the castle, they found themselves suddenly surrounded by a large body of the enemy, under the command of Nourhaddin. In this situation, they endeavoured to cut their way through the Turkish force, but, attacked on every side, few of them escaped to tell the tale of their own defeat. Nourhaddin marched over their necks into Edessa, and, in order to remove for ever that bulwark to the Christian kingdom of Jerusalem, he caused the fortifications to be razed to the ground.

The consternation of the people of Palestine became great and general. The road to the Holy City lay open before the enemy, and continual applications for assistance reached Europe, but more particularly France.

159

The state of that country, however, was the least[1] propitious that it is possible to conceive for a crusade. The position of all the orders of society had undergone a change since the period when the wars of the Cross were first preached by Peter the Hermit; and of the many causes which had combined to hurry the armed multitudes to the Holy Land, none remained but the spirit of religious fanaticism and military enterprise. At the time of the first crusade, the feudal system had reached the acme of its power. The barons had placed a king upon the throne. They had rendered their own dominion independent of his, and though they still acknowledged some ties between themselves and the monarch—some vague and general power of restraint in the king and his court of peers—yet those ties were so loose, that power was so undefined in its nature, and so difficult in its exercise, that the nobles were free and at liberty to act in whatever direction enthusiasm, ambition, or cupidity might call them, without fear of the sovereign, who was, in fact, but one of their own body loaded with a crown.

The people, too, at that time, both in the towns and in the fields, were the mere slaves of the nobility; and as there existed scarcely a shadow of vigour in the kingly authority, so there remained not an idea of distinct rights and privileges among the populace. Thus the baronage were then unfettered by dread from any quarter; and the lower classes—both the poorer nobility, and that indistinct tribe (which we find evidently[2] marked) who were neither among the absolute serfs of

1. Mills says, "The news of the loss of the eastern frontier of the Latin kingdom reached France at a time peculiarly favourable for foreign war." It will be seen that I have taken up a position as exactly the reverse of that assumed by that excellent author as can well be conceived; but I have not done so without much investigation, and the more I consider the subject, the more I am convinced that the moment when the feudal power was checked by the king and assailed by the communes, was not the most propitious to call the nobility to foreign lands—that the moment in which the burghers were labouring up hill for independence, was not a time for them to abandon the scene of their hopes and endeavours—and that the moment when a kingdom was torn by conflicting powers, when the royal authority was unconfirmed, and the nobility only irritated at its exertion, was not the period that a monarch should have chosen to quit his dominions.

2. A curious essay might be written on the classes or castes in Europe at that period. It is quite a mistaken notion which some persons have entertained, that the only distinctions under the monarch, were noble and serf. We find an immense class, or rather various classes, all of which consisted of freemen, interposed between the lord and his slave. Thus Galbertus Syndick, of Bruges, in recounting the death of Charles the Good, Count of Flanders, *A. D.* 1130, mentions not only the *burghers* of the town, but various other persons who were not of the noble race, but were then evidently free, as well as the Brabançois or Cotereaux, (continued next page)

any lord, nor belonging to the military caste—were all glad to engage themselves in wars which held out to them riches and exaltation in this world, and beatification in the next; while they could hope for nothing in their own land but pillage, oppression, and wrong; or slaughter in feuds without an object, and in battles for the benefit of others.

Before the second crusade was contemplated, a change—an immense change had operated itself in the state of society. Just fifty years had passed since the council of Clermont: but the kings of France were no longer the same; the royal authority had acquired force[3]—the latent principles of domination had been exercised for the general good. Kings had put forth their hands to check abuses, to punish violence and crime; and the feudal system began to assume the character, not of a simple confederation, but of an organized *hierarchy*,[4] in which the whole body was the judge of each individual, and the head of that body the executor of its sentence. Louis VI., commonly called Louis the Fat,[5] was the first among the kings of France who raised the functions of royalty above those of sovereignty, and the distinction between the two states is an important one.

The former monarchs of France, including Philip I., under whose reign the first crusade was preached, had each been but sovereigns, who could call upon their vassals to serve them for so many days in the field, and whose rights were either simply personal, that is to say, for their own dignity and benefit, or only general so far as the protection of the whole confederacy from foreign invasion was implied. Louis the Fat, however, saw that in the kingly office was comprised both duties and rights of a different character; the right of punishing private crime,[6] and of opposing universal wrong; the duty of maintaining public order, and of promoting by one uniform and acknowledged power the tranquillity of the whole society and the security of each individual. The efforts of that prince were confined and partial, it is true;[7] but he and his great minister, Suger, seized the just idea of the monarchical form of government, and laid the basis of a well-directed

---

a sort of freebooting soldier of that day. Guibert of Nogent, also, in his own life, and Frodoardus, in the history of Rheims, refer to many of whose exact station it is difficult to form an idea.

3. Rouillard, Histoire de Melun: Vie de Bouchard.

4. I know that I use this word not quite correctly, but I can find none other to express more properly what I mean.

5. Suger in vit. Ludovic VI.

6. Galbert in vit. Carol.

7. Suger in vit. Ludovic VI.

and legitimate authority.

This authority, of course, was not pleasing to the barons, whose license was thus curtailed. Their views, therefore, were turned rather to the maintenance of their own unjust privileges, than to foreign adventures. At the same time, the nobles found themselves assailed by the classes below them, as well as by the power above, and the people of the towns were seen to struggle for the rights and immunities so long denied to them. The *burghers* had,[8] indeed, been permitted to labour in some small degree for themselves. Though subject to terrible and grievous exactions, they had still thriven under the spirit of commerce and industry. Their lords had sometimes even recourse to them for assistance.

The greater part, though of the servile race, had been either freed, or were descended from freed men; and the baron of the town in which they lived, though cruel and tyrannical, was more an exacting protector than a master. At length—the precise time is unknown—the people of the cities began to think of protecting themselves; and, by mutual co-operation, they strove at once to free themselves from the tyranny of a superior lord, and to defend themselves against the encroachments of others. The word *commune*[9] was introduced, and each town of considerable size hastened to struggle for its liberty. At first the horror and indignation of the nobles were beyond all conception; but the spirit of union among them was not sufficiently active to put down that which animated the commons.

Each lord had to oppose his revolted subjects alone; and after long and sanguinary contests,[10] sometimes the baron, the bishop, or the abbot succeeded in subjugating the people; sometimes the *burghers* contrived, by perseverance, to wring from the nobles themselves a charter which assured their freedom.

This struggle[11] was at its height, at the time when the fall of Edessa and the growing power of the Moslems called Europe to engage in a second crusade; but the barons at that moment found their privileges invaded both by the crown and the people; and the latter discovered that they had rights to maintain in their own land—that they were no longer the mere slaves to whom all countries were alike—that prospects were opened before them which during the first crusade they

---

8. Chron. Vezeliac.
9. Guibert Nog. in vit. s.
10. Chron. Vezeliac.
11. Gesta regis Ludovici VII.

hardly dreamed of—that the swords which had before been employed in fighting the quarrels of their lords at home, or raising them to honour and fame abroad, were now required to defend their property, their happiness, and the new station they had created for themselves in society. Thus the period at which aid became imperatively necessary to the Christians at Jerusalem, was when France was least calculated to afford it. Nevertheless, the superstition of a king and the eloquence of a churchman combined to produce a second crusade; but in this instance it was but a great military expedition, and no longer the enthusiastic effort of a nation, or a great popular movement throughout the whole of the Christian world.

One of the strongest proofs of this fact[12] is the scantiness of historians on the second crusade, and the style in which those that do exist, speak of its operations. It is no longer the glory of Christendom that they mention, but the glory of the king; no more the deliverance of the Holy Land, but merely the acts of the monarch.

In pursuance of the general plan of extending the dominion of the crown, which had been conceived by Louis VI., and carried on with such infinite perseverance by his great minister Suger, Louis VII., the succeeding monarch, on hearing of the election of the Archbishop of Bourges by the chapter of that city, without his previous consent, had declared the nomination invalid, and proceeded to acts of such flagrant opposition to the papal jurisdiction, that the church used her most terrific thunders to awe the monarch to her will. Thibalt, Count of Champagne, armed in support of the pope's authority, and Louis instantly marched to chastise his rebellious vassal.

Thibalt was soon reduced to obedience, but the anger of the monarch was not appeased by submission; for, even after the town of Vitry had surrendered, he set fire to the church, in which nearly thirteen hundred people had taken refuge, and disgraced his triumph by one of the direst pieces of cruelty upon record. A severe illness, however, soon followed, and reflection brought remorse. At that time the news of the fall of Edessa was fresh in Europe; and Louis, in the vain hope of expiating his crime, determined to promote a crusade, and lead his forces himself to the aid of Jerusalem.

Deputies were speedily sent to the Pope Eugenius, who willingly

---

12. The only two I know who accompanied this crusade, and wrote any detailed account of it, are Odon de Deuil, or Odo de Diagolo, and Frisingen, or Freysinghen. It is an extraordinary fact, that the Cardinal de Vitry makes no mention of the second crusade.

abetted in the king's design, and commissioned the famous St. Bernard, Abbot of Clairvaux, to preach the Cross through France and Germany. St. Bernard possessed every requisite for such a mission.[13] From his earliest years he had been filled with religious enthusiasm; he had abandoned high prospects to dedicate himself entirely to an austere and gloomy fanaticism; he had reformed many abuses in the church, reproved crime wherever he found it, and raised the clerical character in the eyes of the people, too much accustomed to behold among his order nothing but vice, ignorance, and indolence. He was one of the most powerful orators of his day, endowed with high and commanding talents of many kinds; and in his controversy with the celebrated Abelard, the severe purity of his life and manners had proved most eloquent against his rival.

Thus, when after repeated entreaties[14] he went forth to preach the crusade, few that heard him were not either impressed by his sanctity, persuaded by his eloquence, or carried away by his zeal: and thus, notwithstanding the unfavourable state of France,[15] a multitude of men took the symbol of the Cross, and prepared to follow the monarch into Palestine. In Germany the effects of his overpowering oratory were the same. Those who understood not even the language that he spoke, became awed by his gestures and the dignified enthusiasm of his manner, and devoted themselves to the crusade, though the tongue in which it was preached was unknown to them. Wherever he went his presence was supposed to operate miracles, and the sick are reported to have recovered by his touch, or at his command; while all the legions of devils, with which popish superstition peopled the atmosphere, took flight at his approach.

For some time Conrad, Emperor of Germany, suffered[16] St. Bernard to call the inhabitants of his dominions to the crusade without taking any active part in his proceedings, but at length the startling eloquence of the Abbot of Clairvaux reached even the bosom of the monarch, and he declared his intention of following the Cross himself. At Vezelai Louis VII. received the symbol: but the most powerful obstacle that he found to his undertaking was the just and continued opposition of his minister,[17] Suger, who endeavoured by every means

---

13. William of St. Thierry, Mabillon.
14. Geoffroi de Clairvaux, Continuation of the Life of St. Bernard.
15. Odo of Deuil.
16. Mabillon.
17. Guizot.

to dissuade the monarch from abandoning his kingdom.

All persuasions were vain; and having committed the care of his estates to that faithful servant,[18] Louis himself, accompanied by Eleonor, his queen, departed for Metz, where he was joined by an immense multitude of nobles and knights, among whom were crusaders from England[19] and the remote islands of the northern sea. Ambassadors from Roger, King of Apulia, had already warned Louis of the treachery of the Greeks, and besought him to take any other way than that through the dominions of the emperor; but the French monarch was biassed by other counsels, and determined upon following the plan before laid down.

The Emperor of Germany was the first[20] to set out, and by June reached Constantinople in safety, followed by a large body of armed men, and a number of women whose gay dress, half-military, half-feminine, gave the march the appearance of some bright fantastic cavalcade.

The King of France, having previously received[21] at St. Denis, the consecrated banner as a warrior, and the staff and scrip[22] as a pilgrim, now quitted Metz, and proceeded by Worms and Ratisbon. Here he was met by envoys from the Emperor of the East, charged with letters so filled with flattery and fair speeches, that Louis is reported to have blushed, and the Bishop of Langres to have observed—

Timeo Danaos et dona ferentes.

Here,[23] too, the French beheld, for the first time, the custom of an inferior standing in the presence of his lord. The object of the emperor was to obtain from Louis a promise to pass through his territories without violence, and to yield to him every town from which he should expel the Turks, and which had ever belonged to the Grecian territory.

Part of this proposal was acceded to, and part refused; and the army marched on through Hungary into Greece. The progress of the sec-

---

18. *A. D.* 1147.
19. Odon de Deuil.
20. William of Tyre.
21. Odon de Deuil.
22. See Notes 10.
23. It appears from the passage of Odo of Deuil which mentions the curious servility, as he designates it, of the Greeks never sitting down in the presence of a superior till desired to do so, that the French of that day were not quite so ceremonious as in that of Louis XIV.

ond crusade was of course subject to the same difficulties that attended that of the first, through a waste and deserted land; but many other obstacles no longer existed—the people of the country were more accustomed to the appearance of strangers;[24] the army was restrained by the presence of the king; and the whole account of the march to Constantinople leaves the impression of a more civilized state of society than that which existed at the period of the first crusade. We meet with no massacres, no burning of towns, no countries laid waste: and though there are to be found petty squabbles between the soldiers and the townspeople, frays, and even bloodshed; yet these were but individual outrages, kindled by private passions, and speedily put down by the arm of authority.

The Germans[25] were less fortunate on their way than the French, and some serious causes of quarrel sprung up between them and the Greeks, in which it is difficult to discover who were the chief aggressors. The Greeks call the Germans[26] barbarians, and the Germans accuse the Greeks of every kind of treachery; but it appears evident,[27] that Conrad himself was guilty of no small violence on his approach to Constantinople. A most magnificent garden had been laid out at a little distance from that capital, filled with every vegetable luxury of the day, and containing within its walls vast herds of tame animals, for whose security woods had been planted, caverns dug, and lakes contrived; so that the beasts which were confined in this vast prison might follow their natural habits, as if still at liberty. Here also were several buildings, in which the emperors were accustomed to enjoy the summer: but Conrad, with an unceremonious freedom, partaking not a little of barbarism, broke into this retreat, and wasted and destroyed all that it had required the labour of years to accomplish.

Manuel Comnenus, who now sat on the throne of Constantinople, beheld, from the windows of his palace, this strange scene of wanton aggression; and sent messengers[28] to Conrad, who was connecte with him by marriage,[29] desiring an interview. But the Greek would not trust himself out of the walls of his capital, and the German would not venture within them, so that a short time was passed in negotiation;

---

24. Odo of Deuil.
25. Nicetas.
26. Cinnamus, cited by Mills.
27. Odon de Deuil.
28. *Ibid.*
29. Manuel Comnenus had married Bertha, and Conrad, Gertrude, both daughters of Berenger the elder, Count of Sultzbach.

and then Conrad passed over the Hellespont with his forces, relieving the eastern sovereign from the dread and annoyance of his presence. Manuel, however, furnished the German army with guides to conduct it through Asia Minor; and almost all accounts attribute to the Greek the design of betraying his Christian brethren into the hands of the *infidels*.

After passing the sea, the troops of Conrad proceeded in two bodies,[30] the one under the emperor, and the other under the Bishop of Freysinghen; but the guides with which they had been provided led them into the pathless wilds of Cappadocia, where famine soon reached them. At the moment also when they expected to arrive at Iconium,[31] they found themselves attacked by the army of the *infidels*, swelled to an immense extent by the efforts of the *Sultaun of* the Seljukian Turks, who, on the first approach of the Christian forces, had spared no means to ensure their destruction. The heavy-armed Germans[32] in vain endeavoured to close with the light and agile horsemen of the Turkish host.

The treacherous guides had fled on the first sight of the infidels, and the enemy hovered round and round the German army, as it struggled on through the unknown deserts in which it was entangled, smiting every straggler, and hastening its annihilation by continual attacks. Favoured by the fleetness of their horses, and their knowledge of the localities, they passed and repassed the exhausted troops of the emperor,[33] who now endeavoured to retrace his steps under a continued rain of arrows. No part of the army offered security. The famous Count Bernard, with many others, was cut off fighting in the rear; the van was constantly in the presence of an active foe; and the emperor himself was twice wounded by arrows which fell in the centre of the host. Thus, day after day, thousands on thousands were added to the slain; and when at length Conrad reached the town of Nice, of seventy

---

30. Odon de Deuil.
31. William of Tyre; Odon de Deuil.
32. The Pope, in his exhortation to the second crusade, had not only regulated the general conduct of the crusaders, and formally absolved all those who should embrace the Cross, but he had given minute particulars for their dress and arms, expressly forbidding all that might encumber them in their journey, such as heavy baggage, and vain superfluities, and all that might lead them from the direct road, such as falcons and hunting-dogs. "Happy had it been for them," says Odo of Deuil, "if, instead of a scrip, he had commanded the foot pilgrims to bear a cross bow, and instead of a staff, a sword."
33. Odo of Deuil; Will. Tyr.

167

thousand knights, and an immense body of foot, who had followed him from Europe, scarcely a tenth part were to be found in the ranks of his shattered army.

That he was betrayed into the hands of the Turks by the guides furnished by the emperor no earthly doubt can be entertained; nor is it questionable that Manuel Comnenus was at that time secretly engaged in treaty with the *infidels*. It is not, indeed, absolutely proved that the monarch of Constantinople ordered or connived at the destruction of the Christian forces; but every historian[34] of the day has suspected him of the treachery, and when such is the case it is probable there was good cause for suspicion.

In the meanwhile, Louis the younger led the French host to Constantinople, and, unlike Conrad, instantly accepted the emperor's invitation to enter the city with a small train. Manuel received him as an equal, descending to the porch of his palace to meet his royal guest. He, of course, pretended to no homage from the King of France, but still his object was to secure to himself all the conquests which Louis might make in the ancient appendages of Greece, without acting himself against the *infidels*.

To force the French monarch into this concession, he pursued a plan of irritating and uncertain negotiations, not at all unlike those carried on by his predecessor Alexius,[35] towards the leaders of the former crusade. In the midst of these, however, it was discovered that Manuel had entered into a secret treaty with the Turks; and, indeed, the confidence which the deceitful Greeks placed in the promises of the crusaders forms a singular and reproachful comment on the constant and remorseless breach of their own. There were many of the leaders of the French who did not scruple to urge Louis to punish by arms the gross perfidy of the Greek emperor; and, by taking possession of Constantinople, to sweep away the continual stumbling block by which the efforts of all the crusades had been impeded.

Had Louis acceded to their wishes, great and extraordinary results would, no doubt, have been effected towards the permanent occupation of the Holy Land by the Christian powers; but that monarch was not to be seduced into violating his own good faith by the treachery of another, and after having, on the other hand, refused to aid Manuel in the war which had arisen between him and Roger, King of Apulia, he crossed the Bosphorus, and passed into Asia Minor. Thence advancing

34. Will. Tyr; Odon de Deuil; Gest. Ludovic VII; Nicetas.
35. Odon de Deuil.

through Nicomedia,[36] Louis proceeded to Nice, and encamped under the walls of that city. Here the first reports reached him of the fate of the German Army, for hitherto the Greeks had continued to fill his ears with nothing but the successes of his fellows in arms. For a time the news was disbelieved, but very soon the arrival of Frederic, Duke of Suabia, charged with messages from the German monarch, brought the melancholy certainty of his defeat.

Louis did all that he could to assuage the grief of the Emperor Conrad,[37] and uniting their forces, they now marched on by the sea-coast to Ephesus. Here, however, Conrad, mortified at a companion-ship in which the inferiority of his own troops was painfully contrasted with the multitude and freshness of the French, separated again from Louis; and, sending back the greater part of his army by land, took ship himself and returned to Constantinople, where he was received both with more distinction and more sincerity, on account of the scantiness of his retinue, and the disasters he had suffered.

In the meanwhile, the French proceeded on their way, and after travelling for some days without opposition, they first encountered the Turks on the banks of the Meander.[38] Proud of their success against the Germans, the *infidels* determined to contest the passage of the river; but the French knights, having found a ford, traversed the stream without difficulty, and routed the enemy with great slaughter. The loss of the Christians was so small, consisting only of one knight,[39] who perished in the river, that they as usual had recourse to a miracle, to account for so cheap a victory.

Passing onward to Laodicea they found that town completely deserted, and the environs laid waste; and they here heard of the complete destruction of that part of the German army which had been commanded by the Bishop of Freysinghen.[40] In the second day's journey after quitting Laodicea, a steep mountain presented itself before the French army, which marched in two bodies, separated by a considerable distance. The commander of the first division, named Geoffroy de Rancun,[41] had received orders from the king, who remained

---

36. Will. Tyr.; Odon de Deuil.

37. Odon de Deuil; Freysinghen; William of Tyre.

38. William of Tyre.

39. Odon de Deuil.

40. Odo of Deuil always calls Otho, Bishop of Freysinghen, brother of the Emperor Conrad. He was, however, only a half-brother; his relationship being by the mother's side.

41. Will. Tyrens lib. xvi.; Odon de Deuil.

with the rear-guard, to halt on the summit of the steep, and there pitch the tents for the night. That baron, unencumbered by baggage, easily accomplished the ascent, and finding that the day's progress was considerably less than the usual extent of march, forgot the commands he had received, and advanced two or three miles beyond the spot specified.

The king, with the lesser body of effective troops and the baggage, followed slowly up the mountain, the precipitous acclivity of which rendered the footing of the horses dreadfully insecure, while immense masses of loose stone gave way at every step under the feet of the crusaders,[42] and hurried many down into a deep abyss, through which a roaring torrent was rushing onward towards the sea. Suddenly, as they were toiling up, the whole army of the Turks, who had remarked the separation of the division, and watched their moment too surely, appeared on the hill above. A tremendous shower of arrows instantly assailed the Christians. The confusion and dismay were beyond description: thousands fell headlong at once down the precipice, thousands were killed by the masses of rock which the hurry and agitation of those at the top hurled down upon those below; while the Turks, charging furiously all who had nearly climbed to the summit, drove them back upon the heads of such as were ascending.

Having concluded,[43] that his advance-guard had secured the ground above, Louis, with the cavalry of his division, had remained in the rear, to cover his army from any attack. The first news of the Turkish force being in presence was gathered from the complete rout of the foot-soldiers, who had been mounting the hill, and who were now flying in every direction. The king instantly sent round his chaplain, Odon de Deuil, to seek for the other body under Geoffroy de Rancun, and to call it back to his aid; while in the meantime he spurred forward with what cavalry he had, to repel the Turks and protect his infantry.

Up so steep an ascent the horses could make but little progress, and the Moslems, finding that their arrows turned off from the steel coats of the knights, aimed at the chargers, which, often mortally wounded, rolled down the steep, carrying their riders along with them. Those knights who succeeded in freeing themselves from their dying steeds were instantly attacked by the Turks, who, with fearful odds on their side, left hardly a living man of all the chivalry that fought that day. The king even, dismounted by the death of his horse, was surrounded

42. Odon de Deuil; Will. Tyr.
43. Odon de Deuil.

before he could well rise; but, catching the branches of a tree, he sprang upon a high insulated rock, where, armed with his sword alone, he defended himself, till the night falling freed him from his enemies.

His situation now would have been little less hazardous than it was before, had he not luckily encountered a part of the infantry who had remained with the baggage. He was thus enabled, with what troops he could rally, to make his way during the night to the advance-guard, which had, as yet, remained unattacked. Geoffroy de Rancun had nearly been sacrificed to the just resentment of the people, but the uncle of the king, having been a participator in his fault, procured him pardon; and the army, which was now reduced to a state of greater discipline than before, by the Grand Master of the Templars,[44] who had accompanied it from Constantinople arrived without much more loss at Attalia.[45] Here the Greeks proved more dangerous enemies than the Turks, and everything was done that human baseness and cunning could suggest, to plunder and destroy the unfortunate crusaders.

Much discussion now took place concerning their further progress, and the difficulties before them rendered it necessary that a part of the host should proceed by sea to Antioch. The king at first determined that that part, should be the pilgrims on foot; and that he himself with his chivalry would follow the path by land. The winter season, however, approaching, the scanty number of vessels that could be procured, and the exorbitant price which the Greeks demanded for the passage of each man—being no less than four marks of silver[46]—rendered the transport of the foot impossible. Louis, therefore, eager to reach Jerusalem, distributed what money he could spare among the pilgrims, engaged at an enormous price a Greek escort and guide to conduct them by land to Antioch, left the Count of Flanders to command them, and then took ship with the rest of his knights. The Count of Flanders soon found that the Greeks, having received their reward, refused to fulfil their agreement, and the impossibility of reaching Antioch without their aid being plain, he embarked and followed the king.

The unhappy pilgrims, who remained cooped up beneath the walls, which they were not permitted to enter, on the one hand, and the Turkish Army that watched them with unceasing vigilance, on the other, died, and were slaughtered by thousands. Some strove to force

---

44. Odon de Deuil.
45. William of Tyre.
46. Odon de Deuil.

their passage to Antioch by land, and fell beneath the Moslem scimitar. Some cast themselves upon the compassion of the treacherous Greeks, and were more brutally treated than even by their *infidel* enemies. So miserable at length became their condition, that the Turks themselves ceased to attack them, brought them provisions and pieces of money, and showed them that compassion which their fellow-Christians refused. Thus, in the end, several hundreds attached themselves[47] to their generous enemies, and were tempted to embrace the Moslem creed. The rest either became slaves to the Greeks, or died of pestilence and famine.

In the meanwhile, Louis and his knights[48] arrived at Antioch, where they were received with the appearance of splendid hospitality by Raimond, the prince of that city, who was uncle of Eleonor, the wife of the French monarch. His hospitality, however, was of an interested nature: Antioch and Tripoli hang upon the skirts of the kingdom of Jerusalem as detached principalities, whose connexion with the chief country was vague and insecure. No sooner, therefore, did the news of the coming of the King of France reach the princes of those cities, than they instantly laid out a thousand plans for engaging Louis in extending the limits of their territories, before permitting him to proceed to Jerusalem.

The Prince of Antioch assuredly had the greatest claim upon the king, by his relationship to the queen;[49] and he took every means of working on the husband, by ingratiating himself with the wife. Eleonor was a woman of strong and violent passions,[50] and of debauched and libertine manners, and she made no scruple of intriguing and caballing with her uncle to bend the king to his wishes. The Archbishop

47. Odon de Deuil.
48. William of Tyre; Vertot.
49. Gest. Ludovic. regis; William of Tyre; Vertot.
50. Vertot, a learned man and a diligent investigator, speaks of Eleonor in the following curious terms: "*On pretend que cette princesse, peu scrupuleuse sur ses devoirs, et devenue éprise d'un jeune Turc baptisé, appellé Saladin, ne pouvait résoudre à s'en séparer, &c.*" These reports of course gave rise to many curious suppositions, especially when Richard Cœur de Leon, Eleonor's son by her second marriage, went to war in the Holy Land. On his return to France, Louis VII. instantly sought a plausible pretext for delivering himself from his unfaithful wife without causing the scandal of a public exposure of her conduct. A pretence of consanguinity within the forbidden degrees was soon established, and the marriage was annulled. After this Eleonor, who, in addition to beauty and wit, possessed in her own right the whole of Aquitain, speedily gave her hand to Henry II. of England, and in the end figured in the tragedy of Rosamond of Woodstock.

of Tyre, who was but little given to repeat a scandal, dwells with a tone of certainty upon the immoral life of the Queen of France, and says, she had even consented that her uncle should carry her off, after Louis had formally refused to second his efforts against Cesarea.

However that may be, her conduct was a disgrace to the crusade; and Louis, in his letters to Suger, openly complained of her infidelity.

The king resisted all entreaties and all threats, and, equally rejecting the suit of the Count of Tripoli,[51] he proceeded to Jerusalem, where the emperor Conrad, having passed by sea from Constantinople, had arrived before him. Here the whole of the princes were called to council; and it was determined that, instead of endeavouring to retake Edessa, which had been the original object of the crusade, the troops of Jerusalem, joined to all that remained of the pilgrim armies, should attempt the siege of Damascus. The monarchs immediately took the field, supported by the knights of the Temple and St. John, who, in point of courage, equalled the chivalry of any country, and in discipline excelled them all. Nourhaddin and Saphaddin, the two sons of the famous Zenghi, threw what men they could suddenly collect into Damascus, and hastened in person to raise as large a force as possible to attack the Christian army.

The crusaders advanced to the city, drove in the Turkish outposts[52] that opposed them, and laid siege to the fortifications, which in a short time were so completely ruined, that Damascus could hold out no longer. And yet Damascus did not fall. Dissension, that destroying angel of great enterprises, was busy in the Christian camp. The possession of the still unconquered town[53] was disputed among the leaders. Days and weeks passed in contests, and at length, when it was determined that the prize should be given to the Count of Flanders, who had twice visited the Holy Land, the decision caused so much dissatisfaction, that all murmured and none acted.

Each one suspected his companion; dark reports and scandalous charges were mutually spread and countenanced; the Templars were accused of having received a bribe from the *infidels*; the European monarchs[54] were supposed to aim at the subjugation of Jerusalem; the conquerors were conquered by their doubts of each other; and, retiring from the spot where they had all but triumphed, they attempted

---

51. William of Tyre; Vertot.
52. Gest. regis Ludov. VII.
53. Vertot.
54. William of Tyre; Col. script. Arab.; Vertot.

to storm the other side of the city, where the walls were as firm as a rock of adamant.

Repenting of their folly, they soon were willing to return to their former ground, but the fortifications had been repaired, the town had received fresh supplies, and Saphaddin, *emir* of Mousul, was marching to its relief. Only one plan was to be pursued. The siege was abandoned, and the leaders,[55] discontented with themselves and with each other, retreated gloomily to Jerusalem.

The Emperor of Germany set out immediately for Europe; but Louis, who still hoped to find some opportunity of redeeming his military fame, lingered for several months; while Eleonor continued to sully scenes, whose memory is composed of all that is holy, with her impure *amours*. At length the pressing entreaties of Suger induced the French monarch to return to his native land.

There he found the authority he had confided to that great and excellent minister had been employed to the infinite benefit of his dominions—he found his finances increased and order established in every department of the state;[56]—and he found, also, that the minister was not only willing, but eager, to yield the reins of government to the hand from which he had received them.—During the absence of the king, his brother, Robert of Dreux, who returned before him, had endeavoured to thwart the noble Abbot of St. Denis, and even to snatch the regency from him; but Suger boldly called together a general assembly of the nobility of France, and intrusted his cause to their decision. The court met at Soissons, and unanimously supported the minister against his royal opponent; after which he ruled, indeed, in peace; but Robert strove by every means to poison the mind of the king against him; and it can be little doubted, that Louis, on his departure from Palestine, viewed the conduct of Suger with a very jealous eye.

The effects of his government, however, and the frankness with which he resigned it, at once did away all suspicions. The expedition was now over, but yet one effort more was to be made, before we can consider the second crusade as absolutely terminated.

Suger had opposed the journey of the king to the Holy Land, but he was not in the least wanting in zeal or compassionate enthusiasm in favour of his brethren of the east.[57] Anything but the absence of a

---

55. William of Tyre; Freysinghen, reb. gest. Fred.; Gest. reg. Lud. VII.
56. Guil. Monach. in *vit. Suger. Ab. Sanct. Dion.; Gest. reg. Lud. VII.*
57. Guil. Monach. in *vit. Sug.*

monarch from his unquiet dominions he would have considered as a small sacrifice towards the support of the kingdom of Jerusalem; and now, at seventy years, he proposed to raise an army at his own expense, and to finish his days in Palestine.—His preparations were carried on with an ardour, an activity, an intelligence, which would have been wonderful even in a man at his prime; but, in the midst of his designs, he was seized with a slow fever, which soon showed him that his end was near.

He saw the approach of death with firmness; and, during the four months that preceded his decease, he failed not from the bed of sickness to continue all his orders for the expedition, which could no longer bring living glory to himself. He named the chief whom he thought most worthy to lead it; he bestowed upon him all the treasures he had collected for the purpose; he gave him full instructions for his conduct, and he made him swear upon the Cross to fulfil his intentions. Having done this, the Abbot of St. Denis waited calmly the approach of that hour which was to separate him from the living; and died, leaving no one like him in Europe.

With his life appears to have ended the second crusade, which, with fewer obstacles and greater facilities than the first, produced little but disgrace and sorrow to all by whom it was accompanied.[58]

---

58. All the writers of that day attempt to excuse St. Bernard for having preached a crusade which had so unfortunate a conclusion. The principles upon which they do so are somewhat curious. The Bishop of Freysinghen declares, that it was the vice of the crusaders which called upon their heads the wrath of Heaven: and, to reconcile this fact with the spirit of prophecy which elsewhere he attributes to the Abbot of Clairvaux, declares that prophets are not always able to prophesy.—*Freysing. de rebus gestis Fred. Imperat.* Geoffroy of Clairvaux, who was a contemporary, and wrote part of the Life of St. Bernard, would fain prove that the crusade could not be called unfortunate, since, though it did not at all help the Holy Land it served to people heaven with martyrs.

CHAPTER 11

Progress of Society

Before proceeding to trace the events which occurred in the Holy Land between the second and third crusades, it may be as well to keep our eyes upon Europe for a few moments, and to remark the advance of society towards civilization. Prior to the period of the first expedition to Palestine, Germany had been occupied alone in struggling against the papal authority, and in fighting for dominions in Italy, the limits of which were always sufficiently vague to admit of disputes and aggressions on all parts. Apulia and the southern portion of Italy had been subjected, as we have seen, by the Normans; and the rest of that country, with the exception of some small republican cities, was divided into feudal baronies, the right of homage over which was very uncertain. Engaged in private wars and feuds, where personal interest was the sole object, unmixed with any refining principle, the chivalry of Italy made but small progress.

From time to time a great and distinguished chief started up, and dignified his country; but the general feeling of knightly zeal was not extended far in Italy, or was wasted in the petty purposes of confined and unimportant struggles. In Germany also chivalry advanced but little. There was much dignified firmness in the character of the people; and—under the walls of Damascus—in the wars with the pope, and with the Norman possessors of Calabria—the German knights evinced that in the battle-field none were more daring, more powerful, or more resolute; but we find few instances where enthusiasm was mingled with valour, and where the ardour of chivalric devotion was joined to the bold courage of the Teutonic warrior.

In Spain the spirit was at its height; but Spain had her own crusades; and it was quite enough for the swords of her gallant band of knights to free their native land, inch by inch, from her Saracen invaders. Military orders[1] were there instituted in the middle of the twelfth century; and the knights of Calatrava and St. James might challenge the world to produce a more chivalrous race than themselves; still the object of all their endeavours was the freedom of their native country from the yoke of the Moors, and they engaged but little in any of those great expeditions which occupied the attention and interest of the world. It is to France, then, and to England, under the dominion of its Norman monarchs, that we must turn our eyes; and here, during the course of the twelfth century, we shall find great and extraordinary progress.

Previous to the epoch of the crusades, France, though acknowledging one king, had consisted of various nations, whose manners, habits, and languages differed in the most essential points.[2] The Provençal was as opposite a being to the Frank of that day, as the Italian is now to the Russian. The Norman and the Breton also descended from distinct origins, and in most cases these separate tribes hated each other with no slight share of enmity.

The character of the Norman was in all times enterprising, wandering, cunning, and selfish; that of the Breton, or Armorican, savage, ferocious, daring, and implacable; but imaginative in the highest degree, as well as superstitious. The Provençal was light, avaricious, keen, active, and sensual; the Frank, bold, hardy, persevering, but vain, insolent, and thoughtless.[3] Distinctive character lies more generally in men's faults than their virtues; and thus, all these different races possessed the same higher qualities in common. They were brave to a prodigy; energetic, talented, enthusiastic; but during the eleventh, and the beginning of the twelfth centuries, the rude state of society in which chivalry had arisen, continued to affect it still.

The first crusade, however, gave an impulse to all those countries that joined in it, which tended infinitely to civilize Europe, by uniting nations and tribes, which had long been separated by different interests, in one great enterprise, wherein community of object, and community of danger, necessarily harmonized many previously discordant feelings, and did away many old animosities, by the strong power of mutual assistance and mutual endeavour. The babel of languages which Fulcher describes in the Christian camp before long began to form itself into two more general tongues. Latin, notwithstanding all

---

1. Existing orders of knighthood.
2. Fulcher; Raoul Glaber.
3. Robert; Fulcher; Raimond d'Agiles.

the support it received in the court, in the church, and in the schools, was soon confined to the cloister; and the *langue d'oc*, or Provençal, became the common language of all the provinces on the southern side of the Loire, while the *langue d'oil* only was spoken in the north of France.

The manners and habits of the people, too, were gradually shaded into each other; the distinctions became less defined: the Provençal no longer looked upon the Breton as a savage; and the Frank no longer classed the Provençal with the ape. A thousand alliances were formed between individuals of different tribes, and the hand of kindred smoothed away the remaining asperities of national prejudice. Such assimilations tend of course to calm and mollify the mind of man; so that the general character of the country became of a less rude and ferocious nature. At this time, too, sprang up that greatest of all the softeners of the human heart, poetry; and immense was the change it wrought in the manners and deportment of that class which constituted the society of the twelfth century. The poetry of that age bore as distinct and clear a stamp of the epoch to which it belonged, as any that the world ever produced; and it is absurd to trace to an earlier day the origin of a kind of poesy which was founded upon chivalry alone, and reflected nothing but the objects of a chivalrous society.

It is little important which of the two tongues of France first boasted a national poet, and equally unimportant which gave birth to the most excellent poetry. The *langue d'oc* was the most mellifluous; the *langue d'oil* was the most forcible; but neither brought forth anything but the tales, the songs, the satires, the ballads of chivalry.

It is more than probable that some musical ear in Provence first applied to his own language the melody of regularly arranged syllables, and the jingle of rhyme. No sooner was this done than the passion spread to all classes. Chivalrous love and chivalrous warfare furnished subjects in plenty; and the *gai savoir*, the *biau parler*, became the favourite relaxation of those very men who wielded the lance and sword in the battlefield. The *troubadours* were multiplied to infinity; the language lent itself almost spontaneously to versification; and kings, warriors, and ladies, as well as the professed poets, occasionally practised the new and captivating art, which at once increased chivalrous enthusiasm, by spreading and perpetuating the fame of noble deeds, and softened the manners of the age, by the influence of sweet sounds and intellectual exercises. The songs themselves soon became as various as those who composed them, and were divided into *sirventes*,

Tensons, *pastourelles*, and *nouvelles*, or *contes*.[4]

The *conte*, or tale in verse, needs no description, and the nature of the *pastourelle* also is self-evident. The *sirvente* deserves more particular notice. It was in fact a satire, of the most biting and lively character; in which wit and poetry were not used to cover or to temper the reprobation of either individual or general vice, but rather, on the contrary, to give point and energy to invective. The keen bitterness of the *troubadours* spared neither rank nor caste; kings, and nobles, and priests, all equally underwent the lash of their wit; and it is from these very *sirventes* that we gain a clear insight into many of the customs and manners of that day, as well as into many, too many, scenes of grossness and immorality, from which we would fain believe that chivalry was free. The *tensons*, or *jeux partis*, were dialogues between two persons on some subject of love or chivalry, and in general show far more subtilty than poetical feeling. To these were added occasional epistles in verse; and *plaintes*, or lamentations, in which the death or misfortune of a friend was mourned with a touching simplicity that has since been too often imitated with very ineffective art.

Other compositions, such as the *aubade* and the *serenade*, were in use, the difference of which from the common *lay* consisted merely in their metrical construction: the word *alba* being always repeated at the end of each *stanza* of the aubade, and the word *ser* continually terminating each division of the serenade.[5] Such was the poesy of the *langue d'oc* and the *troubadours*. The *langue d'oil* had also its poets, the *trouveres*, and its poesy, which differed totally from that of the *langue d'oc*. The art was here more ambitious than with the Provençals; and we find, among the first productions of the *trouveres*, long and complex poems, which would fain deserve the name of epics. The first of these, both in date and importance, is the Norman romance of Rou, which bears a considerable resemblance, in its object and manner, to the fragments of old Scandinavian poetry which have come down to us, but has a continuous and uniform subject, and strong attempts at unity of design.

The romance of the Rose also, commenced by Guillaume de Lorris,[6] and concluded by Jean de Meung, is one of the most extraordinary compositions that the world ever produced, and stands

---

4. Raynouard, Poesies des Troubadours; Millot, Hist. des Troubadours; Le Grand d'Aussi Fabliaux.

5. Raynouard.

6. Oeuvres de Maroc.

perfectly alone—an allegory in twenty-two thousand verses! Various subjects, quite irrelevant to the object of the song, are introduced in its course; and the poet mingles his tale with satire and sarcasm, which were fully as often misdirected as deserved. Besides these were all the famous romances of chivalry which probably originated in the fabulous but interesting story of Charlemagne's visit to the Holy Land, falsely attributed to the archbishop Turpin. This work bears internal evidence of having been written after the first crusade, and, we have reason to suppose, was translated into French,[7] from the Latin manuscript of some monkish author.

In all the romances of the Round Table, we trace the end of the twelfth, and the beginning of the thirteenth century. They could not have been composed prior to that epoch; for we find many customs and objects mentioned, which were not known at an earlier period; and it is probable, from various circumstances, that they are not referable to a later age. Besides these, multitudes of *Fabliaux*[8] have descended to us from the Trouveres, and in this sort of composition, it is but fair to say, we find more originality, variety, and strength, though less sweetness and less enthusiasm, than among the compositions of the *troubadours*. At this period also we meet with an institution in Provence, of which I shall speak but slightly, from many motives, though undoubtedly it had a great influence upon the character of chivalry: I mean the Court of Love, as it was called, where causes concerning that passion were tried and judged as seriously, as if feelings could be submitted to a tribunal. Could that be the case, the object of such a court should certainly be very different from that of the Provençal Court of Love, the effect of which was anything but to promote morality. It tended, however, with everything else, to soften the manners of the country, though all the mad absurdities to which it gave rise were a scandal and a disgrace to Europe.

Besides all these causes of mitigation, the constant journeys of the people of Europe to the Holy Land taught them gradually the customs of other nations; and in that age there was much good to be learned by a frequent intercourse with foreigners. The great want of Europe was civilization; the vices of the day were pretty equally spread through all countries, and the very circumstance of mingling with men of different habits and thoughts promoted the end to be desired, without bringing any great importation of foreign follies or crimes. Many useful arts, and many sciences, previously unknown, were also

7. Fauchet.
8. Le Grand d'Aussi.

obtained from the Saracens themselves; and though in the crusades Europe sacrificed a host of her noblest knights, and spent immense treasures and energies, yet she derived, notwithstanding, no small benefit from her communication with Palestine.

The state of that country, in the meanwhile, was every day becoming more and more precarious. The nations by whom it was surrounded were improving in military discipline, in political knowledge, and in the science of timing and combining their efforts, while the Christians were losing ground in everything but courage. The military orders of the Temple and St. John were the bulwarks of the Latin kingdom of Jerusalem; but at the same time, by their pride, their disputes, and their ambition, they did nearly as much to undermine its strength at home as they did to support it with their swords in the field of battle.

It would be endless to trace all the events in Palestine which brought about the third crusade, and to investigate minutely the causes which worked out the ruin of the Christian dominion in the Holy Land. The simple facts must be enough in this place.

Although the crusade which went forth for the express purpose of delivering Edessa never even attempted that object, Joscelyn of Courtenay did not neglect to struggle for his lost territory, and gained some splendid successes over the *infidels*, which were all in turn reversed, by his capture and death in prison.[9] After his failure, the difficulty of keeping Edessa was so apparent, that the monarch of Jerusalem[10] determined to yield it to the Emperor Manuel Comnenus, on condition of his defending it against the Turks. Manuel, therefore, received the principality; but the weak and cowardly Greeks soon lost what the valiant Franks could not maintain; and before a year was over, Nourhaddin the Great, Sultaun of Aleppo, was in full possession of Edessa and all its dependencies. Baldwin III., however, who had cast off the follies of his youth, and now displayed as great qualities as any of his race, more than compensated for the loss of that principality by the capture of Ascalon.[11]

After this great success, eight years of varied warfare followed; and at the end of that period Baldwin died, leaving behind him the character of one of the noblest of the Latin kings. His brother Almeric ascended the vacant throne, but with talents infinitely inferior, and

9. Bernard, the Treasurer; James of Vitry; William of Tyre.
10. William of Tyre; Bernard.
11. William of Tyre.

a mind in no degree calculated to cope with the great and grasping genius of Nourhaddin, who combined, in rare union, the qualities of an ambitious and politic monarch with the character of a liberal, frugal, and unostentatious man.

Almeric was ambitious also; but his avarice was always a check on his ambition, and he suffered himself often to be bribed, where he might have conquered. At this time[12] the Fatimite *califs* of Egypt had fallen into a state of nonentity. The country was governed by a *vizier*, and the high office was struggled for by a succession of military adventurers.

Such a state of things awakened the attention of the monarchs of Jerusalem and Aleppo, and each resolved to make himself master of Egypt. An opportunity soon presented itself. Shawer, the *vizier* of Egypt, was expelled from his post by Dargham, a soldier of fortune. The disgraced *vizier* fled to the court of Nourhaddin, and prayed for assistance against the usurper. Nourhaddin willingly granted a request which yielded the means of sending his troops into Egypt; and two Curdish refugees, uncle and nephew, who had risen high in his army,[13] under the names of Assad Eddyn Chyrkouh, and Salah Eddyn or Saladin, were despatched with considerable forces to expel Dargham, and to re-establish Shawer. Dargham saw the gathering storm, and to shelter himself from its fury called the Christians from Palestine to his aid. But the movements of the Moslems were more rapid than those of Almeric; and, before the King of Jerusalem could reach Cairo, Chyrkouh had given battle to Dargham, and defeated and killed him, and Shawer was repossessed of the authority he had lost.

Shawer soon found that his power was fully as much in danger from his allies as it had been from his enemies; and, to resist the Turks whom he had brought into Egypt, he was obliged to enter into a treaty with the Christians. Almeric marched immediately to Cairo, and after a multitude of manœuvres and skirmishes, forced Chyrkouh and Saladin to quit the country; displaying, through the whole of this war, more scientific generalship than was at all usual in that age. No sooner were the Turks gone, than the Latin monarch[14] broke his truce with the Egyptians, and Shawer was once more obliged to apply to Nourhaddin. Chyrkouh again advanced into the Fatimite dominions with increased forces, obliged Almeric to retreat with great loss, took

12. Cardinal of Vitry; William of Tyre.
13. Cardinal of Vitry; Will. of Tyre.
14. Bernard; William of Tyre.

possession of Cairo, beheaded Shawer, and installed himself in the office of *vizier* to Adhad, *calif* of Egypt, though he still retained the title of lieutenant for Nourhaddin of Aleppo.

Not long after these successes, Chyrkouh died, and Nourhaddin, doubtful of the fidelity of the Turkish *emirs*, gave the vacant post to Saladin, the nephew of the late *vizier*, in which choice he was as much guided by the apparently reckless and pleasure-seeking despotism of the young Curdish chief, as by the military skill he had shown when forced unwillingly into action. Saladin, however, was scarcely invested with supreme power in Egypt when his real character appeared. He cast from him the follies with which he had veiled his great and daring mind; and, by means of the immense treasures placed at his command, soon bound to his interests many who had been at first disgusted by his unexpected elevation.

The *califs* of Egypt had been always considered as *schismatics* by the *califs* of Bagdat, to whom Nourhaddin still affected homage; and Saladin was forthwith instructed to declare the Fatimite dynasty at an end, and to re-establish in Egypt the nominal dominion of the Abassides. This was easily accomplished; Adhad, the *calif*, either died before the revolution was completed, or was strangled in the bath; the people little cared under whose yoke they laboured. The children of the late *calif* were confined in the *harem*; and Motshadi, *calif* of Bagdat, was prayed for as God's vicar on earth.

Saladin's ambitious projects became every day more and more apparent, and Nourhaddin was not blind to the conduct of his officer. Submission quieted his suspicions for a time; and, though repeated causes for fresh jealousy arose, he was obliged to forego marching into Egypt in person, as he undoubtedly intended, till death put a stop to all his schemes. No sooner was Nourhaddin dead, than Almeric attacked his widow at Paneas,[15] and Saladin began to encroach upon other parts of his territories: but Saladin was the only gainer by the death of the great *sultaun*, and made himself master, by various means, of the whole of his Syrian dominions, while internal dissensions and changes in the government of Palestine gradually weakened every bulwark of the Latin throne. Almeric[16] died in returning from Paneas, and his son, Baldwin IV, surnamed the Leper, succeeded him. Had his corporeal powers been equal to the task of royalty, it is probable that Baldwin would have been a far greater monarch than his father; but,

---

15. William of Tyre; James of Vitry; Guillelm de Nangis; Chron. *ann.* 1174.
16. William of Tyre.

183

after many struggles for activity, he found that disease incapacitated him for energetic rule, and he intrusted the care of the state to Guy of Lusignan, who had married his sister Sybilla, widow of the Marquis of Montferrat, to whom she had borne one son.[17]

Guy of Lusignan soon showed himself unworthy of the charge, and Baldwin,[18] resuming the government, endeavoured to establish it in such a form that it might uphold itself after his death, which he felt to be approaching. With this view he offered the administration to the Count of Tripoli,[19] during the minority of his sister's child; but the count refused to accept it, except under condition that the charge of the young prince should be given to Joscelyn de Courtenay, the surviving branch of the Courtenays of Edessa, and son of the unhappy count who died in a Saracen prison. He also stipulated that the castles and fortresses of the kingdom should be garrisoned by the Hospitallers and Templars; and that in case the boy should die in his youth, the question of succession should be determined by the Pope, the Emperor of Germany, the King of France, and the King of England.[20] Not many years after this the king died, and Baldwin V. succeeded, but his death followed immediately upon his accession.

Without abiding by the dispositions of the former monarch, no sooner was the young king dead, than the Grand Master of the Temple, Renauld of Chatillon, Count of Karac, and the Patriarch of Jerusalem joined to raise Sybilla to the throne, in spite of the formal protest of all the other barons and the Grand Master of the Hospital. The gates of Jerusalem were shut;[21] and it was only by sending one of their followers, disguised as a monk, that the nobles assembled with the Count of Tripoli at Naplousa could gain any tidings of what passed. Sybilla was crowned in form; and then the patriarch, pointing to the other crown which lay upon the altar, told her that it was hers to dispose of, on which she immediately placed it on the head of Guy of Lusignan.[22] After this some of the barons refused to do homage to the new king, and some absented themselves from his court; but the imminent dan-

---

17. Jacob. Vitr.

18. Bernard the Treasurer says, that the monarch wished to annul the marriage between his sister and Guy. "*Si grans haine estoit entre le roy et le cuens de Jaffe que chascun jor cressoit plus et plus et jusque a tant estoit la chose venue que le roy queroit achaison par quoy il peut desevrer tot apertement le mariage qui iert entre lui et sa seror.*"

19. William of Tyre; Bernard the Treasurer: James of Vitrv.

20. Bernard the Treasurer; James of Vitry.

21. Bernard the Treasurer.

22. Rog. of Hovedon.

ger in which the country was placed at length brought back a degree of concord, when concord could no longer avail.

Saladin had by this time made himself master of all Syria;[23] and had not only consolidated into one great monarchy dominions which for ages had been separated into petty states, but also, by the incessant application of a powerful and expansive mind, he had drawn forth and brought into action many latent but valuable resources which had previously been unknown or forgotten. He had taught the whole interests of his people to centre in his own person, and he now determined to direct their energies to one great and important enterprise. That enterprise was the conquest of Palestine, and with an army of fifty thousand horse, and near two hundred thousand foot, he advanced towards Jerusalem, and laid siege to Tiberias.[24] Within the walls of that fortress the Countess of Tripoli held out against the Saracens, while her husband joined Guy of Lusignan, and brought his forces to the field in defence of the Holy Land.

The conduct of the Count of Tripoli is very obscure.[25] That from time to time he had treated with the Saracens is evident, and almost every European authority, except Mills, accuses him of having, in this instance, betrayed his countrymen into the hands of the infidels. Whether with or against his advice matters little to the general result— the Christians marched down to meet Saladin at Tiberias.[26] Beyond doubt it was by the counsel of the Count of Tripoli that they pitched their tents in a spot where no water was to be found. The troops suffered dreadfully from thirst; and in the morning, when they advanced to attack Saladin in the cool of the dawn, the wary monarch retired before them, resolved not to give them battle till the heat of the risen sun had added to their fatigues. To increase the suffocating warmth of a Syrian summer's day, he set fire to the low bushes and shrubs which surrounded the Christian camp; so that when the battle did begin, the Latin forces were quite overcome with weariness and drought.

The contest raged throughout the day, the Christians fighting to reach the wells which lay behind the Saracen power,[27] but in vain; and night fell, leaving the strife still doubtful. The next morning the Latins and Turks again mixed in combat. The Count of Tripoli[28] forced his

23. William of Tyre; William de Nangis.
24. Bernard; William of Nangis.
25. Will. Neub.
26. Bernard.
27. William of Nangis.
28. Bernard the Treasurer; William of Nangis.

185

way through the Saracens, and escaped unhurt; but the scimitars of the Moslems mowed down whole ranks of the Christians, for their immense superiority of numbers allowed them to surround the height upon which the king and the chief of his army were stationed, and to wage the warfare at once against every face of the Latin host. Such a conflict could not long endure. Multitudes of the *infidels* fell, but their loss was nothing in proportion to their number, when compared with that which their adversaries underwent.

The Grand Master of the Hospital[29] alone clove his way from the field of battle, after having staid till victory had settled upon the Paynim banners. He reached Ascalon that night, but died on the following day of the wounds he had received. The king—Renault de Chatillon, Count of Karac, who had so often broken faith with the Moslems—and the Grand Master of the Temple, whose whole order was in abhorrence among the Mussulmans—were taken alive and carried prisoners to the tent of Saladin. That monarch remained for some time on the field, giving orders that the Knights of St. John[30] and those of the Temple, who had been captured, should instantly embrace Islamism, or undergo the fate of the scimitar. A thousand acts of cruelty and aggression on their part had given cause to such deadly hatred; but at the hour of death not one knight could be brought to renounce his creed; and they died with that calm resolution which is in itself a glory.

After this bloody consummation of his victory, Saladin entered the tent where Lusignan and his companions expected a similar fate: but Saladin, thirsty himself, called for iced sherbet, and having drank, handed the cup to the fallen monarch, a sure pledge that his life was secure. Lusignan in turn passed it to Renaul of Chatillon,[31] but the *sultaun*, starting up, exclaimed, "No hospitality for the breaker of all engagements!"[32] and before Chatillon could drink, with one blow of his scimitar, Saladin severed his head from his body.

Tiberias surrendered immediately. City after city now fell into the power of the victor, and at length, after an obstinate defence, Jerusalem once more was trodden by the Moslems.[33] But the conduct of the *infidel sultaun* on this occasion shames the cruelty of the crusaders. When

29. Vertot.
30. Rog. of Hovedon; William of Nangis.
31. William of Nangis; Bernard the Treasurer.
32. Some writers state that Saladin proposed to Chatillon to abjure Christianity, which he boldly refused: but others do not mention the circumstance, and the act of Saladin seems to me to have been more one of hasty passion than of deliberation.
33. Bernard.

the people could hold out no longer, Saladin, who had at first offered the most advantageous terms, insisted that the city should now throw itself upon his mercy.

He then agreed upon a moderate ransom for the prisoners, and promised to let each man carry forth his goods without impediment. When this was done, with extraordinary care he saw that neither insult nor injury should be offered to the Christians; and, having taken possession of the town, he placed a guard at one of the gates to receive the ransom of the inhabitants as they passed out. Nevertheless, when the whole wealth which could be collected in the town had been paid down, an immense number of the poorer Christians remained unredeemed. These were destined to be slaves; but Bernard the treasurer relates, that Saif Eddyn, the brother of the monarch, begged the liberty of one thousand of these, and that about the same number were delivered at the prayer of the Patriarch and of Baléan de Ibelyn,[34] who had commanded in the place, and communicated with the Curdish monarch on its surrender.

After this Saladin declared that his brother, the Patriarch, and Ibelyn had done their alms, and that now he would do his alms also; on which he caused it to be proclaimed through the city,[35] that all the poor people who could give no ransom might go forth in safety by the gate of St. Lazarus; but he ordered that if any attempted to take advantage of this permission who really could pay for their deliverance, they should be instantly seized and cast into prison. Many of the nobler prisoners also he freed at the entreaty of the Christian ladies; and in his whole conduct he showed himself as moderate in conquest, as he was great in battle.

Antioch and the neighbouring towns, as well as the greater part of the county of Tripoli,[36] were soon reduced to the Saracen yoke, and with the exception of Tyre, which was defended by the gallant Conrad, Marquis of Montferrat, the whole of Palestine became subject to the victor of Tiberias.

Such was the sudden and disastrous termination of the Christian dominion in the Holy Land;[37] a misfortune which all the contemporary writers attribute to the vices of the inhabitants. Without presuming to assign it, as they do, to the special wrath of Heaven, we may

---

34. Bernard the Treasurer; Continuation of William of Tyre.
35. William of Nangis.
36. Bernard.
37. James of Vitry; Bernard; William of Tyre.

nevertheless believe that the gross and scandalous crimes of the people of Jerusalem greatly accelerated its return to the Moslem domination. After the successes of the first crusade, the refuse of European populations poured into Palestine in hopes of gain, and brought all their vices to add to the stock of those that the country already possessed.

The clergy were as licentious as the laity, the chiefs as immoral as the people. Intestine quarrels are sure to follow upon general crime; and unbridled passions work as much harm to the society in which they are tolerated, as to the individuals on whom they are exercised. The Latins of Palestine retained their courage, it is true; but they knew no confidence in each other. Virtue, the great bond of union, subsisted not among them, and each one caballed, intrigued, and strove against his neighbour. The ambition of the two great military orders bred continual hatred and opposition,[38] and the discord that existed between the Hospitallers and the clergy caused another breach in the harmony of the state.

During the time that the kingdom of Jerusalem was thus dividing itself, by passions and vices, into ruinous factions and enfeebled bodies, Saladin and those that preceded him were bending all their energies to consolidate their power and extend their dominion. Zenghi was a great warrior, Nourhaddin a great monarch,[39] and Saladin added to the high qualities of both, not only a degree of civilization in his own person which neither had known, but, what was still more, the spirit of civilization in his heart.

Saladin was as superior to any of the princes of Palestine in mind as he was in territory; and with clear and general views of policy, keenness and strength of perception in difficulties, consummate skill in war, innumerable forces, and the hearts of his soldiers, it was impossible that he should not conquer. There can be no doubt that the Latins were a more powerful and vigorous race of men than the Turks. The event of every combat evinced it; and even in their defeats, they almost always left more dead upon the field of the enemy's forces than of their own. Their armour, too, was weightier,[40] and their horses heavier and more overpowering in the charge. But the Turkish horseman and the Turkish horse were more active and more capable of bearing long fatigue, privation, and heat than the European; and this in some degree made up for the slighter form and lighter arms of the Saracen.

---

38. Bernard; Albert.
39. William of Tyre.
40. Albert of Aix; Fulcher; Robert.

In war, also, as a science, the Turks had improved more than the Christians. We find that the troops of Saladin employed means in their sieges that they had acquired from the crusaders; that they stood firmly the charge of the cavalry; that they now fought hand to hand with the mailed warriors of Europe, and mixed all the modes of chivalrous warfare with those they had practised before.

We do not perceive, however, that the Latins adopted their activity or their skill with the bow; and at the same time it must be remarked, that the armies of the Moslem fought as a whole, under the absolute command of one chief; while the Christians, divided in the battle as in the time of peace, were broken into separate corps under feudal leaders, who each consulted his own will fully as much as that of his sovereign.

Many other causes might be traced for the Christian fall and the Mussulman triumph; but perhaps more has been already said than was required. Whatever were the causes the result was the same—Jerusalem was taken by the Moslem, and consternation spread through Christendom.

CHAPTER 12

The News of the Fate of Palestine Reaches Europe

We have seen the solicitations of the church, and the eloquence of two extraordinary men, produce the first and second crusades; but many other incitements were added to clerical exhortations before the inveterate enmity of the French and English could be sufficiently calmed to permit of anything like a united expedition for the recovery of the Holy Land. The Italian merchants,[1] who at that time carried on the commerce of the world, were the first that brought to Europe the terrible news of the Battle of Tiberias, the capture of Jerusalem, and the fall of Palestine: but very soon after, William of Tyre,[2] the noble historian of the crusades, set out in person to demand assistance in behalf of his afflicted country from all the princes of Christendom.

He first landed in Sicily, where William, king of that country, who had married Joan of England, received him with kindness, and instantly took measures for furnishing such assistance to the Christians of the Holy Land, that the small territory yet unconquered might be successfully defended till further succour could arrive. Three hundred knights and a considerable naval force were despatched at once; and William of Sicily was continuing zealously his preparations, when death cut him off in the midst; and the crown was seized by Tancred, natural son of Roger I.

From Sicily, the Archbishop of Tyre proceeded to Rome; but he only arrived in time to witness the death of Pope Urban III.,[3] whose

---

1. There is a letter in Hovedon from a Templar to Henry II., giving an account of the state of Jerusalem and the Holy Land, dated 1179.
2. Bernard the Treasurer; William of Nangis, *A. D.* 1188; B. Peterborough.
3. William de Nangis; Jacob. Vit. lib. i.

mind was so deeply affected by the loss of the Holy Land, and the capture of the sepulchre, that his enfeebled constitution gave way under the shock, and he literally died of grief. Gregory VIII., who succeeded, lost not a moment in preaching a new crusade; and during his short pontificate of but two months, he left no means untried to heal the dissensions of Christendom, and to turn the arms of the princes who now employed them against each other to the service of God, as it was then considered, in the deliverance of that land which had been sanctified by his advent.

The first who took the Cross was the famous Frederic Barbarossa,[4] who conducted a magnificent army across Hungary and Greece, saw through and defeated the perfidious schemes of the Greek emperor, Isaac Angelus,[5] passed on into Asia Minor, overthrew in a pitched battle the Saracen forces which had been called against him by the base and cowardly Greek, and took the city of Iconium itself. Such splendid successes, with so little loss, had never before attended any Christian host; but the light that shone upon the German arms was soon changed to darkness by the death of Frederic, who, bathing imprudently in the Orontes,[6] returned to his tent in a dying state, and soon after expired[7] at seventy years of age. After the decease of the emperor, while Henry, his eldest son, who had remained in Germany, assumed the imperial crown, Philip Duke of Suabia led on the host towards Antioch.

But the very name of Frederic had been a subject of such fear, even to Saladin himself,[8] that he had ordered the towns of Laodicea, Ghibel, Tortosa, Biblios, Berytes, and Sidon to be dismantled at the approach of the Germans. Now, again, the Saracens resumed the offensive; and, between war and famine, the Teutonic crusaders were reduced to a small body when they reached Antioch. Their force was still sufficient to give them the command of that city, and proved a most serviceable aid to the Christian troops, who were slowly beginning to rally throughout Palestine. A new military institution was soon

---

4. Bernard the Treasurer.
5. A. D. 1189, 1190.
6. I have followed James of Vitry. Some say that Frederic's death proceeded from bathing in the Cydnus, and some in the Calycadnus. The matter is of little moment; but, as he was descending towards Antioch at the time, it is not improbable that the Cardinal de Vitry was right. Emadeddin, in the collection of Arabic historians by Reinaud, calls this river the Selef.
7. Jacob. Vit.; Hist. Hieros. ab.; Bernardus; Lection. Canisius Antiquæ.
8. James of Vitry.

after attached, by the Duke of Suabia, to the German hospital, which had been founded at Jerusalem many years before by some northern merchants, and had since been greatly enlarged by the Hanseatic[9] traders of Bremen and Lubec. On this establishment he grafted the Order of the Knights of the Holy Cross, or the Teutonic knights of the Hospital of St. Mary,[10] which soon greatly increased, and was sanctioned by papal authority.

I must now return to France and England, where private feuds had prevented the distresses of Palestine from producing so immediate an effect as they had wrought with the Germans. Henry II. had, as we have already seen, espoused Eleonor, the repudiated wife of Louis VII., and had obtained with her the whole of Aquitain.[11] This, in addition to Normandy, which he also held as a feudatory of the French crown, rendered the kingly vassal a greater territorial lord than even the sovereign to whom he did homage for his continental lands. Such a state of things, was alone quite sufficient to cause endless dissensions; but soon more immediate matter was found. Louis VII. died. Philip Augustus succeeded, yet in his youth; and Henry II., after having himself, in execution of the feudal duty of the dukes of Normandy, lifted the crown with which Philip's brow was to be decorated, endeavoured to strengthen his own party in France as much as possible against the young monarch.

His second son, Geoffrey, he married to Constance, Dutchess of Brittany: his eldest son, Henry, espoused Marguerite, sister of Philip, and received with her the lordship of Gisors,[12] and the territory of the Vexin. Prince Henry died early, leaving no children; and the land, by his marriage contract, reverted to the crown of France; but his father refused to yield it. War broke out in consequence, and was raging fiercely when the news of the fall of Jerusalem reached Europe. The tidings were so unexpected, each one felt so deep and religious a devotion for the Holy Land, every knight had there so many relations or friends, that the news found a thousand avenues open to the hearts of all who heard it.

The world, too, was then mad with song. Nations in that early age had all the zealous passions of youth. That fresh ardour—that wild spirit of pursuit, which almost every one must have felt in his own

9. Pet. de Dusburg.; Chron. Ord. Teuton.
10. Existing Orders of Knighthood; James of Vitry.
11. Vit. Ludovic VII.; Roger de Hovedon.
12. Rigord de gest. Phil Aug.; Hovedon; Robert, de Monte.

young days, was then the character of society at large. Europe was as an enthusiastic boy, and whatever it followed, love, religion, song, it followed with the uncontrolled passion, the fiery desire which burns but in the days of boyhood among nations as among men. Poetry had now become both the great delight, and the great mover of the day; and all the eloquence of verse found a fit subject in the sorrows of Palestine. The *troubadours*[13] and the *trouveres* vied with each other, which should do most to stimulate the monarchs and the chivalry of Europe to lay aside their private quarrels, and to fly to the deliverance of the Holy Land.

The *plainte* was heard from castle to castle, mourning over the loss of Jerusalem. The *sirvente* and the *fabliau* were spread far and wide, lashing with all the virulence of indignant satire those whom feuds or interests withheld from the battles of the Cross. The papal authority enjoined, with its menaces and its inducements, peace to Europe and war to the Saracen: but even superstition and zeal effected little, when compared with the power of the new passion for song. The first crusade had been the effect of a general enthusiasm; the second of individual eloquence; but this was the crusade of poetry. The first two were brought about by the clergy alone; but this was the work of the *troubadours*.

A truce between Henry II. and Philip Augustus was agreed upon, and a meeting was fixed between Trie and Gisors,[14] for the purpose of considering the manner of settling all difficulties, and the best means of delivering Jerusalem. The whole of the barons of France and England were present at this parliament, which was held in the month of January, and mutual jealousies and hatred had nearly turned the assembly, which met to promote peace, to the purposes of bloodshed. At length the Cardinal of Albano and William, Archbishop of Tyre, presented themselves to the meeting; and the oriental prelate having related all the horrors he had himself beheld in the Holy Land—the slaughter of Tiberias, the fall of Jerusalem, the pollution of the temple, and the capture of the sepulchre—the symbol of the Cross was unanimously adopted by all; private wars were laid aside, and a mode of proceeding was determined on which promised to furnish vast supplies for the holy enterprise to which the kings and barons bound themselves.

The first of the measures resolved was to enforce a general contribution from all persons who did not take the Cross, whether clergy or laity,

---

13. Geoffroi Rudel in Raynouard; Millot; Ducange.
14. William of Nangis, *A. D.* 1188; Rigord.

towards defraying the expense of the crusade. This consisted of a tenth of all possessions, whether landed or personal, and was called *Saladin's tithe*. Each lord, clerical or secular, had the right of raising this tax within his own feoff. The lord of the commune could alone tithe his burghers, the archbishop his see, the abbot the lands of the monastery, the chapter the lands of the church. Any knight having taken the Cross, and being the legitimate heir of a knight or a widow[15] who had not taken the Cross, was entitled to lay the tax upon the lands of the other; while all who refused or neglected to pay their quota were given absolutely to the disposal of him who had the right to require it.

At the same time that such inflictions were adjudged to those who rejected the call to the Holy Land, many immunities were accorded to such as followed the crusade. Great facilities were given to all the crusaders for the payment of their anterior debts; but they were by no means, as has been frequently asserted,[16] liberated from all engagements during the time they were occupied in the expedition. Such were the regulations which were first brought forward at Gisors. Each of the monarchs proposed them afterward to a separate court of their barons and clergy, Philip at Paris, and Henry, first at Rouen, to his Norman council, and afterward to his English vassals at Geddington, in Northamptonshire.

All seemed now to tend rapidly towards the great enterprise; nothing was seen in the various countries but the symbol of the Cross, which in England was of *ermine* or white, of *gules* or red for France, and of *synople* or green for Flanders.

But the whole current of feeling was suddenly turned, by an aggression of Richard, Duke of Guienne, afterward King of England, upon the territories of the Count of Toulouse. Philip Augustus flew to arms to avenge his vassal and friend; Richard met him with equal fierceness, and the feuds between France and England were renewed with increased violence.[17] Many of the French and English knights, several of the clergy of the two countries, together with a great multitude of Germans, Italians, and Flemings, waited not for the tardy journey of the crusading monarchs, but passed over into the Holy Land, and joined themselves to Guy of Lusignan, who had now collected the remnants of all the military orders, and with those princes

---

15. Rigord in vit. Philip August.; Guil. de Nangis, *A. D.* 1188.

16. See Rigord, who gives minutely the statutes on this occasion.

17. Branche des royaux Lignages, ann. 1189-90, Guil. de Nangis Rigord. William the Breton.

and knights who had escaped the Moslem scimitar, was engaged in besieging Acre.

His forces[18] gradually increased till they became immense; and, owing to the skill of those by whom he was accompanied, rather than his own, the camp of Lusignan was fortified in such a manner that no efforts of the Saracens could penetrate its lines. Saladin pitched his tents on the mountains to the south, not long after the Christians had undertaken the siege, and innumerable battles in the open field succeeded, in which neither army gained any material advantage that was not compensated by some following reverse.

The fleet of the Saracens supplied the town,[19] and the fleet of the Christians brought aid to the camp, so that the conflict seemed to be interminable, from the equal zeal and force of the contending parties.

In the meanwhile, the war between Henry and Philip continued; and, from a personal dispute between Richard Cœur de Lion and the French monarch, had so changed its character, that Richard, accompanied by his brother John, went over to the faction of the enemy, and did homage to the crown of France.[20] Henry, abandoned by his children and the greater part of his nobles, found himself forced to sign an ignominious peace; and after one of the violent fits of passion to which he so often yielded himself, was taken ill, and concluded a long life of vice and crime before the altar of the Lord,[21] which he had once caused to be stained with blood.[22]

Richard and Philip were already in alliance; and no sooner had the new monarch of England ascended the throne, than the preparations for the crusade were resumed with activity. Ample treaties were entered into between the French and English kings; and as the clergy, though willing enough to preach the crusade, were in general unwilling to aid it by the payment of Saladin's tenth, Richard had recourse to the most arbitrary[23] extortions, to furnish the sums necessary for his enterprise. Philip Augustus, the Count of Flanders, and Richard Cœur de Lion met at Nonancourt, on the confines of Normandy, and engaged mutually to live in peace and defend each other, as true allies, till a period of forty days after their return from Palestine.[24] Richard

---

18. Bernard the Treasurer; James of Vitry.
19. Continuation of William of Tyre, *Anon.*
20. R. de Diceto; Roger de Hovedon; Matthew Paris. Ann. 1188.
21. Henry died before the altar of the church of Chinon.
22. Hovedon.
23. Brompton; Hovedon.
24. Diceto.

also published a code of laws or regulations for the government of his troops during the expedition.

By these it was enacted, that whoever slew a brother crusader should be tied to the corpse and buried alive; or, if the murder were perpetrated at sea, should be plunged with the dead body into the waves. A man who drew his knife upon another, or struck him so as to produce blood, was destined to have his hand cut off. Other chastisements were instituted for simple blows, abusive language, and blasphemy;[25] and if anyone were discovered in committing a robbery, he was sentenced to have his head shaved and to be tarred and feathered. This is, I believe, the first mention in history of that curious naval punishment.

Each of the crusading monarchs now made large donations to abbeys, churches, and religious communities,[26] and performed various acts of grace to bring down the blessing of Heaven upon their enterprise. They took every measure that could be devised for the security and good of their respective realms during their absence, and then proceeded towards Lyons, where, finding that the followers of their camp were becoming somewhat more numerous than was desirable, and remembering the vices and irregularities of the former crusades, they instituted several new laws; among which it was strictly enjoined that no woman should be permitted to accompany either army, except washerwomen, and such as had accomplished fifty years. Here, also, the two kings separated,[27] and Philip, traversing the Alps, soon arrived at Genoa,[28] where he hired vessels to carry him to Messina, the general rendezvous, which place he reached with no other impediment than a severe storm.

Richard, in the meantime, hurried on to Marseilles, where he waited a few days for the fleet which was to have joined him from England; but his impatient spirit could never brook delay, and after a pause of little more than a week, he hired all the vessels he could find, and proceeded to Genoa. Leaving that city he touched at several places on the coast of Italy, and near the mouth of the Tiber was encountered by Octavian, Bishop of Ostia, who demanded various sums, stated to be due to the church of Rome from the English monarch, as fees, on the election of the Bishop of Ely, and the deposition of the

---

25. Rymer, col. diplom.

26. Brequegny, coll. ann. 1188; Rigord in *vit. Phil. Aug.*

27. Benedict of Peterborough.

28. Rigord says nothing of any illness which Philip suffered at Messina.

Bishop of Bourdeaux. Richard replied by boldly reproaching the prelate with the simoniacal avarice of his church, and sent him indignantly from his presence.

In the Gulf of Salernum, the English king was met by his fleet, and soon anchored before Messina, causing all the horns of his armament to blow as he entered the port. The noise was so great, that the inhabitants crowded to the walls, where they beheld the thousand banners of England covering the sea with all the gay and splendid colours of chivalrous blazonry.[29] Richard was fond of such display, and, perhaps, so slight a thing as this first woke that jealousy in the bosom of Philip Augustus which afterward proved ruinous to the crusade. Nevertheless that monarch came down to meet Richard, with Tancred, the usurping King of Sicily, who had everything to fear from the anger of the hasty sovereign of England.

After dispossessing Constantia, the heiress of the crown, Tancred had imprisoned Joan, sister of Richard, the widow of the last king William the Good. He had freed her, it is true, on the news of Richard's arrival; but the first act of the English monarch[30] was to demand the restitution of his sister's dowry, and the legacies which had been bequeathed by William of Sicily to Henry II. of England. These together amounted to forty thousand ounces of gold,[31] and for some time Richard's application was met by nothing but quibbling and evasion.

The best intelligence had hitherto reigned between the French and English, but not so with Richard's knights and the people of Sicily. The Anglo-Normans were dissolute and reckless, and the Sicilians soon proceeded from squabbling and opposition, to seek bloody revenge. It is probable that both parties were in fault. Everything at Messina was charged at a most exorbitant price,[32] and the Normans were very apt to take what they could not buy. The Sicilians cheated them, and they plundered the Sicilians, till at length some of the Norman soldiers were killed.[33] Hugh Lebrun, a favourite of Richard, was wounded; and Richard himself, finding the peasantry supported by Tancred in the attack on his soldiers, lost command of his temper, fell upon the people who had come forth from Messina, stormed the

---

29. Hovedon; Brompton.
30. Benedict of Peterborough.
31. Rigord; Benedict of Peterborough.
32. Rigord.
33. Vinesauf.

walls of the city; and in an inconceivably short time, the banner of the King of England was flying over the capital of Sicily.[34]

Philip Augustus, who had interfered on many occasions to quiet the differences between the Normans and the Sicilians, could not bear to see the English standard on the towers of Messina, and a coolness rose up between the two monarchs from that moment. All angry discussion, however, was removed by the conduct of Richard, which was calm and moderate, far beyond his usual habits. He offered to give up the guard of the city to either the Knights of the Temple or of St. John, till his claims on Tancred had been fairly met. This tranquillized the matter for a time; but Eleonor, Richard's mother, now arrived in Sicily,[35] bearing with her the beautiful Berengaria, of Navarre. The King of England had been affianced to Alice of France, the sister of Philip; but criminal intercourse, it was supposed, had existed between the French princess and Henry II., and Richard had long meditated breaking off formally an alliance he never intended to fulfil. The sight of Berengaria decided him.[36]

Some letters were shown to him by Tancred, King of Sicily, in which Philip Augustus promised aid to the Sicilians in case of their warring with the English. Richard, with the papers in his hand, cast himself on horseback, and galloped to the tent of the French monarch. Philip declared the letters were forged, and that Richard's anger was a mere pretence to break off a marriage which suited not his taste. War between the two sovereigns seemed inevitable, and how it was averted does not very clearly appear. Probably the higher barons interposed; but at all events the concessions were on the side of Philip, who, by a formal treaty, renounced all pretensions to Richard's hand, on the part of his sister;[37] confirmed him in all the feoffs he held from the crown of France; and, leaving him and Berengaria to conclude their

---

34. Ben. Abb. Peter.; R. Hovedon.

35. Rigord.

36. Rigordus states positively that Berengaria had arrived before the treaty was signed between Philip and Richard. Mills says, that Richard remained in Sicily after Philip's departure, to wait for Berengaria; but Rigord lived at the time, and was one of the most diligent inquirers who have left us records of that age. The *Branche des royaux Lignages* makes Richard say to the King of France, "*Sire vostre suer espousai De laquele atan le don hui; Mes onc nul jour ne la connui Et j'ai puis prise Bérangarre Qui fille est au roy de Navarre.*"—1226. William the Breton, also, who was afterward chaplain to Philip Augustus, represents Richard as saying, "*Et jam juncta thoro est mihi Berengaria, regis Filia Navarræ.*"

37. Rigord in vit. Phil. Aug.; Hovedon; Rymer.

marriage, he set sail with his fleet for Acre.

The appearance of the French before that place caused great rejoicing among the Christians, for notwithstanding every effort on the part of the assailants the city still held out; and, girt in themselves by the army of Saladin, the scarcity[38] was little less in their camp than in the town. Before the coming of their allies, the crusaders under the walls of Acre had done all that human ingenuity could invent to force the garrison to yield. They had turned the course of the river which supplied the city with fresh water; they had been incessant in their attacks and, during nearly two years, had never relaxed one moment in their endeavours.[39] It was apparent, therefore, that nothing but assault by a large force could carry the fortress, and this the arrival of Philip gave the possibility of attempting. That monarch, however, either from some engagement to that effect, or from the scantiness of the succour he brought, which, according to Boha Eddin, consisted only of six large ships,[40] determined to wait the arrival of Richard Cœur de Lion, contenting himself with battering the walls in the meanwhile.

The coming of the King of France had spread as much alarm among the Saracens as joy among the Christians; but his inactivity calmed their apprehensions; and the escape of a magnificent white falcon which Philip had brought from Europe, was considered by the infidels as an evil omen for the French monarch. The bird flew into the besieged city, and was thence sent to Saladin, who would not be prevailed upon to part with it, though Philip offered a thousand pieces of gold for his favourite falcon.[41]

Richard remained some time in Sicily, enjoying the idleness and luxury of a delicious climate, and a fertile and beautiful land; but the preaching of a wild enthusiast, called Joachim, together with various celestial phenomena, which the superstition of the age attributed to Divine wrath, awoke the monarch from his dream of pleasure, and af-

---

38. Bernardus.

39. Various knights are mentioned by Bernard the Treasurer, as having signalized themselves greatly, both prior to the siege and after its commencement. One in particular, whom he calls the Green Knight, even raised the admiration of the Saracens to such a height that Saladin sent for him, and made him the most brilliant offers, in hopes of bringing him to join the Moslems. It is more than probable that this Green Knight was the famous Jacques d'Avesnes, and was so called from the colour of the cross which he wore.

40. *Auteurs Arabes, rec. de Reinaud; Branche des loyaux Rignages*; Rigord in *vit. Phil. August.*

41. Boha Eddin, rec. de Reinaud.

ter having submitted to an humiliating penance,[42] he set sail for Acre. A tempest soon dispersed his fleet, and three of the vessels were lost upon the rocky shores of Cyprus. The monarch of that island, one of the Comneni of Constantinople, had rendered himself independent of Greece, and had taken the title of emperor. In the madness of insatiable greediness, he pillaged the crews and passengers of the English vessels stranded on his coast, and refused a refuge to the bride and sister of Richard himself, when driven by the storm into the port of Limisso.

At Rhodes[43] the lion-hearted king heard of the disasters of his fleet, and the inhospitality of the Emperor of Cyprus, and no sooner had he gathered together his ships, than he sailed for Limisso, and demanded reparation and apology.

With infinite moderation, the more admirable in the conduct of a violent and irritable monarch, he three times required satisfaction before he proceeded to any act of aggression. At length, finding it not to be obtained but by the sword, he landed on the island, drove the coward Greeks[44] before him, took the ungenerous usurper Isaac, and reduced the whole country to his sway. His wrath had now been roused, and all temper was forgotten: he taxed the unfortunate inhabitants of the country to an enormous extent and then, after having spent some time at Limisso, where he celebrated his marriage with Berengaria, he once more set sail for Acre. In the passage the fleet of the English monarch came suddenly upon a large vessel bearing the arms of the King of France. Something suspicious in the appearance of the ship induced Richard to pursue her, and it was soon discovered that she was filled with Saracen troops.

The attack was instantly ordered;[45] the *infidels* defended themselves with the greatest bravery; the sea was covered with Greek fire, and a rain of arrows fell upon the decks of the low European galleys from the high sides of the Arabian vessel. But resistance against the whole fleet of the English king was vain; and the Emir Jacob, who commanded, ordered the ship to be sunk by cutting through the bottom with hatchets. Before this could be completely accomplished, however, the English and Normans were masters of the vessel, and ere she went down a great part of her cargo was saved. This principally consisted of military stores for the camp of Saladin: and, among other

---

42. Brompton, *A. D.* 1191; Ben. Abb. Peterborough, 1191.
43. Hovedon; Ben. Abb. Peterborough.
44. Hovedon; Brompton; Will. Newb.
45. Boha Eddin; Walter Vinesauf; Hovedon; Benedict of Peterborough.

implements of destruction, the English were surprised and horrified to find a number of large earthen vases filled with poisonous reptiles, from the bites of which it was known that the Christians near Acre suffered most dreadfully. Whether these animals were or were not really destined by Saladin as the means of a new and direful mode of warfare, such was the purpose which the Christian monarch[46] attributed to those who carried them; and giving way to his wrath, he ordered all the prisoners to be put to death. Some few were saved, who were afterward ransomed according to the universal custom of the day.[47]

But little time now elapsed ere Richard, with a hundred sail, arrived before the city of Acre, and the shouts of joy that welcomed him made his proud heart beat with more than wonted ardour. All the Chivalry of Europe were upon the sandy plain between Ptolemais and the mountains of Carouba:[48] the Templars, the Hospitallers, the Knights of France, of England, of Germany, of Italy, of Flanders, and of Burgundy. Thousands of banners floated on the wind; and every sort of arms, device, and ensign glittered through the camp. On the inland hills lay the millions of Saladin, with every accessory of eastern pomp and eastern luxury. There, too, was the pride of all the Saracen tribes, called into the field by their great monarch to meet the swarming invasion of the Christians.[49] One wing of the Moslem army was commanded by Malek Adel Saif Eddin,[50] brother of Saladin, and the other by that monarch's nephew, Modaffer. Through the host were seen banners of green, and black, and yellow; and armour of as many kinds, and of as great magnificence, as that of the Europeans.

Nor was the chivalrous courtesy of the day confined to the Christian camp. In times of truce the adverse nations mingled together in friendship; and at one moment they sent mutual presents, and reciprocated good offices, while at another they met in bloody and impetuous

46. Peterborough; Vinesauf; James, Cardinal of Vitry, lib. i.

47. Mills speaks of the conduct of Richard in the following terms: "The sanguinary and ungenerous Richard killed or cast overboard his defenceless enemies; or, with an avarice equally detestable, saved the commanders for the sake of their ransom." That author, however, says not one word of the Saracens' fighting under false colours, or of the horrible cargo which they carried in their ship, though he afterward himself alludes to the sufferings of the crusaders from the bites of reptiles. Is this historical justice?

48. Bernard the Treasurer.

49. Boha Eddin, rec. Hist. Arabes de Reinaud.

50. His name, literally translated, means *the just king, the sword of the faith*. From Saif Eddin the Christians composed the word Saphaddin, by which he is generally designated in the chronicles of the time.

strife. Saladin himself seems to have conceived the highest respect for the character of Richard; and when he was not opposing him in the field, he was always desirous of showing that the Moslems were not to be outdone in generous sentiment by any of the Christian knights.

It would be endless to recount all the transactions of the siege of Acre. The *spirit* of the whole of this crusade (which I could wish to dwell upon more than anything else) has been already fully, perfectly, and feelingly displayed, in that most beautiful composition, The Talisman; wherein Sir Walter Scott, however he may have altered some historical facts to suit the purposes of fiction, has given a more striking picture of the human mind in that age—of the character of nations as well as individuals—than any dull chronicle of cold events can furnish.

Richard Cœur de Lion, soon after his arrival before Acre, was seized with the fever of the country, and in the attack made upon the town by Philip Augustus the English monarch was not present.[51] Philip murmured highly, and his assault was repulsed from the want of sufficient forces to follow up his first advantage. Richard in his turn attempted to storm the city without the aid of France, and notwithstanding efforts of almost incredible valour, was likewise repelled. Mutual necessity brought some degree of concord; and it was agreed that while one army assailed the walls the other should guard the camp, but still the endeavours of both were ineffectual to take the town by storm; and continual disputes were every day springing up between the two monarchs and the two hosts. Philip strove to seduce the vassals of Richard to follow his banner, as the sovereign of their sovereign, and paid three pieces of gold per month to each of the Norman knights who would join his standard:[52] Richard gave four pieces of gold to all who came over from Philip, and many a French feudatory joined himself to the English king.

The siege of Acre still advanced, notwithstanding, less indeed by the presence or efforts of the two sovereigns, than by the simple fact of the city being cut off from all supplies. It had now held out for many months; and for long had endured but little privation from its communication with the sea; but as one article of the first necessity after another became exhausted, that means of receiving provisions was not sufficiently productive or regular for the supply of a great city. Even when ships arrived the town was in a state of scarcity, and a day's

---

51. Vinesauf; Hovedon.
52. Chron. St. Denis.

delay brought on a famine. Acre could resist no longer,[53] and after a short truce, which was asked in the hope of assistance from Egypt, it surrendered to the monarchs of France and England, on very rigorous terms.

All the Christian prisoners within the town were to be freed, together with one thousand men and two hundred knights, chosen from those that Saladin detained in captivity; two hundred thousand pieces of gold were to be paid, and the true Cross was to be restored to the Christians. Such was the only capitulation granted to the people of Acre, who were also to remain in the hands of the crusaders till the stipulations had been fulfilled by Saladin; and in case the conditions were not accomplished within forty days, the prisoners were left to the disposal of their conquerors.

Saladin neglected to fulfil any of the terms which depended on him; the ransom was not paid; the wood of the Cross was not restored; and Richard[54] cruelly commanded his prisoners to be put to death.[55] After the capture of the city, the Archduke of Austria boldly placed his banner on one of the towers but no sooner was it seen by Richard, than with his own hand he tore it down, and rending it to pieces,[56] trampled it under his feet. The insult was neither forgotten nor unrevenged, though from that moment the banners of the kings[57] only continued to float from the walls of Acre. Thus new dissensions were added to those which had already arisen, and the two monarchs, by taking possession of the whole spoil and dividing it between them, gave high disgust to the rest of the crusaders.

Another more tangible cause of animosity soon sprang up. Sybilla, the wife of Guy of Lusignan, through whom alone he possessed the title of King of Jerusalem, died during the siege of Acre, but he still pretended a right to the throne. Conrad of Montferrat, lord of Tyre,

---

53. James of Vitry; Hovedon; Vinesauf; Ben. of Pet.; Bernard the Treasurer.

54. Rigord; William of Nangis; James of Vitry; Bernardus; Vinesauf; Hovedon. All these authors give different accounts of the numbers sacrificed.

55. Bernard the Treasurer affirms that Philip caused the prisoners to be executed; but most of the other historians agree, that this piece of cruelty was committed by Richard alone.

56. Rigord.

57. Bernard the Treasurer says, that the English king lodged in the house of the Templars, and that Philip Augustus occupied the citadel; "*Le Roi de France ot le chastel d'Acre, et le fist garnir et le Roi d'Angleterre se herberja en la maison du Temple.*" Most authorities, however, are opposed to this statement, declaring that Richard lodged in the palace, and Philip with the Templars.

had seized upon Isabella, sister of Sybilla, and wife of the weak and cowardly Humphrey de Thoron; and having obtained, by one means or another, a divorce between her and her husband, had married her; on which marriage, he also claimed the empty vanity of the crown. Richard, with the Pisans and the Hospitallers, maintained the cause of Lusignan; Philip Augustus, with the Genoese and the Templars, supported Conrad; and the schism was only healed by Lusignan acknowledging Conrad to be heir to the nominal kingdom, while Conrad allowed Lusignan to retain the title for his life.

Soon after this, the crusade received[58] its deathblow, by the defection of Philip Augustus. No doubt can exist that that monarch had really lost his health since his sojourn in the Holy Land; but as little doubt is there that his chief motive in returning to Europe was his disgust[59] at the overbearing conduct of Richard, and his jealousy at the great superiority of his rival in all military exercises. Philip Augustus was an expert and able general, a brave and distinguished knight; but Richard was the wonder of his day, and what Philip might have admired in an inferior, he could not bear in a fellow-king. He therefore proclaimed aloud his illness, and his intention to return to Europe, most unwisely—as James of Vitry observes—for the interest of the crusade; for Saladin[60] had been so much depressed by the fall of Acre, that beyond all question immense concessions might have been obtained, had the monarchs but made a demonstration of acting in concert.

As bound to him by treaties, Richard's permission was demanded by the King of France. At first Richard exclaimed, with a burst of honest indignation, "Eternal shame on him and on all France, if for any cause he leave the work unfinished!"[61] but he added afterward, "Well, let him go, if his health require it, or if he cannot live without seeing Paris." With this surly leave, Philip hastened his departure, after having made over to Conrad of Tyre his share in the city of Acre, and having sworn, in the most solemn manner, to respect Richard's possessions in Europe—an oath which he soon found occasion to break.

The Duke of Burgundy,[62] with ten thousand men, was left behind to support Richard; and that monarch, after repairing the fortifications of Acre, having seen the churches purified, and the Christian

58. Bernard the Treasurer; Rigord; William the Breton; Branche des royaux Lignages.
59. Rigord; Robert of Gloucester.
60. James of Vitry; Boha Eddin; Emad Eddin; Recueil de Reinaud.
61. Benedict of Peterborough.
62. Bernard the Treasurer; James of Vitry, &c.

religion restored, marched out with considerable force, and took the road by the seaside towards Ascalon. Vessels laden with provisions followed along the shore; but, on the other hand, the Moslems, who had now recovered confidence at the dissensions which they knew reigned among the Christians, pursued the army as it marched, and harassed it by continual attacks.

Richard[63] refrained from anything like a general engagement, as long as such conduct was possible; but near Azotus he found himself compelled to fight, and he accordingly drew out his men in battle array. Eudes, Duke of Burgundy, commanded the left, and the famous Jacques d'Avesnes the right, of the crusaders, while Richard himself appeared in the centre.

Saladin[64] led the attack against the Christian army, and the right gave way. At the same time the left repulsed the Moslems, and with the usual impetuous courage of the French, who composed it, followed up their success till they were cut off from the main body. Richard advanced to the aid of the Duke of Burgundy, but only so far as to save him from being destroyed. With wonderful coolness he waited till the Saracens had exhausted their arrows, and wearied their horses with rapid evolutions, so that the knights murmured at the unwonted inactivity of their monarch.

At length, seeing that Saladin had weakened his left wing to attack the Duke of Burgundy, that the hail of missiles was passed, and that there existed some confusion in the enemy's[65] lines, the king commanded his knights to charge, and leading them on himself, he with his own hand overthrew all that opposed him. The *infidels* whom he slew, and the feats that he performed, are almost incredible; but certain it is, that his voice, his eye, his look, brought inspiration to the Christians and dismay to the hearts of the Moslems. The Saracen host fled amain, and Richard remained master of the field, having to mourn few of his distinguished soldiers besides Jacques d'Avesnes who was slain towards the end of the battle.[66]

The road both to Ascalon and Jerusalem was now open to the host of the Cross;[67] but either from treachery, as some have supposed, or from envy, as others have imagined, Richard was continually op-

---

63. Hovedon; James of Vitry; Vinesauf.

64. Vinesauf; Boha Eddin.

65. Hovedon; Vinesauf.

66. James of Vitry; *Trivet Annales*.

67. Bernard the Treasurer.

posed in the council of war: the operations of the crusaders became vacillating, uncertain, and ill-judged, and the kingdom of Jerusalem was virtually cast away. The army, instead of following its advantages, proceeded to Jaffa,[68] wasted time in fortifying that city, and suffered the Saracens to recover from their panic. Various attacks were soon made upon the Christians; a party of Templars was surrounded by the foe, and would have been cut to pieces, with the Earl of Leicester and some English who had come to their aid, had not Richard, with his lion-heart, rushed, almost unarmed, into the fight; and, scattering the enemy like a whirlwind, delivered his friends from their peril.

On another occasion, he had himself nearly been taken prisoner while falconing, and would certainly have fallen into the hands of the Saracens, had not one of his followers, named William de Pratelles,[69] exclaimed, "I am the king!" and thus drawn the attention of the enemy to himself. After this, various treaties[70] were entered into, which ended in nothing, and probably were devised by the Saracens merely for the purpose of gaining time to recruit their forces. It was even proposed that Joan of Sicily, the English monarch's sister, should be given in marriage to Saphaddin, or Saif Eddin; and that Jerusalem should be yielded to the parties in this strange alliance. All these negotiations, however, terminated as they began, and hostilities were often commenced and suspended, equally without cause. Richard advanced to Ramula, and nothing opposed his proceeding to Jerusalem; but at a council of war it was determined that the army should retire upon Ascalon.[71]

This was done, and Ascalon was once more fortified; but here the troops were cut off from supplies, new divisions arose, and many desertions took place. The Duke of Burgundy retreated to Acre; the Genoese and Pisans broke out into open warfare, and one party, supported by Conrad of Montferrat, would have destroyed the other, had not Richard marched to the spot, forced Conrad to withdraw, and re-established peace between the contending nations. Conrad, frustrated in the views he had entertained, rejected all conciliation from Richard, and allied himself with Saladin. That monarch immediately hastened once more to attack the divided army of the Cross;[72] but

68. James of Vitry.

69. This gentleman was taken prisoner, but was of course ransomed immediately by Richard.

70. Hovedon; Boha Eddin.

71. Vinesauf; James of Vitry.

72. Hovedon; William of Nangis, ann. 1192; Vinesauf.

Conrad was stabbed by two of a class of men called the Assassins,[73] at the moment that Richard, to obtain concord, had consented to his coronation as king of Jerusalem, in opposition to the claim of Guy of Lusignan.

The French attributed the death of Conrad to Richard, and all parties flew to arms; but in the midst of this confusion, Henry Count of Champagne came forward, married the widow of Conrad, was proclaimed king of Jerusalem[74] with the consent of all, and the united host once more prepared to march and conquer the kingdom for which they had just been providing a king.

During this time, Richard Cœur de Lion, while waging the war for Jerusalem, was neglecting all his best interests in Europe. John, his brother, was striving for the crown of England, and Philip Augustus was stripping him of his territories in France. Messenger after messenger brought naught but tidings of danger, and pressing solicitations for his return.

---

73. For many years a horde of plunderers had been established in the mountains of Phœnicia, in the neighbourhood of Tortosa and Tripoli, who, in the end, obtained the name of Assassins, from the small dagger which was their only weapon, and which was called *hassassin*. Their religion was a corrupted species of Islamism, and their government a fanatical despotism. Their chief was called sometimes the Ancient, sometimes the Lord of the Mountains, and among the Christians he obtained the name of the Old Man of the Mountains. By working on the excitable imaginations of an illiterate and fanatical race, the lords of this extraordinary tribe had obtained over them an influence unknown to any other power which was ever brought to sway the mind of man. The will of the Old Man of the Mountains was absolute law to each of his subjects. Whatever were his commands, whether to slay themselves or another, they asked no questions—paused not to consider of justice or injustice—but obeyed; and when sent to execute the will of their lord upon anyone, they followed their object with a keen sagacity and unalterable perseverance, that placed the life of each individual in the hands of their remorseless monarch. Nothing could turn them aside from the pursuit; no difficulties were too great for them to surmount; and when they had struck the victim, if they escaped, it was well; but if they were taken, they met torture and death with stoical firmness, feeling certain of the joys of Paradise as a compensation for their sufferings. The number of this tribe was about sixty thousand, all conscientious murderers, whom no danger would daunt, and no human consideration could deter. Such were the men who slew Conrad of Montferrat; and yet the French with the wild inconsistency of their national hatred, attributed the deed to Richard, who never found aught on earth that could induce him to cover his wrath when it was excited, or to stay him from the open pursuit of revenge, which was always as bold and unconcealed as it was fierce and evanescent. From this tribe we have derived the word *assassin*.—See James of Vitry; Matthew of Paris; William of Tyre; Ducange ou Joinville.
74. Bernard the Treasurer; James of Vitry; William of Nangis.

Still Richard advanced towards Jerusalem,[75] but his force was too small to attempt a long-protracted siege. He found himself far from resources, and in a country where supplies could be obtained but with the greatest difficulty.[76] The marches before him were barren and hot; little water was to be procured and at Bethlehem a council of twenty persons was appointed to inquire into the possibility of proceeding. Certain information was received that the Turks had destroyed all the wells and cisterns round the Holy City, and it was determined to abandon the enterprise. Richard felt the disappointment with all the bitterness of broken hope and crushed ambition. He was led to a hill from whence he could behold Jerusalem; but the sight and its memories were too much, and, covering his eyes with his shield,[77] the warrior monarch turned away with a swelling heart to concert measures for gaining something, at all events, to compensate the loss of Jerusalem.

But discord was in the bosom of the crusade; the soldiers murmured,[78] the chiefs rebelled, and the only thing that could save the army was immediate retreat. Such, then, after many plans had been proposed and rejected, was the ultimate step. The great body of the forces, with Richard and the Duke of Burgundy, fell back upon Acre; but a smaller part threw itself into Jaffa; and Saladin, recovering his energies as the crusaders lost theirs, collected his power and prepared to reap the fruits of their disunion. The hope of saving the Holy Land was now gone, and Richard determined to abandon an endeavour which jealousies and treacheries had rendered infeasible; and, returning to Europe, to give his thoughts to the consolidation and security of his own dominions.

Before he set out, however, the news reached him that Saladin had attacked Jaffa with immense forces; and that the only hope of the garrison was in aid from him.[79] Sending the bulk of the army by land,

75. Bernard; Vinesauf; Matthew Paris.
76. Little doubt can exist that one great cause of the abandonment of the crusade were the differences between Richard and the Duke of Burgundy. The Frenchman was jealous of the fame which the English king would have acquired by taking Jerusalem, and consequently took care that he should not effect that object. Such is the account given by Bernard the Treasurer—a Frenchman, who always showed a manifest tendency to exculpate his countrymen, whenever there existed a fair excuse. See the Chronicle in old French, published in the collection of Martenne and Durand. It was generally attributed to Hugh Plagon, but has since been proved to be the original of Bernard the Treasurer.
77. Vinesauf.
78. Hovedon; Vinesauf.
79. The French refused to march to the assistance of Jaffa.

he took advantage of a favourable wind, and set sail with a very small retinue for the besieged city. When he arrived at Jaffa, he perceived that the gates were already in the hands of the Saracens, and that the Christians were fighting to the last, to sell their lives dearly. To use the words of Bernard the Treasurer:—

> When King Richard found that the place was taken, he sprang on shore, with his shield round his neck, and his Danish axe in his hand, retook the castle, slew the Saracens that were within the walls, and drove those that were without back to their camp, where he halted on a little mound—he and his men. Saladin asked his troops why they fled; to which they replied, that the King of England had come to Jaffa, had slain much people, and retaken the town. Then Saladin asked, 'Where is he?' And they replied, 'There, sire, upon that hillock with his men.' 'What!' cried Saladin, 'the king on foot among his servants! This is not as it should be.' And Saladin sent him a horse,[80] charging the messenger to say, that such a man ought not to remain on foot in so great danger.

The attempts of the Saracens were vain to recover the position they had lost, and their terror at the tremendous name of Richard made that name a host. This victory again placed the King of England in a commanding situation, and he took advantage of it to demand peace. Saladin gladly met his advances. A treaty was entered into, and a truce was concluded for three years and eight months, during which period the Christians were to enjoy the liberty of visiting Jerusalem, as pilgrims, exempt from all grievance. Tyre and Jaffa, with the whole district between them, were yielded to the Latins, who, on their part, agreed to demolish the fortifications of Ascalon. The troops of the Cross were permitted to resort as palmers to Jerusalem, where the *sultaun* received and treated them with courteous hospitality. Richard would not visit the city he could not capture; but the Bishop of Salisbury was entertained in the *sultaun's* own palace, and obtained from the generous Saracen leave to establish three societies of Latin priests, in Jerusalem, in Bethlehem, and in Nazareth. Various other splendid acts of kingly magnanimity closed Saladin's communication with the crusaders.

On the 25th of October, *A. D.* 1192, Richard set sail for Europe. The fruits of his crusade were but small, as far as the recovery of the Holy Land was concerned; but in his own person he acquired a de-

---

80. Bernard the Treasurer.

gree of military glory that enmity could not wrest from him, and ages have not been able to dim.

He had many faults and many failings; and his own pride contributed as much as the jealousy of his enemies to create disunion among the allies, and frustrate the object of the expedition. But he had also to contend with many wrongs and difficulties, and possessed many bright and noble qualities. He carried the heart of a lion to his grave;[81] and for centuries after the women of Palestine scared their children with his name.[82]

---

81. Bernard the Treasurer.

82. The Queen Berengaria and Joan of Sicily left Acre on the 29th of September, previous to the departure of Richard, who set out on the 25th of October, 1192. After encountering a violent storm, which scattered his fleet and wrecked the greater number of his vessels, Richard, with his single ship, touched at Zara, where he landed, accompanied only by two priests and a few knights of the Temple, whose garb he had assumed. From Zara, Richard endeavoured to make his way through Germany in disguise, but in vain. The news of his journey had already spread; the unforgiving Archduke of Austria, whose banner he had trampled on at Acre, caused every road to be narrowly watched. One after another of his companions were sent away by the king, till at length, with a single squire, he arrived at a small town near Vienna; where, taking up his abode at a petty lodging, Richard despatched his follower for provisions. The squire was recognised by some of the spies of the archduke, and Richard was taken and cast into prison. The royal captive was speedily given into the hands of the emperor of Austria, who concerted with Philip Augustus the means of detaining him in secrecy. His confinement, nevertheless, was soon known in England, and means were used to discover his precise situation. General tradition gives the merit of having ascertained his lord's prison to his favourite troubadour Blondel, or Blondiau; and we may be surely allowed to regret that no grave historian has confirmed the tale. However that may be, the place of the king's confinement was discovered, and England began to cry loudly for justice from all Christendom. Knightly honour and religious feeling were invoked, and the infamy of detaining a traveller, a pilgrim, and a crusader was proclaimed with the loud and powerful voice of a people's indignation. Henry at length felt himself obligated to yield some appearance of justice for detaining an independent monarch; and Richard was brought before the diet at Worms, where he was charged with imaginary crimes, the chief of which was the assassination of Conrad, Marquis of Montferrat. Had the least shadow of reason been left on the side of the emperor, Richard's fate would have been sealed; but the English monarch defended himself with so much eloquence and justice, that no doubt remained on the minds of those who heard him, and his ransom was agreed upon at one hundred thousand marks of silver. This money was obtained with difficulty, and John and Philip strove to raise greater sums to tempt the cupidity of the emperor to retain the lion-hearted monarch. The avaricious Henry hesitated on their proposals, and thus was the liberty of the noble king of England set up to auction, till the Germanic body indignantly interfered, the ransom was paid, and Richard returned to England.

CHAPTER 13

Death of Saladin

For some time the Christians of the Holy Land enjoyed an interval of repose. Saladin was a religious observer of his word; and during the short space that intervened between the departure of Richard Cœur de Lion and the death of his great adversary, the Latins received the full benefit of the treaty which had been executed between those monarchs.

A year had scarcely elapsed ere Saladin was seized with a mortal sickness; and, finding his end approaching, he commanded the black standard, which had so often led the way to victory, to be taken down, and replaced by the shroud which was to wrap his body in the grave. This was then borne through the streets, while the criers called all men to behold what Saladin, the mighty conqueror, carried away with him of all his vast dominion.[1] Saladin died, a monarch in whose character, though the good was not unmixed with evil, the great qualities so far preponderated, that they overbalanced the effects of a barbarous epoch and a barbarous religion, and left in him a splendid exception to most of the vices of his age, his country, and his creed.

At that period the principle of hereditary succession was not very clearly ascertained either in Europe or in Asia; and the vast monarchy which Saladin had been enabled to consolidate was broken in pieces at his death. Saif Eddin, his brother, took possession of the greater part of Syria, and strengthened himself by the soldiers of his dead relative, who both loved and esteemed him. Three of the great monarch's sons seized upon such portions of their father's dominions as they could reach; and civil dissensions followed, highly detrimental to the power of the Moslem, and favourable to the security of the Christians.

---

1. William of Nangis.

This, indeed, was the moment when a crusade was most practicable, and Pope Celestine III. exhorted all Christendom to snatch the opportunity. In most instances his call fell upon cold and unwilling ears. Philip Augustus was too deeply engaged in those vast and magnificent schemes which, however impeded by the prejudices of the day, rendered his reign a great epoch in the history of nations.[2] Richard Cœur de Lion had learned the danger of quitting his own kingdom, and the vanity of hoping for union among ambitious men. Henry of Germany alone, moved by wild schemes for aggrandizing his territories, assented at once to the crusade; but finding that Sicily seemed ready to receive him, he deemed the nearer conquest the more advisable; and on the same principle he had taken the Cross, he abandoned it again. Not so his subjects; an immense number of the vassals followed eagerly the road which he had quitted;[3] and several Teutonic bishops, with the Dukes of Saxony, Brabant, and Bavaria, set out from Germany, and reached Acre in safety.

The Christians of Palestine were at that moment in the enjoyment of peace,[4] and they beheld the coming of new crusaders with horror and despair. Had the troops that arrived been sufficient, indeed, to give anything like certainty to their enterprise, all the Latins of the Holy Land would willingly have concurred; but the prospect of new and desolating wars, waged by scanty forces, was, notwithstanding the dissensions of their enemies, a hopeless and painful anticipation. Nevertheless, the Germans began their operations at once;[5] and Saif Eddin, with his whole attention suddenly directed to the Christians, showed, by the energetic activity of his movements, that the spirit of Saladin survived in his brother. Jaffa was taken by assault,[6] with a great slaughter of the Christians, and all promised a speedy destruction to the small remains of the Latin kingdom. Fresh succours, however, were received from Europe; the hopes of the Christians revived; and, under the command of the Duke of Saxony, they marched on towards Beritus.

Saif Eddin hastened to meet them, and attacked the Latin forces near Sidon; but his army was completely routed by the firm and steady gallantry of the Germans; and the way to Jerusalem was once more

---

2. Rigord; William the Breton.
3. Will. of Nangis, ann. 1196.
4. James of Vitry.
5. Bernard the Treasurer.
6. Bernard; Will. of Nangis, ann. 1197.

open to the followers of the Cross. But the crusaders embarrassed themselves with the siege of the castle of Thoron. The Saracens had time to recover from their panic; civil dissensions were forgotten; and while the garrison of Thoron held out with persevering valour, the *Sultaun of* Egypt advanced to join his uncle, and repel the Christian invasion. Vague rumours of immense preparation on the part of the *infidels* reached the besieging army. The crusaders were, as usual, disunited among themselves; the Saracens within the castle were fighting with the coinage of despair; and, at last, a sudden panic seized the leaders of the German army.[7] They abandoned the camp in the night, and, flying to Tyre, left their soldiers to follow as they could.[8]

A complete separation ensued between the Germans and the Latins, each accusing the other of treachery; while the Syrian Christians remained at Tyre, the Teutonic crusaders proceeded to Jaffa. Thither Saif Eddin pursued them; and another battle was fought, in which the Germans were once more victorious, though victory cost them the lives of many of their princes. Almost at the same time news reached their camp of the death of the emperor Henry. From that moment, none of the German nobles remembered aught but the election of a new emperor; and as soon as vessels could be procured, the principal barons set off for Europe. They left behind them in Jaffa about twenty thousand of the inferior soldiers, and a few knights; but the town was surprised by the Saracens on the night of the following festival of St. Martin; and the Germans, plunged in revelry and drunkenness,[9] were slaughtered to a man.

Such was the end of the German crusade in Palestine; and before proceeding to speak once more of the affairs of Europe, it may be as well to touch upon the brief and uninteresting series of events that followed in that country. Henry, Count of Champagne, who had married Isabella, the heiress of Jerusalem, had proved but an indolent monarch; and in the year 1197, at the precise moment when the Saracens had newly captured Jaffa, he was killed by falling from a window. His loss was attended by no evil consequences;[10] for the Saracens were soon involved once more in civil dissensions by the death of Saladin's second son, Malek el Aziz, *Sultaun of* Egypt, and the truce with the Christians was willingly renewed. Isabella, the queen, whose grief was

---

7. James of Vitry.
8. Hovedon.
9. Fuller's Holy War; Bernard the Treasurer.
10. James of Vitry; Bernard; Will. of Nangis; A. D. 1198.

not even so stable as that of the dame of Ephesus, was easily prevailed on, by the Grand Master of the order of St. John,[11] to give her thrice-widowed hand to Almeric of Lusignan, now—by the cession of Richard of England—King of Cyprus.

This marriage was certainly a politic one, as Cyprus afforded both a storehouse and a granary to Palestine; but the peace with the Saracens remained unbroken till the bigoted Simon de Montfort, detaching himself from another body of knights,[12] which I shall mention hereafter, arrived at Acre, and made some feeble and ineffectual incursions on the Mussulman territory. After his fruitless attempts, the truce was once more established, and lasted till the death of Almeric and Isabella, when the crowns of Jerusalem and Cyprus were again separated.

The imaginary sovereignty of the Holy City now became vested in Mary,[13] the daughter of Isabella, by Conrad of Tyre, while the kingdom of Cyprus descended to the heirs of Lusignan. According to feudal custom it was necessary to find a husband for Mary who could defend her right, and on every account it was determined to seek one in Europe. The choice was left to Philip Augustus; and he immediately fixed upon Jean de Brienne, a noble, talented, and chivalrous knight, who willingly accepted the hand of the lady of Palestine, and that thorny crown which was held out to him from afar.

The news of his coming, and the prospect of large European reinforcements to the Christians,[14] depressed the mind of Saif Eddin, who had already to struggle with vast and increasing difficulties. He tendered the most advantageous terms of peace; but at that time the two great military orders may be said to have governed Palestine.[15] They were then, as usual, contending with jealous rivalry;[16] and the Templars, having for the moment the superiority, the offers of the sultaun were refused, because the Hospitallers counselled their acceptance. Jean de Brienne arrived, and wedded Mary, but the succour that he brought was very far inferior to that which the Latins had anticipated, and the war which had begun was confined to predatory

---

11. Vertot; Bernard.

12. James of Vitry.

13. Bernard; A. D. 1205.

14. Sanut. cap. 3.

15. Hovedon.

16. The power of the orders of the Temple and the Hospital had, by this time, become immense. Riches flowed in upon riches, and donation was added to donation. In the year 1244, Matthew Paris declares the Templars possessed in Europe nine thousand manors, and the Hospitallers nineteen thousand.

excursions on the territory of the enemy.[17]

I must now retrograde in my history for some years, and speak of the affairs of Europe. No crusade, as we have seen, had been desired by the Christians of Palestine[18] since they had enjoyed the comforts of peace, and no crusade had reached that country; but, nevertheless, one of the most powerful expeditions which Europe had ever brought into the field had set out for the purpose of delivering Jerusalem.[19]

This crusade was, in the first place, instigated by the preaching of a man less mighty than St. Bernard in oratory,[20] and less moved by enthusiasm than Peter the Hermit; but it was encouraged by one of the most talented and most ambitious of the prelates of Rome. Foulque of Neuilly would have produced little effect, had he not been supported by Innocent III.; and the influence of neither the one nor the other would possibly have obtained the object desired, had not the young and enterprising Thibalt, Count of Champagne, embraced the badge of the Cross with his court and followers, at a grand tournament[21] to which he had invited all the neighbouring princes.

In the midst of their festivities, Foulque appeared, and called the whole assembly to the crusade. Partly, it is probable, from the love of adventure, partly from religious feeling, Thibalt, in his twenty-second year, assumed the Cross. The Count of Blois, who was present, followed his example; and of eighteen hundred knights who held vassalage under the lord of Champagne, scarcely enough were left to maintain the territories of their sovereign. Nothing, except fear, is so contagious as enthusiasm: the spirit of crusading was revived in a wonderfully short time. The Count of Flanders, with various other persons, took the Cross at Bruges, and many more knights joined them from different parts of France, among whom was Simon de Montfort, who afterward proved the detestable persecutor of the Albigeois.

After holding two general conferences at Soissons and at Compiegne, it was determined to send messengers to Italy for the purpose of contracting with one of the great merchant states to convey the armament to the Holy Land.[22] The choice of the city was left to the deputies; and they proceeded first to Venice, furnished with full powers from the crusading princes to conclude a treaty in their name.

17. *A. D.* 1210.
18. James, Cardinal de Vitry.
19. *A. D.* 1202.
20. Rigord.
21. Ducange; *Villehardouin chronique.*
22. Villehardouin.

Venice was at that time governed by the famous Henry Dandolo, who, with the consent of the Senate, agreed not only to carry the crusaders to Palestine for a certain sum, but also promised to take the Cross himself and aid in their enterprise.[23]

Well satisfied with this arrangement, the deputed barons returned to France, but found the Count of Champagne sick of a disease which soon produced his death. After having been refused by Eudes, Duke of Burgundy, and Thibalt, Count of Bar, the office of commander of the expedition was offered to Boniface, Marquis of Montferrat, and accepted. The new chief of the crusade repaired to Soissons, to confer with the rest of the knights, and then proceeded to Italy to prepare for his departure. All these delays retarded their departure till the year 1202, when they set out in several bodies for Venice, and arrived safely at that city with very little difficulty.[24]

Innocent III. had made infinite efforts in favour of the crusade: and, with the daring confidence of genius, had even taxed the unwilling clergy, while he merely recommended charitable subscriptions among the laity. Under such circumstances it will be easily conceived that the voluntary donations amounted to an equal sum with the forced contributions; but what became of the whole is very difficult to determine. Certain it is, that when the crusaders arrived at Venice, not half the money could be raised among them which they had agreed to pay for the use of the republic's transports,[25] although the chiefs melted down their plate to supply those who had not the means to defray their passage.

This poverty was attributed to the fact of various large bodies having, either by mistake or perversity, taken the way to the Holy Land[26] by other ports, and carried with them a large part of the stipulated sum; but it does not appear that the Pope, into whose hands flowed the full tide of European alms, made any effort to relieve the crusaders from their difficulties. In this distress the Venetians offered to compromise their claim, and to convey the French to Palestine, on condition that they should aid in the recapture of the city of Zara, in Sclavonia, which had been snatched from the republic some time before by the King of Hungary.[27] With this stipulation, Dandolo, though aged and

---

23. Ducange, *Hist. de Constantinople sous les Français.*
24. Vit. Innocent III.
25. Villehardouin.
26. Ducange.
27. Villehardouin.

stone blind, agreed to take the Cross; and so deeply affected were the knights, both with his forbearance and gallant enthusiasm, that the iron warriors of Europe were melted to tears by the old man's noble daring.

The news of this undertaking having reached Rome, the most vehement opposition was raised to any change of destination; and Innocent[28] launched the thunders of the church at the refractory crusaders. Many of the chiefs—terrified by the excommunication pronounced against those who should quit the direct road to the Holy Land, to attack the possessions of a Christian prince—remained in Italy;[29] but the greater part made every preparation to second the Venetians against Zara.

Before their departure, the crusaders received envoys, the event of whose solicitations afterward gave a new character to their expedition. At the death of Manuel Comnenus, emperor of the east, Andronicus, his brother, seized upon the throne and murdered his nephew, Alexius II., who had succeeded. Either urged by indignation or ambition, Isaac Angelus, a distant relation of the slaughtered prince, took arms against the usurper, overthrew and put him to death; after which he in turn ascended the throne of Constantinople.[30] His reign was not long; for, at the end of two years, a brother, named Alexius, whom he had redeemed from Turkish captivity, snatched the crown from his head, and, to incapacitate him from ruling, put out his eyes.

His son, named also Alexius, made his escape from prison, and fled to Italy, where he endeavoured to interest the Pope in his favour. But the church of Rome entertained small affection for the schismatic Greeks; and though Innocent wrote an impotent letter[31] to the usurper, he showed no real favour to the unhappy prince. The young exile then turned to Philip of Suabia (then Emperor of Germany), who had married his sister Irene; and at the same time hearing of the crusade, which was delayed at Venice,[32] he sent deputies from Verona to the chiefs, to solicit their aid against his treacherous uncle. The barons of France met his prayers with kindness; and the envoys were accompanied, on their return to the court of Philip of Suabia,[33] by a

28. Baronius; Gesta Innocent III.
29. Villehardouin.
30. Villehardouin; Ducange, *Hist. de Constantinople sous les Français.*
31. Ducange, notes on Villehardouin.
32. Philip Mouskes.
33. Villehardouin.

party of the crusaders, who were instructed to receive any proposition which Alexius might think fit to make.

In the meanwhile, the knights embarked on board the Venetian galleys, round the decks of which they ranged their shields, and planted their banners; and having been joined by Conrad, Bishop of Halberstadt, with a large body of German soldiers, a finer armament never sailed from any port.[34]

The chain which protected the harbour of Zara was soon broken through; the crusaders landed, pitched their tents,[35] and invested the city on all sides. The besiegers, as usual, were much divided among themselves; and those who had unwillingly followed the host to Zara, against the commands of the Pope,[36] still kept up a continual schism in the camp, which produced fatal consequences to the people of the city. The morning after the disembarkation, a deputation of citizens came forth to treat with Dandolo for the capitulation of the town. The *doge* replied that he could enter into no engagement without consulting his allies, and went for that purpose to the tents of the French chiefs.

During his absence, those who opposed the siege persuaded the deputies from Zara that the crusaders[37] would not assist the Venetians in an assault. With this assurance the *doge's* reply was not waited for; the envoys returned, and the city prepared for defence. At the same time, the Abbot of Vaux Cernay presented himself to the assembled barons, and commanded them, in the name of the Pope, to refrain from warring against Christians while engaged under the banners of the Cross. On this the *doge* angrily remonstrated; the greater part of the knights embraced his cause; and Zara, after being furiously attacked, surrendered at discretion.

The town was now occupied during the winter by the army of the crusade; and the chiefs of the French forces sent a deputation to Rome to obtain pardon for their disobedience. This was easily granted; but the Venetians, who seemed to care little about excommunication, remained under the papal censure. Notwithstanding the forgiveness they had obtained, many of the most celebrated knights quitted Zara,[38] and made their way to the Holy Land. Such desertions took place especially after the return of the deputies sent to Philip of

---

34. It consisted of three hundred vessels of a large size, besides palanders and storeships.
35. November, 1202.
36. Gunther; Villehardouin.
37. Ducange; Villehardouin.
38. Alberic; *A. D.* 1202.

Suabia; and it was difficult to keep the army[39] together, when it became known that its destination was likely to be changed from Acre to Constantinople.

Alexius, however, offered, in case of his being re-established in his father's dominions,[40] to place the Greek church under the authority of the Roman *pontiff*, to turn the whole force of the eastern empire against the *infidels* of Palestine, and either to send thither ten thousand men, and there maintain five hundred knights during his life, or to lead his forces towards Jerusalem in person. Besides this he promised to pay two hundred thousand marks of silver[41] to the crusading army, and to place himself in the hands of the chiefs till the city of Constantinople was retaken.

These offers were so advantageous that the greater part of the barons embraced them at once: but many exclaimed loudly against the proposed interruption of the main purpose of the crusade, and many abandoned the host altogether.

Alexius the usurper trembled at the news of the treaty between his nephew and the crusaders, and sent instant ambassadors to Rome,[42] in order to engage the pontiff in his interest. Such of the chiefs as were opposed to the measure talked loudly of the papal injunction to refrain from all wars with the Christians;[43] but it does not appear that Innocent exerted himself strenuously to turn the Latins from their design. It was far too much his desire to bring the Greek church under the domination of the Roman see, for him to dream of thwarting an enterprise backed with the solemn conditions I have mentioned; and it was not at all likely that the clear-sighted prelate should renounce absolute engagements, as Mills has supposed,[44] for the vague hope of

---

39. Villehardouin.
40. Ducange.
41. Villehardouin.
42. Ducange.
43. Gunther in Canisius.
44. Mills says, that Innocent issued decrees and bulls against the expedition to Constantinople, and founds his reasoning on a passage of Baluzius: but it is extremely probable that the anger of the Pope was a mere menace of the party opposed to the enterprise rather than an existing fact. Baluzius was not present any more than Ducange; and surely, for everything where research is concerned, Ducange is the better authority of the two: yet Ducange makes no mention of the opposition of the Pope, and absolutely states that the legate counselled the attack on Constantinople. See *Ducange, Hist. de Constantinople sous les Francais.*
Geoffroy de Villehardouin, who was not only present, but one of the chief actors in what he relates, speaks fully of the Pope's wrath at the attack (continued next page)

wringing the same from a treacherous usurper.

At length, after the Venetians had demolished Zara,[45] to prevent its falling again into the hands of their enemies, the expedition, having been joined by the prince Alexius, set sail, and at the end of a short and easy passage came within sight of Constantinople.[46]

The allies were instantly met by ambassadors from the emperor, who, mingling promises with threats, endeavoured to drive them again from the shore, but in vain. The crusaders demanded the restoration of Isaac, and submission from the usurper, and prepared to force their landing; but before they commenced hostilities, they approached the walls of Constantinople, and sailed underneath them, showing the young Alexius to the Greek people, and calling to them to acknowledge their prince. No sympathy was excited, and the attack being determined on, the chiefs held a council on horseback, according to the custom of the ancient Gauls, when the order of their proceedings was regulated. The army was portioned into seven divisions, the first of which was commanded by the Count of Flanders, and the last by the Marquis of Montferrat. Having procured a number of flat-bottomed boats, one of which was attached to every galley, the knights entered with their horses, armed at all points, and looking, as Nicetas says, like statues of bronze.[47] The archers filled the larger vessels, and it was the general understanding that each should fight as he came up.

The old Mareschal of Champagne writes:—

> The morning was beautiful,[48] the sun beginning to rise, and the Emperor Alexius waited for them with thick battalions and a great armament. On both sides the trumpets were sounded, and each galley led on a boat. The knights sprang out of the barks, while the water was yet to their girdle,[49] with their helmets laced and their swords in their hands; and the good archers, the sergeants, and the crossbowmen did the same wherever they happened to touch. The Greeks, at first, made great show of resistance, but when they saw the lances levelled they turned

of Zara, but mentions no opposition to the enterprise against Constantinople, though that enterprise was in agitation at the time the deputies were sent to Rome. Philippe Mouskes, Bishop of Tournay, a contemporary, states that the first application of the young Prince Alexius to the crusaders was made by the advice of the Pope.

45. Villehardouin.
46. June, 1203.
47. Nicetas, lib. iii. cap. 5.
48. Villehardouin.
49 *Ibid.*

their backs and fled.

The tents and camp equipage of the fugitives fell immediately into the hands of the crusaders; and siege was laid to the tower of Galata, which guarded one end of the great chain wherewith the mouth of the harbour was closed. Before night the Greeks had recovered from their panic, and some severe fighting took place ere the fort could be taken and the barrier removed; but at length this being accomplished, the Venetians entered the port. After ten days of continual skirmishing, a general attack was determined upon; and it was agreed that the Venetians[50] should assail the city by sea, while the French attempted to storm the walls by land. The enterprise began on the land side against the barbican; but so vigorously was every inch of ground disputed by the Pisans, the English and Danish mercenaries who guarded the fortifications, that though fifteen French knights obtained a footing for some time on the ramparts, they were at length cast out, while four of their number were taken.

In the meanwhile, the fleet of the Venetians advanced to the walls; and after a severe fight of missiles between the defenders and the smaller vessels which commenced the assault, the galleys themselves approached the land; and, provided with high towers of wood, began to wage a nearer warfare with those upon the battlements. Still the besieged[51] resisted with extraordinary valour, and the galleys were beaten off; when the blind chief of the republic, armed at all points, commanded, with tremendous threats in case of disobedience, that his vessel should be run on shore;[52] and then, borne out with the standard of St. Mark before him, he led the way to victory. Shame spread through the rest of the fleet; galley after galley was brought up close under the walls, and all the principal towers round the port were in a moment stormed and taken. Alexius made one great effort to recover the twenty-five towers which the Venetians had captured; but, with remorseless resolution, Dandolo set fire to the neighbouring buildings, and thus raised up a fiery bulwark to his conquest.[53]

As a last resource, the emperor now issued forth to give battle to the French: and so infinite was the superiority of his numbers, that the hearts of the pilgrims almost failed them. The gallant Doge of Venice no sooner heard of their danger, than, abandoning the ram-

---

50. Dandolo, Chron.; Villehardouin.
51. Epist. Innocent III.
52. Villehardouin.
53. Ducange; Villehardouin; Nicetas.

parts he had so nobly won, he brought his whole force[54] to the aid of the French, declaring that he would live or die with his allies. Even after his arrival, however, the disparity was so great, that the crusaders dared not quit their close array to begin the fight, and the troops of Alexius hesitated to attack those hardy warriors whose prowess they had often witnessed. The courage of the Latins gradually increased by the indecision of their enemy, while the fears of the Greeks spread and magnified by delay and at length Alexius abandoned the last hope of courage, and retreated into the city.

The weary crusaders hastened to disarm and repose themselves, after a day of immense fatigues; but Alexius, having no confidence either in his own resolution, or in the steadiness of his soldiery, seized what treasure he could carry, and abandoned Constantinople to its fate.[55] The coward Greeks, deserted by their chief, drew forth the miserable Isaac from his prison; and having robed the blind monarch in the long-lost purple, they seated him on the throne, and sent to tell the Franks that their object was accomplished. The crusaders would hardly believe the tidings, but despatched four of their body to ascertain the truth. The envoys found Isaac enthroned in the palace of Blachernæ,[56] and surrounded by as large and splendid a court as if fortune had never ceased to smile upon him.

They now represented to the restored Emperor the conditions of their treaty with his son; and Isaac, after some slight hesitation, accepted them as his own. He also agreed to associate the young Alexius in the throne; but as all these hard terms, especially that which implied the subjection of the Greek church to the Roman prelate, deeply offended his subtle and revengeful subjects, he prayed the crusaders to delay their departure till complete order was re-established.[57] This was easily acceded to; and the Franks and Venetians, during their stay, wrote to Innocent III., excusing their having again turned from the road to Jerusalem.[58] The Pope willingly pardoned both; but intimated, that to make that pardon efficacious, they must be responsible that the schism in the church should be healed by the submission of the Greeks to the see of Rome.

At first, the harmony between the Franks and the Greeks appeared

---

54. Villehardouin.
55. Nicetas.
56. Ducange; Villehardouin.
57. *Ibid.*
58. Gest. Innoc. III.

to be great. The young Alexius paid several portions of the money which had been stipulated;[59] and while the presence of the Latin army kept the capital in awe, he proceeded to reduce the provinces to obedience. When this was completed, however, and the tranquillity of the empire seemed perfectly restored, his conduct changed towards his benefactors.

A fire which broke out in the city[60] was attributed to the French, who were at the very moment engaged in serious dispute with a party of Greeks, exasperated by an insult to their religion. The very domineering presence of the crusaders was a continual and irritating reproach, and the Greeks began to testify no small hatred towards their armed guests. Alexius himself, ungrateful in his own nature, contending with his father about their divided sovereignty, and hesitating between the people he was called to govern and those who upheld him in the government, refused or evaded the fulfilment of many of the items in his treaty with the Latins. The chiefs soon found that they were deceived, and formally summoned the young monarch to accomplish his promises.

The messengers who bore the haughty demand to a despotic court hardly escaped with their lives; and the same desultory warfare which had been waged by the emperors against each body of crusaders that had passed by Constantinople was now commenced against the Count of Flanders and his companions.[61] A thousand encounters took place, in which the Franks were always victorious; and though the Greeks directed a number of vessels, charged with their terrific fire, against the Venetian fleet, the daring courage and conduct of the sailors freed them from the danger, and only one Pisan galley was consumed.

In the meanwhile the Greeks of the city, hating and despising a monarch who had seated himself among them by the swords of strangers, and who had drained their purses to pay the troops that held them down;[62] seeing, also, that his ingratitude, even to his allies, had left him without the support by which alone he stood, suddenly rose upon Alexius, and cast him into prison. Isaac himself died, it is said, of fear; and the Greeks at first elected a nobleman of a different family, named Nicholas Canabus; but he was mild and weak, a character which little suited the times or country in which he assumed so high

---

59. Ducange.
60. Nicetas.
61. Villehardouin.
62. Nicetas.

a station.

A rival, too, existed in a man who had shown unremitting enmity to the Latins, and after a short struggle, Alexius Ducas, a cousin of the late monarch, a bold, unscrupulous villain,[63] was proclaimed emperor. Among his first acts—though at what exact period remains in doubt[64]—the new Alexius, who was more commonly called Murzuphlis, caused the preceding Alexius to be put to death. The manner of his fate is uncertain: but the usurper had the cunning impudence to yield his victim's body a public funeral.

War was now determined between the crusaders and Murzuphlis, and the attack of the city was resolved; but previous to that attempt, the crusaders, who were in great want of provisions, despatched Henry, brother of the Count of Flanders, with a considerable force to Philippopoli, in order to take possession of the rich magazines which it contained. Returning loaded with spoil, he was attacked by Murzuphlis; but the Greeks scattered like deer before the Latins,[65] and Henry rejoined his companions not only rich in booty, but in glory also. Negotiations were more than once entered into, for the purpose of conciliating the differences of the Greeks and the Latins; but all proved ineffectual; and early in the spring the armies of France and Venice prepared for the attack. The first step was, as usual, a treaty between the allies to apportion the fruits of success.

By this it was determined that the whole booty should be divided equally between the French and Venetians;[66] that six persons from each nation should be chosen to elect an emperor; that the Venetians should retain all the privileges they had hitherto enjoyed under the monarchs of Constantinople; and that, from whichever of the two nations the emperor was selected, a patriarch should be named from the other. There were various other conditions added, the principal of which were, that one-fourth of the whole conquest should be given to the new emperor, besides the palaces of Bucoleon and Blachernæ, while the rest was divided among the French and Venetians; and that twelve persons should be selected from each nation, to determine the feudal laws by which the land was to be governed, and to allot the

---

63. Nicetas; Villehardouin; Gest. Innoc. III.
64. Villehardouin intimates that Murzuphlis put Alexius to death immediately after having seized the crown; and the Chronicle in the Rouchy dialect, No. 148, *Bibliothéque de l'Arsenal,* says, "*Et ne demeura gaires après que Morcuffle estrangla le josne empereur Alexes en la prison.*"
65. Nicetas.
66. Ducange; Villehardouin.

territory in feoffs among the conquerors.

On the 8th of April, 1204, the whole army, having embarked on board the ships,[67] as had been previously concerted, attacked the city by water. The vessels approached close to the walls, and a tremendous fight began between the assailants and the besieged: but no hope smiled on the Franks; they were repelled in every direction; and those who had landed,[68] were forced to regain their vessels with precipitancy, approaching to flight. The Greeks rejoiced in novel victory, and the Franks mourned in unwonted defeat. Four days were spent in consultations regarding a further attempt; and the chiefs, judging that no one vessel contained a sufficient number of troops to effect a successful assault on any particular spot,[69] it was resolved to lash the ships two and two together, and thus to concentrate a greater force on each point of attack.

On the fourth day the storm was recommenced, and at first the fortune of battle seemed still in favour of the Greeks; but at length, a wind springing up, drove the sea more fully into the port, and brought the galleys closer to the walls.[70] Two of those lashed together, called the *Pilgrim* and the *Paradise*, now touched one of the towers, and, from the large wooden turret with which the mast was crowned, a Venetian and a French knight named Andrew d'Arboise sprang upon the ramparts of the city.[72]

The crusaders rushed on in multitudes; and such terror seized the Greeks, that the eyes of Nicetas magnified the first knight who leaped on the walls to the unusual altitude of fifty feet.[72] One Latin drove before him a hundred Greeks;[73] the defence of the gates was abandoned; the doors were forced in with blows of axes; and the knights, leading their horses from the ships, rode in, and took complete possession of the city. Murzuphlis once, and only once, attempted to rally his troops before the camp he had formed, in one of the open spaces of the town. But the sight of the Count of St. Pol, with a small band of followers, was sufficient to put him to flight; and a German having set fire to a part of the buildings[74] no further effort was made to oppose

67. Villehardouin; Ducange.
68. Gunther; Ducange.
69. Villehardouin.
70. Ducange.
71. 2nd April, 1204.
72. Nicetas.
73. Gest. Inn. iii.
74. Gunther; Villehardouin.

the victorious crusaders.

The fire was not extinguished for some time; and the Latin host, in the midst of the immense population of Constantinople, like a handful of dust in the midst of the wilderness, took possession of the purple tents of Murzuphlis, and keeping vigilant guard, passed an anxious and a fearful night, after all the fatigues and exploits of the day. Twenty thousand was the utmost extent of the Latin numbers;[75] and Constantinople contained, within itself, four hundred thousand men capable of bearing arms. Each house was a citadel, which might have delayed and repelled the enemy; and each street was a defile, which might have been defended against a host. But the days of Leonidas were passed; and the next morning the Latins found that Murzuphlis had fled, and that their conquest was complete. Plunder and violence of course ensued;[76] but there was much less actual bloodshed than either the nature of the victory or the dangerous position of the victors might have occasioned.

Fear is the most cruel of all passions; and perhaps the fact that not two thousand persons were slain in Constantinople after the storm, is a greater proof of the courage of the Latins than even the taking of the city. Many noble and generous actions mingled with the effects of that cupidity and lust which follow always upon the sack of a great town. Nicetas mentions a striking example which happened to himself, wherein a noble Venetian dedicated his whole attention to protect an ancient benefactor;[77] and a body of Frenchmen, in the midst of the unbounded licentiousness of such a moment, were moved by a father's agony to save his daughter from some of their fellows. This is the admission of a prejudiced and inveterate enemy; and it is but fair to suppose, that many such instances took place. The great evils that followed the taking of the eastern capital, originated in the general command to plunder.

Constantinople had accumulated within it the most precious monuments of ancient art,[78] and these were almost all destroyed by the barbarous hands of an avaricious soldiery. Naught was spared; the bronzes, which, valueless as metal, were inestimable as the masterpieces and miracles of antique genius, were melted down,[79] and struck

---

75. Villehardouin; Ducange.
76. Nicetas; Gunther.
77. Nicetas.
78. See Notes 11.
79. Nicetas.

into miserable coin; the marble was violated with wanton brutality; all the labour of a Phidias or a Lysippus was done away in an hour; and that which had been the wonder and admiration of a world left less to show what former days had been, than the earth after the deluge.

In this the Latins were certainly *barbarians*; but in other respects— unless subtilty, deceit, vice, and cowardice can be called civilization, and courage, frankness, and honour can be considered as barbarism— the Latins deserved not the opprobrious name by which the Greeks designated them.

The plunder of the city was enormous. In money[80] a sufficient sum was collected to distribute twenty marks to each knight, ten to each servant of arms, and five to each archer. Besides this, a vast quantity of jewels and valuable merchandise was divided between the French and Venetians; and the republic, who understood the value of such objects better than the simple Frankish soldiers, offered to buy the whole spoil from their comrades, at the rate of four hundred marks for a knight's share, and in the same proportion to the rest. The booty— with a few individual instances of concealment,[81] which were strictly punished with death when discovered—was fairly portioned out; and, after this partition, the twelve persons selected to choose an emperor proceeded to their deliberations. They were bound by oath to elect without favour the best qualified of the nobles; and after a long hesitation, between the Marquis of Montferrat and the Count of Flanders, they named the latter.[82]

In all probability the determining consideration was, that Baldwin, by his immediate connexion with France, was more capable of supporting the new dynasty than the *marquis*, whose Italian domains could not afford such effective aid. To prevent the evil consequences of rivalry, the island of Crete and the whole of Asiatic Greece were given to Montferrat, who afterward, with the consent of Baldwin, exchanged them for the Sclavonian territory. Baldwin was then raised upon a buckler,[83] and carried to the church of St. Sophia. After a brief space of preparation, he was formally proclaimed, and crowned as emperor; and, according to old usage, a vase filled with ashes,[84] and a tuft

---

80. Villehardouin; Ducange.

81. Villehardouin.

82. Nicetas; Ducange; Villehardouin; Alberic.

83. Ducange.

84. The cardinal legate invested Baldwin with the purple with his own hands, and Innocent confirmed, in all points but those of ecclesiastical government, the treaty by which the Venetians and the Franks had bound (continued next page)

of lighted wool, were presented to the new monarch, as a symbol of the transitory nature of life and the vanity of greatness—emblems too applicable to himself and his dominions; for ere two years had passed, Baldwin had gone down into the grave; and less than the ordinary life of one man elapsed before the dynasty that he established was again overthrown.

themselves. He also took the greatest interest in the new state, and wrote to all the prelates of France and Germany to support it by their preaching and influence. This may be added to other proofs, that Innocent never seriously opposed the expedition against the schismatic empire of the Greeks. The truth in all probability is, that he made a show of turning the crusaders from their purpose, both to preserve consistency and to afford room for any after-exertion of his authority that he might judge necessary: but that, at the same time, the cardinal legate very well understood that he was to promote the enterprise, and to be slightly blamed for it afterward, in order to screen his superior from the charge of that ambitious craving for which, however, he was notorious. It would be difficult to believe that Innocent, who triumphed over Philip Augustus, the greatest monarch of the day, and forced him to abandon his dearest wishes, would confine himself to idle threats, if he entertained any serious disinclination to the attack of Constantinople.

CHAPTER 14

Divisions Among the Moslems

The fifth crusade had ended, as we have seen, without producing any other benefit to Palestine than a deep depression in the minds of the Turks, from the knowledge that the weak dynasty of the Greeks had been replaced by a power of greater energy and resolution. The famine also, which about this time desolated the territories of the Egyptian *sultaun*, and the contests[1] between the remaining Attabecs and the successors of Saladin, crippled the efforts of the Moslems; while the courageous activity of Jean de Brienne[2] defeated the attempts of Saif Eddin. Nevertheless, many bloody disputes concerning the succession of Antioch, and the fierce rivalry of the orders of the Temple and Hospital, contributed to shake the stability of the small Christian dominion that remained.

Each year,[3] two regular voyages of armed and unarmed pilgrims took place, from Europe to the Holy Land: these were called the *passagium Martii*, or the spring passage; and the *passagium Johannis*, or the summer passage which occurred about the festival of St. John. A continual succour was thus afforded to Palestine: and that the spirit of crusading was by no means extinct in Europe is evinced by the extraordinary fact of a crusade of children[4] having been preached and adopted towards the year 1213. Did this fact rest alone upon the authority of Alberic of Three Fountains Abbey, we might be permitted to doubt its having taken place, for his account is, in several particulars, evidently hypothetical; but so many coinciding authorities exist,[5] that

1. Reinaud rec. des Hist. Arabes.
2. Vertot.
3. Ducange.
4. Alberic. Mon. Trium Fontium.
5. Jacob. de Voragine; Albert Stadensis.

belief becomes matter of necessity.

The circumstances are somewhat obscure; but it seems certain that two monks, with the design of profiting by a crime then too common, the traffic in children, induced a great number of the youth of both sexes to set out from France for the Holy Land, habited as pilgrims, with the scrip and staff. Two merchants of Marseilles,[6] accomplices in the plot, as it would seem, furnished the first body of these misguided children with vessels, which, of course, were destined to transport them for sale to the African coast. Several of the ships were wrecked on the shores of Italy, and every soul perished, but the rest pursued their way and accomplished their inhuman voyage. The two merchants, however, were afterward detected in a plot against the emperor Frederic, and met the fate they deserved. Another body, setting out from Germany, reached Genoa after immense difficulties; and there the Genoese, instead of encouraging their frantic enthusiasm, wisely commanded them to evacuate their territory; on which they returned to their homes, and though many died on the road, a great part arrived in safety,[7] and escaped the fate which had overtaken the young adventurers from France.

When Innocent III. heard of this crusade, he is reported to have said, "While we sleep, these children are awake:" and it is more than probable, that his circumstance convinced him, that the zealous spirit which had moved all the expeditions to the Holy Land was still active and willing. Certain it is, that he very soon afterward sent round an encyclical letter, calling the Christian world once more to arms against the Moslems. Indulgences were spread, and extended in their character: a council of Lateran was held, and Innocent himself declared[8] his intention of leading the warriors of Christ to the scene of his crucifixion. De Courçon, an English monk, who had become cardinal, preached the new crusade with all the pomp of a Roman prelate, and a great number of individuals were gathered together for the purpose of succouring Palestine. But the kings of the earth had now more correct views of policy; and policy never encourages enthusiasm except as an instrument.

Only one king therefore could be found to take the Cross—this was Andrew,[9] monarch of Hungary; and the Dukes of Austria and Bavaria, with a multitude of German bishops and nobles, joined his

---

6. Albericus.

7. Jacob. de Voragine; Albert. Stadensis.

8. Gest. Innocent III: Labbe concil. Matthew Paris, A. D. 1213.

9. Chron. Godefrid Mon.; Bonfinius.

forces, and advanced to Spalatro. Innocent III. was by this time dead, but the expedition sailed in Venetian ships to Cyprus, and thence, after having given somewhat too much rein to enjoyment, proceeded to Acre, carrying with it a large reinforcement from France and Italy. The Saracens had heard less of this crusade than of those which had preceded it, and were therefore less prepared to oppose it. The Christian army advanced with success, and many thousands of the infidels felt the European steel; but the crusaders, not contented with plundering their enemies, went on to plunder their friends; and serious divisions began, as usual, to show themselves, which were only healed by the influence of the clergy, who turned the attention of the soldiers from pillage and robbery to fasts and pilgrimages.

When the host was once more united, its exertions were directed to the capture of the fort[10] built by the Saracens on Mount Thabor. After overcoming infinite difficulties in the ascent of the mountain, the Latins found themselves opposite the fortress: the soldiers were enthusiastic and spirited; and it is more than probable that one gallant attack would have rendered the greatest benefit to the Christian cause, by obtaining possession of such an important point. The leaders,[11] however, seized with a sudden fear of being cut off, abandoned their object without striking a blow, and retired to Acre. The rest of the season was passed in excursions, by which the Christians obtained many prisoners and much spoil; and in pilgrimages, wherein thousands were cut to pieces by the Saracens. The kings of Cyprus and Hungary then turned their course to Tripoli, where the first died, and the Hungarian monarch[12] was suddenly seized with the desire of returning to his own dominions;[13] which he soon put in execution, notwithstanding the prayers and solicitations of the Syrian Christians.

Still the Latins of Palestine were not left destitute. The Duke of Austria remained, with all the German crusaders; and the next year a large reinforcement arrived from Cologne; nor would these have been so tardy in coming, had they[14] not paused upon the coast of Portugal

---

10. Bernard the Treasurer.

11. Jacob. Vitriae; Bernardus.

12. Bernardus.

13. Mere restlessness is stated by Mills to have been the cause of Andrew's abandonment of the enterprise, but this was anything but the case. Andrew, it is true, was of a weak and unstable character; but there were far too many dissensions in Hungary, and tragic horrors in his own family, to permit of his remaining in Palestine without total ruin to himself and his dominions.—See *Bonfinius*.

14. Godefrid. Moc.; James of Vitry.

to succour the queen of that country against the Moors. The efforts of the Christians had proved hitherto so fruitless for the recovery of Jerusalem, while the Saracens could bring vast forces from Egypt continually to the support of their Syrian possessions, that the Latins now resolved to strike at the very source of their power.

Damietta was supposed to command the entrance of the Nile, and consequently to be the key of Egypt; and thither the crusaders set sail, for the purpose of laying siege to that important city. They[15] arrived in the month of May, and landed on the western bank of the river opposite to the town. A tower in the centre of the stream, connected with the walls by a strong chain, was the immediate object of attack; but the first attempt was repulsed with great loss, though made by the Hospitallers, the Teutonic Order, and the Germans, united. An immense machine[16] of wood was now constructed on board two of the vessels, which, lashed together, were moved across to the point of assault, and, after a long and courageous resistance, the garrison of the castle was forced to surrender at discretion.[17] The besieging party then abandoned themselves to joy and revelry; they looked upon the city as taken; and the news of the death of Saif Eddin increased their hopes of the complete deliverance of the Holy Land.

The victories which Saif Eddin had gained over the Christians were indeed but small, nor had he struck any one great blow against the Attabecs, but he had gradually, and almost imperceptibly, extended his dominions in every direction, and left a large territory and full treasury to his successors. His high qualities were different from those of Saladin, and his character was altogether less noble and striking, but he possessed more shrewdness than his brother; and if his mind had not the same capability of expanding, it had more powers of concentration. To Saif Eddin succeeded his two sons, Cohr Eddin and Camel, the first of whom took possession of Syria and Palestine in peace.

But Egypt, which the second had governed for some time, instantly broke out into revolt on the news of his father's death, and had the Franks pushed the war in that country with vigour, greater effects would have been produced than were ever wrought by any preceding crusade. They neglected their opportunity; spent their time in rioting

---

15. Bernardus; James of Vitry.
16. Matthew Paris.
17. The whole of the siege of Damietta, and the events that followed, I have taken from James of Vitry and the old French of Bernard the Treasurer, with the *Recueil des Hist. Arabes.*.

and debauchery under the yet unconquered walls of Damietta: and, after the arrival of large reinforcements from France, England, and Italy, under the Cardinals Pelagius and Courçon, the Earls of Chester and Salisbury, and the Counts of Nevers and La Marche, they only changed their conduct from revelling to dissension.

At length they awoke from their frantic dreams, and prepared to attack the city itself; but before they could accomplish their object, Cohr Eddin had entered Egypt, put down rebellion, and re-established his brother Camel in full possession of his authority. The siege of Damietta now became, like the first siege of Antioch, a succession of battles and skirmishes. For three months the various nations that composed the besieging force as well as the Templars, the Hospitallers, and the Teutonic knights, vied with each other in deeds of glory; nor were the Saracens behind their adversaries in courage, skill, or resolution. But famine took up the sword against the unhappy people of Damietta. Pestilence soon joined her, and the fall of the city became inevitable.[18]

Cohr Eddin, fearful that Jerusalem might be turned to a post against him, had destroyed the walls of that town; but now that he saw the certain loss of Damietta, and calculated the immense advantages the Christians might thence gain, he with the best policy agreed to make a vast sacrifice to save the key of his brother's dominions. Conferences were opened with the Christians, and the Saracens offered, on the evacuation of Egypt by the Latins, to yield the whole of Palestine, except the fortresses of Montreal and Karac, to restore all European prisoners, and even to rebuild the walls of Jerusalem for the Christians. The King of Jerusalem, the English, the French, and the Germans looked upon their warfare as ended, and their object achieved, by the very proposal; but the Cardinal Pelagius, the two military Orders, and the Italians, opposed all conciliation, contending that no faith was to be put in the promises of *infidels*.

Heaven only knows whether the Saracens would have broken their engagements, or whether calm moderation might not have restored Palestine to the followers of the Cross; but moderation was not consulted, and the walls of Damietta were once more attacked. It was no longer difficult to take them, and when the crusaders entered the city, they discovered nothing but a world of pestilence. Death was in every street; and of seventy thousand souls, not three thousand were

---

18. James of Vitry, Bernard the Treasurer.

found alive.[19]

Discord, of course, succeeded conquest; and after having cleansed and purified Damietta, a winter was spent in dissensions, at the end of which a great part of the army returned to Europe; and Jean de Brienne, offended by the arrogance of Pelagius, retired to Acre. Concessions soon brought him back, and hostilities were resumed against the Moslems, but the legate overbore all counsel; and instead of directing their[20] arms towards Palestine, which was now open to them, the crusaders marched on towards Cairo. The forces of the *sultaun* had greatly increased, but he still offered peace, on conditions as advantageous as those that had been previously proposed. The legate insultingly rejected all terms, wasted his time in inactivity, the Nile rose, the sluices were opened, and Pelagius found himself at once unable to advance, and cut off from his resources at Damietta. There is nothing too mean for disappointed pride, and the legate then sued in the humblest language for permission to return to Acre.

The Sultaun of Egypt, with admirable moderation, granted him peace, and the King of Jerusalem became one of the hostages that Damietta should be given up. The troops would still have perished for want, had not the noble *sultaun* been melted by the grief of John of Brienne, who wept while recounting the distress in which he had left his people. The Saracen mingled his tears with those of the hostage king, and ordered the army of his enemy to be supplied with food.[21] Damietta was soon after yielded, and the hostages exchanged. John of Brienne retired to Acre, wearied of unceasing efforts to recover his nominal kingdom; and Pelagius passed over into Europe, loaded with the hatred and contempt of Palestine.

John of Brienne had received the crown of Jerusalem as his wife's dowry, and it was destined that the marriage of his daughter should restore the Holy City to the Christians. The emperor Frederick II. had often vowed in the most solemn manner to lead his armies into

---

19. This pestilence seems to have been somewhat like the sea scurvy. It was not at all confined to the city, though it raged more furiously within the walls. Nevertheless, many of the soldiers of the Cross were attacked by it. James of Vitry, describing its effects, says, "A sudden pain took possession of the feet and legs: soon after, the gums and the teeth became affected with a sort of gangrene, and the sick persons were not able to eat: then, the bones of the legs became horribly black; and thus, after having suffered long torments, during which they showed much patience a great number of Christians went to repose in the bosom of the Lord."
20. James of Vitry; Bernardus.
21. *Recueil des Hist. Arabes;* Matthew Paris; Bernard the Treasurer.

Palestine, and had as often broken his oath. At length it was proposed to him that he should wed Violante, the beautiful heiress of the Syrian kingdom; and it was easily stipulated that John of Brienne should give up his rights on Palestine to his daughter's husband. Frederic eagerly caught at the idea. By the intervention of the Pope the treaty was concluded between the king and the emperor; and Violante, having been brought to Europe, was espoused by her imperial lover.[22]

Many causes combined to delay the new crusade, though it was preached by two succeeding popes with all the zeal and promises that had led to those that went before. France and Italy remained occupied entirely by intestine dissensions; but England showed great zeal, and sent sixty thousand men at arms to the field.[23] The emperor collected together immense forces, and proceeded to Brundusium; but there, being taken ill of a pestilential disease which had swept away many of his soldiers, he was obliged to return after having put to sea. Gregory IX. was now in the papal chair; and—wroth with the emperor for many a contemptuous mark of disobedience to the ecclesiastical authority—he now excommunicated him for coming back, however necessary the measure.

Frederic was angry, though not frightened; and, after having exculpated himself to Europe by a public letter,[24] he sent his soldiers to plunder the Pope's territories while he recovered his health. At length, in 1228, he set sail from Brundusium, still burdened with the papal censure, which he was too much accustomed to bear to feel as any oppressive load. He arrived without difficulty at Acre; but all men wondered that so great an enterprise should be undertaken with so small a force as that which could be contained in twenty galleys; and it soon appeared that Frederic had long been negotiating with Camel, Sultaun of Egypt, who, fearful of the active and ambitious spirit of his brother Cohr Eddin,[25] had entered into a private treaty with the German monarch.

The emperor, on his arrival in Palestine, found that the revengeful Pope had laid his injunction upon all men to show him no obedience, and afford him no aid while under the censure of the church.[26] None, therefore, at first, accompanied him in his march but his own

---

22. Bernard.
23. Matthew Paris.
24. Matthew Paris, ad. ann. 1228.
25. Bernardus.
26. Rainaldus; Sanut.; William of Nangis, 1232.

forces and the Teutonic knights. The Hospitallers and Templars soon followed, and, too fond of active warfare to remain neuter, joined themselves to the army on some verbal concession on the part of Frederic. About this time Cohr Eddin died; and Camel,[27] freed from apprehension,[28] somewhat cooled towards his Christian ally. He was, nevertheless, too generous to violate his promises, and after Frederic had advanced some way towards Jerusalem, a treaty was entered into between the German monarch and the Saracens, whereby the Holy City and the greater part of Palestine was yielded to the Christians, with the simple stipulation that the Moslems were to be allowed[29] to worship in the temple, as well as the followers of the Cross.[30]

Frederic then proceeded to Jerusalem to be crowned; but the conditions he had agreed to had given offence to the Christians of Judea, and the Pope's excommunication still hung over his head. All the services of the church were suspended during his stay; he was obliged to raise the crown from the altar himself and place it on his own brow; and he discovered, by messengers from the Sultaun of Egypt, that some individuals[31] of the military Orders had offered to betray him into the hands of the Saracens. Frederic now found it necessary to depart,[32] and after having done justice upon several of the chief contemners of his authority, he set sail for Europe, leaving Palestine[33]

---

27. Bernard the Treasurer; Cont. of William of Tyre.

28. For some curious particulars concerning the disputes between the emperor and the Templars, see the old French of Bernard the Treasurer.

29. Bernard.

30. This story is doubtful. Matthew Paris says, that the Templars and Hospitallers gave information to the sultaun that Frederic would, on a certain day, make a pilgrimage to bathe in the River Jordan. It was not at all likely, however, that two Orders which were always at enmity should unite for such a purpose.

31. Matthew Paris, ann. 1229.

32. There were many motives which induced Frederic to return to Europe besides disgust at the ungrateful conduct of the Syrian Christians. The Pope, not content with using the spiritual sword against him, had unsheathed the temporal one, and was waging a furious war against the imperial lieutenant in Italy. It would seem a strange fact that John of Brienne, ex-king of Jerusalem, and father-in-law of the emperor, was in command of the papal forces which ravaged his son-in-law's territories, had we not good reason to believe that Frederic's conduct to Violante (who was now dead) had been of a nature that so chivalrous a man as John of Brienne was not likely to pass unnoticed, when his daughter was the sufferer. However, it is but just to remark that the reason why his crusade did not entirely restore the Holy Land to the dominion of the Christians, is to be found in the vindictive and unchristian enmity of Pope Gregory IX. towards the Emperor Frederic.

33. Matthew Paris.

in a far more favourable state than it had known since the fatal Battle of Tiberias.

Soon after the departure of Frederic, a new aspirant to the crown of Jerusalem appeared in the person of Alice, Queen of Cyprus, the daughter of Isabella and Henry, Count of Champagne, and half sister of Mary, through whom John of Brienne had obtained the throne. Her claims were soon disposed of; for the three military Orders,[34] uniting in purpose for once, adhered to the Emperor of Germany, and Alice was obliged to withdraw. After this struggle the attention of the Christians was entirely turned to the general defence; and the right of the emperor, who had now made his peace with the Pope, was universally recognised.[35]

Nevertheless, the truce which he had concluded with Camel, the Sultaun of Egypt, did not in all instances save the Latins of Palestine from annoyance and warfare. The whole country was surrounded by a thousand petty Mahommedan states not included in the peace, and the Moslems left no opportunity unimproved for the purpose of destroying their Christian neighbours. Their incursions on the Latin territory were incessant; and many large bodies of pilgrims were cut to pieces, or hurried away into distant lands as slaves.

A truce had been agreed upon also, between the Templars and the Sultaun of Aleppo; but at the death of that monarch both parties had again recourse to arms, and the Templars were defeated with such terrible slaughter that all Europe was moved with compassion. Even their ancient rivals, the Hospitallers, sent them immediate succour; and from the commandery of St. John, at Clerkenwell,[36] alone, a body of three hundred knights took their departure for the Holy Land.

A council likewise was held about this time at Spoletto, where another crusade was announced; and Gregory IX., who combined in his person every inconsistency that ambition, bigotry, and avarice can produce, sent the Dominican and Franciscan friars to stimulate Europe to take the Cross. No sooner had the crusade been preached, and the enthusiastic multitudes were ready to begin the journey, than Gregory and his agents persuaded many to compromise their vow;[37] and, by paying a certain sum towards the expenses of the expedition, to fill the papal treasury, under the pretence of assisting their brother Christians.

34. Sanutus.
35. Regist. Greg. Noni, Vertot Preuves.
36. Matthew Paris, 1237.
37. Matthew Paris; Sanutus.

Those who would not thus yield to his suggestions he positively prohibited from setting out, and engaged the Emperor Frederic to throw impediments in their way, when they pursued their purpose.

Nevertheless, the King of Navarre, the Duke of Burgundy, the Count of Brittany, and the Count de Bar proceeded to Palestine in spite of all opposition; and their coming was of very timely service to the defenders of the Holy Land, for no sooner had the period of his truce with the Christians expired, than Camel, finding that preparations for war were making on their part, anticipated their efforts, retook Jerusalem, routed all the forces that could be opposed to him, and overthrew what was called the Tower of David. He died shortly after this victory, and on the arrival of the crusaders, a prospect of success seemed open before them.

But the operations of the chiefs were detached, and though the Count of Brittany gained some advantages towards Damascus, the rest of the French knights were completely defeated in a pitched battle at Gaza, and most of their leaders were either killed or taken. The King of Navarre was glad to enter into a disgraceful treaty with the Emir of Karac, which was conducted through the intervention of the Templars;[38] and the rest of the Latins formed alliances with what neighbouring powers they could. The Hospitallers, however, would not subscribe to the truce with the Emir of Karac[39] through jealousy towards the Templars, and there was no power in the state sufficiently strong to force them to obedience.

Shortly after this event, the King of Navarre returned to Europe, and Richard, Earl of Cornwall, with many knights and large forces, arrived in Palestine. Their expedition had been sanctioned by all the authorities of Europe, except the Pope. Henry III. conducted them in person to the shore; the prayers and benedictions of the people and the clergy followed them, and their journey through France was accompanied by shouts and acclamations. On his arrival in Palestine, Richard instantly marched upon Jaffa, but he was met by envoys from the Sultaun of Egypt—who was now at war with the Sultaun of Damascus—offering an exchange of prisoners, and a complete cession of the Holy Land,[40] with some unimportant exceptions.

Richard instantly accepted such advantageous proposals; Jerusalem was given up to the Christians, the rebuilding of the walls was com-

---

38. Sanutus, lib. iii.

39. The Emir of Karac was but a dependant of the Sultaun of Damascus.

40. Matthew Paris; Litteræ Comit. Richardi.

menced, the churches were purified, and the earl returned to Europe with the glorious title of the deliverer of Palestine. The Templars would not be parties to this treaty, as the Hospitallers had refused to participate in the other; and thus, one of the great military Orders remained at war with the Sultaun of Damascus,[41] and the other with the Sultaun of Egypt.

While these events had been passing in Palestine, a new dynasty had sprung up in the north of Asia, and threatened a complete revolution in the whole of that quarter of the world. Genjis Khan and his successors had overturned all the northern and eastern governments of Asia; and, spreading over that fair portion of the earth precisely as the Goths and Huns had spread over Roman Europe, had reduced the more polished and civilized nations of the south, by the savage vigour and active ferocity of a race yet in the youth of being. Among[42] other tribes whom the successors of Genjis had expelled from their original abodes, was a barbarous and warlike horde called the Corasmins; and this people, wandering about without a dwelling, destroying as they went, and waging war against all nations, at length directed their course towards Palestine. So quick and unexpected had been their arrival, that the Christians employed in the re-edification of the city-walls never dreamed of invasion till fire and massacre had swept over half the Holy Land.[43]

No troops were collected, no preparations made, the fortifications of the city were incomplete, and the only resource of the people of Jerusalem was to retire in haste to the shelter of Jaffa, under the guidance of the few Templars and Hospitallers who were on the spot. Some few persons remained, and made an attempt at defence; but the town was taken in a moment, and every soul in it put to the sword.[44] The bloodthirsty barbarians, not satisfied with the scanty number of victims they had found, artfully raised the banner of the Cross upon the walls, and many of the Latins who had fled returned. Seven thousand more were thus entrapped and massacred; and the Corasmins exercised every sort of barbarous fury on those objects they thought most sacred in the eyes of the Christians.

At length the fugitives at Jaffa received a succour of four thousand

---

41. Sanutus; Vertot.
42. Bibliothéque Oriental; Joinville; Ducange; Sanutus, 217; Continuation of William of Tyre.
43. Joinville; Matthew Paris; Bernard in Martenne.
44. Joinville; Matthew Paris; Epist. Fred. Imper.

men from their allies, the Sultauns of Emissa and Damascus,[45] and resolved to give battle to the barbarians. The Patriarch of Jerusalem precipitated the measures of the army, and after a dreadful struggle the Latins were defeated, the Grand Masters of the Temple and St. John slain, the three military Orders nearly exterminated, and the Sultaun of Emissa forced to fly for shelter to his fortifications. Walter de Brienne, the lord of Jaffa, was taken; and to force that town to surrender, the Corasmins hung the gallant knight by the arms to a cross, declaring to the garrison that he should there remain till the city was yielded. Walter heard, and raising his voice, unmindful of his own agonies, solemnly commanded his soldiers to hold out the city to the last.[46] The barbarians were obliged to retire, and Walter was sent captive into Egypt.

The Sultaun of Emissa soon raised the standard a second time against the barbarians and after several struggles, in which the monarch of Egypt sometimes upheld, and sometimes abandoned the Corasmins, they were at length entirely defeated, and not one, it is said, escaped from the field of battle.[47] Barbaquan, their leader, was slain; and thus Asia was delivered of one of the most terrible scourges that had ever been inflicted on her.

At this time a monarch reigned over France who combined in a remarkable degree the high talents of his grandfather Philip Augustus with the religious zeal or, perhaps I may say, fanaticism of his father, Louis VIII. Louis IX. was in every respect an extraordinary man; he was a great warrior, chivalrous as an individual, and skilful as a general: he was a great king, inasmuch as he sought the welfare of his people more than the aggrandizement of his territories: he formed the best laws that could be adapted to the time, administered them often in person, and observed them always himself: he was a good man, inasmuch as he served God with his whole heart, and strove in

---

45. Ducange; Joinville; Bernard.
46. Bernard; Joinville, Matthew Paris.
47. The whole of these events are extremely obscure in history. I have followed Joinville more than any other author, because I find his account more clear and satisfactory. Ducange's valuable notes have greatly aided me; but even that indefatigable investigator has not been able to arrive at precise certainty. The accounts in Matthew Paris do not well harmonize with those of persons who had more immediate means of information. Vincent of Beauvais states, that the Corasmins were finally exterminated, not in a battle, but in separate bodies by the peasantry. Their whole number seems to have been about twenty thousand men. Bernard the Treasurer, in Martenne, corroborates the statement of Vincent of Beauvais.

all his communion with his fellows to do his duty according to his sense of obligation. Had he been touched with religious fervour to the amount of zeal, but not to the amount of fanaticism, he would have been perhaps too superior to his age.

Previous to the news of the Corasminian irruption, St. Louis had determined to visit the Holy Land, in consequence of a vow made during sickness.[48] It appears, that after the signal defeat which he had given to Henry III. of England at Saintonge, Louis's whole attention was turned to the sufferings of the Christians in Palestine; and so deeply was his mind impressed with that anxious thought, that it became the subject of dreams, which he looked upon as instigations from heaven. The news of the destruction of the Christians by the barbarians, the well-known quarrels and rivalry of the two military Orders, and the persuasions of Innocent IV., who then held the thirteenth œcumenical council at Lyons, all hastened Louis's preparations. William Longsword and a great many English crusaders[49] joined the French monarch from Great Britain; and after three years' careful attention to the safety of his kingdom, the provision of supplies, and the concentration of his forces, Louis, with his two brothers, the Counts of Artois and Anjou, took the scrip and staff, and set sail for Cyprus. The third brother of the king, Alphonso, Count of Poitiers, remained to collect the rest of the crusaders, and followed shortly after.[50]

The queen-consort of France, and several other ladies of high note, accompanied the monarch to the Holy Land.[51] At Cyprus, Louis spent eight months in healing the divisions of the military Orders, and endeavouring to bring about that degree of unity which had been unknown to any of the crusades. At length, early in the spring, he set sail from Cyprus with an army of fifty thousand chosen men. A tremendous storm separated the king's fleet, and, supported by but a small part of his troops he arrived at Damietta, where the Sultaun of Egypt, with his whole force, was drawn up to oppose the landing of the Christians. The *sultaun* himself was seen in golden armour, which shone, Joinville says, like the sun itself; and so great was the noise of drums and trumpets that the French were almost deafened by the sound. After some discussion, it was determined that the landing should be attempted without waiting for the rest of the army.

---

48. Joinville; Bernard in Martenne; Guillaume Guiart.
49. Matthew Paris; Joinville.
50. Joinville.
51. Guillaume Guiart; Joinville.

Among the first who reached the shore was Joinville, Seneschal of Champagne, who, accompanied by another baron, and their men-at-arms, landed in the face of an immense body of Turkish cavalry, that instantly spurred forward against them. The French planted their large shields[52] in the sand, with their lances resting on the rim, so that a complete *chevaux-de-frise* was raised, from which the Turks turned off without venturing an assault. St. Louis himself soon followed, and in his chivalrous impatience to land, sprang into the water up to his shoulders, and, sword in hand, rushed on to charge the Saracens.

Intimidated at the bold actions of the French, the Moslems fled from the beach; and as the crusaders advanced, the unexpected news of the death of their *sultaun* reached the Saracens, upon which they abandoned even the city of Damietta itself, without waiting to destroy the bridge, though they set fire to the bazaars.[53]

At Damietta Louis paused for the arrival of his brother, the Count of Poitiers, and the rest of the forces; and here, with the usual improvidence that marked all the crusades, the army gave itself up to luxury and debauchery, which the king neither by laws nor example could check. At length the reinforcements appeared, and Louis, leaving the queen at Damietta, marched on towards Cairo; but near Massoura he found his advance impeded by the Thanisian canal, on the other side of which the Saracens were drawn up to oppose his progress under the command of the celebrated Emir Ceccidun. No other means of passing the canal seemed practicable, but by throwing a causeway across. This was accordingly commenced, under cover of two high moveable towers, called *chats chatiels*, or cat-castles, which were scarcely raised before they were burnt by quantities of Greek fire, thrown from the *pierriers* and *mangonels*.

At length an Arabian peasant agreed, for a large bribe, to point out a ford. The Count of Artois, with fourteen hundred knights, was directed to attempt it. He succeeded, repulsed the Saracens on the banks, and pursued them to Massoura. The panic among the Moslems was general, and Massoura was nearly deserted. The more experienced and prudent knights of all classes advised the Count of Artois to pause for the arrival of the king and the rest of the army. The count, with passionate eagerness, accused his good counsellors of cowardice. Chivalrous honour thus assailed forgot reason and moderation; each one more ardently than another advanced into Massoura: the Moslems,

---

52. Joinville; *Branche des royaux Lignages.*
53. Joinville.

242

recovered from their fear, returned in great numbers; the fight began in earnest, and almost the whole of the imprudent advance-guard of the Christians was cut to pieces.

The Count of Artois fell among the first;[54] and when Louis himself arrived, all was dismay and confusion. The battle was now renewed with redoubled vigour; Louis fought in every part of the strife, and the French and Saracens seemed emulous of each other in the paths of glory and destruction. The sun went down over the field of Massoura, leaving neither army assuredly the victors; but the Saracens had been repulsed, and Louis remained master of the plain.

Sickness and famine soon began to rage in the Christian camp. The Moslems had now interrupted the communication with Damietta; and every soldier in the army was enfeebled by disease. Negotiations were begun for peace; but were broken off, because the sultaun would receive no hostage for the evacuation of Damietta but Louis himself; and it was determined to attempt a retreat. Many strove to escape by the river, but were taken in the attempt; and the host itself was incessantly subject to the attacks of the Saracens, who hung upon its rear during the whole march, cutting off every party that was detached, even to procure the necessaries of life. In this dreadful state Louis long continued to struggle against sickness, fighting ever where danger was most imminent, and bearing up when the hardiest soldiers of his army failed.

At length he could hardly sit his horse; and in the confusion of the flight—which was now the character of the retreat—he was separated from his own servants, and attended only by the noble Geoffroy de Sergines, who defended him against all the attacks of the enemy. He was led to a hut at the village of Cazel, where he lay, expecting every moment that the plague would accomplish its work. He was thus taken by the Saracens,[55] who assisted in his recovery and treated him with honour. The greater part of the army fell into the Moslems' power, but an immense number were slain and drowned in attempting their escape.

Several difficulties now arose with regard to the ransom of the king; the Saracens demanding the cession of various parts of Palestine still in the hands of the Christians. This, however, Louis refused; and conducted himself in prison with so much boldness, that the *sultaun* declared he was the proudest *infidel* he had ever beheld. To humble

54. Joinville; Guillaume Guiart; Ducange
55. Joinville; Ducange, Guillaume Guiart.

him to his wishes, the torture of the *bernicles* was threatened;[56] but the monarch remained so unmoved, that his enfranchisement was at last granted on other terms. Ten thousand golden *besants* were to be paid for the freedom of the army; the city of Damietta was to be restored to the Saracens, and a peace of ten years was concluded. During the interval which followed these arrangements, the *sultaun* was assassinated, and the fate of St. Louis was again doubtful; but the murderers agreed to the same terms which had been before stipulated. Nevertheless, some acts of cruelty were committed; and a great number of the sick were massacred at Damietta. The treasure which the king possessed on the spot not being sufficient to furnish the whole ransom, his friends were obliged to seize upon the wealth of the Grand Master of the Temple, who basely refused to lend a portion to redeem his fellow-Christians.

At length the first part of the sum was paid; the great body of the foreign nobles who had joined in the crusade returned to Europe, and Louis himself retired to Acre. The Saracens had already broken the treaty with Louis by the murder of the sick at Damietta, and by the detention of several knights and soldiers, as well as a large body of Christian children. The promise of peace, therefore, was not imperative; and the Sultaun of Damascus eagerly courted the French king to aid him in his efforts against the people of Egypt.[57] The news of this negotiation immediately brought deputies from Egypt, who submitted to the terms which Louis thought fit to propose; and that monarch, without mingling in the wars that raged between the two Moslem countries, only took advantage of them to repair the fortifications of Jaffa and Cesarea. After having spent two years in putting the portion of Palestine that yet remained to the Latins[58] into a defensible state, he set sail for France, where his presence was absolutely required.

Before proceeding to trace the after-fate of the Holy Land,[59] it may be as well to conduct St. Louis to his last crusade. Sixteen years after his return to Europe, that monarch once more determined on rearing the banner of the Cross. Immense numbers flocked to join him, and England appeared willing to second all the efforts of the French king. Edward, the heir of the English monarchy, assumed the Cross; and large sums were raised throughout Britain for defraying the

---

56. See Notes 12.
57. Ducange; Joinville; Guillaume Guiart.
58. *A. D.* 1254.
59. *A. D.* 1270.

expenses of the war.

In 1270, St. Louis, accompanied by the flower of his national nobility, and followed by sixty thousand chosen troops, set sail for Palestine, but was driven by a storm into Sardinia. Here a change in his plans took place; and it was resolved that the army should land in Africa, where the King of Tunis some time before had professed himself favourable to the Christian religion. St. Louis had been long so weak, that he could not bear the weight of his armour,[60] nor the motion of a horse, for any length of time; but still his indefatigable zeal sustained him; and after a short passage, he arrived on the coast of Africa, opposite to the city of Carthage.

Although his coming had been so suddenly resolved,[61] a large Mahommedan force was drawn up to oppose his landing; but the French knights forced their way to the shore, and after a severe contest, obtained a complete victory over the Moors. Siege was then laid to Carthage, which was also taken; but before these conquests could be turned to any advantage, an infectious flux began to appear in the army. St. Louis was one of the first attacked. His enfeebled constitution was not able to support the effects of the disease, and it soon became evident that the monarch's days were rapidly drawing to their close. In this situation, with the most perfect consciousness of his approaching fate, St. Louis called his son Philip,[62] and spoke long to him on his duty to the people he left to his charge; teaching him with the beautiful simplicity of true wisdom. The king then withdrew his thoughts from all earthly things, performed the last rites of his religion, and yielded his soul to God.[63]

Scarcely was the monarch dead, when Charles of Sicily arrived with large reinforcements, and unknowing the event, approached Carthage with martial music, and every sign of rejoicing. His joy was soon turned into grief by the tidings of his brother's fate;[64] and the courage of the Moors being raised by the sorrow of their enemies, the united armies of France and Sicily were attacked by a very superior power.

After a variety of engagements, Philip, now King of France, and Charles, of Sicily, compelled the defeated Moors to sue for peace; and

---

60. Joinville.
61. Guillaume Guiart.
62. Joinville.
63. *Branche des royaux et Lignages; Sermon de Robert de Saincereaux.*
64. Charles, King of Sicily, was brother to St. Louis.

collecting his troops, the new monarch returned to Europe, driven from the coast rather by the pestilence that raged in his army,[65] than by the efforts of the *infidels*.

Prince Edward of England had taken the Cross, as I have already said, with the intention of following Louis IX. to the Holy Land; and with the small force he could collect, amounting to not more than fifteen hundred men, he arrived in the Mediterranean, but hearing that Louis had turned from the direct object of the crusade, he proceeded to Sicily, where he passed the winter.

As soon as spring rendered navigation possible, he set sail, and arrived at Acre, where he found the state of Palestine infinitely worse than it had been since the first taking of Jerusalem.

Disunion and violence had done far more to destroy the Christians of the Holy Land than the swords of the *infidels*. The two military Orders had been constantly opposed to each other, and had often been engaged in sanguinary warfare. The knights of St. John had ever the advantage; and at one time the Templars of Palestine had nearly been exterminated. The clergy attempted to encroach upon the privileges of both. The different Italian republics, who had secured to themselves various portions of territory, and various commercial immunities, were in continual warfare; and while the Saracens and the Mamelukes were gradually taking possession of the whole soil—while the fortresses of Cesarea, Jaffa, and Saphoury fell into the hands of the infidels, as well as all the cities and feoffs of the Latins, except Acre and Tyre—the sands of Palestine were often wet with Christian blood, shed by the hands of Christians. Antioch also fell almost without resistance, and the citizens were either doomed to death or led into captivity.

Such was the state of the Holy Land at the time of Prince Edward's arrival. His name, however, was a host; the disunion among the Christians was healed by his coming;[66] every exertion was made to render his efforts effectual; and he soon found himself at the head of a small but veteran force, amounting to seven thousand men. With this he advanced upon Nazareth, and after a severe conflict with the Moslems, he made himself master of that city, in which all the Saracens that remained were slaughtered without mercy. The climate put a stop to his successes. It was now the middle of summer, and the excessive heat brought on a fever, from which Edward was recovering, when a strange messenger desired to render some despatches to the prince's

---

65. Guillaume Guiart; William of Nangis.
66. Hemingford; Langtoft; Matthew Paris, continuation.

own hand.

He was admitted; and as the young leader lay in his bed, without any attendants, he delivered the letters, and for a moment spoke to him of the affairs of Jaffa. The instant after, he drew a dagger from his belt, and before Edward was aware, had stabbed him in the chest. The prince was enfeebled, but was still sufficiently vigorous to wrench the weapon from the assassin, and to put him to death with his own hand. His attendants, alarmed by the struggle, rushed into the apartment, and found Edward bleeding from the wound inflicted by a poisoned knife. Skilful means[67] were instantly used to preserve his life;[68] and an antidote, sent by the Grand Master of the Temple, is said to have obviated the effects of the poison. Edward's natural vigour, with care, soon restored him to health; and the Sultaun of Egypt, daunted by the courage and ability of the English prince, and engaged in ruinous wars in other directions, offered peace on advantageous conditions, which were accepted. Edward and his followers returned to Europe, and the Christians of Palestine were left to take advantage of a ten years' truce.

Such was the end of the last expedition. In 1274, Gregory X., who had himself witnessed the sorrows of Palestine, attempted to promote a new crusade, and held a council for that purpose at Lyons, where many great and noble personages assumed the Cross. The death of the Pope followed shortly afterward, and the project was abandoned, on the loss of him who had given it birth. In Palestine, all now tended to the utter expulsion of the Christians. The Latins themselves first madly broke the truce, by plundering some Egyptian merchants near Margat. Keladun, then Sultaun of Cairo, hastened to revenge the injury, and Margat was taken from the Christians, after a gallant defence.[69] Tripoli, which had hitherto escaped by various concessions to the Moslems, fell shortly after Margat; and in the third year from that period, two hundred thousand Mahommedans were under the walls of Acre, the last possession of the Christians. The Grand Master of St. John had collected together a small body of Italian mercenaries, but no serviceable support could be won from the kings of Europe.

The Grand Master[70] of the Temple, however, with the rest of the

67. The popular version of this story is, that Eleonora, the wife of the prince, who had accompanied him to Palestine, sucked the poison from the wound, at the risk of her own life. Camden sanctions this account.
68. Hemingford; Langtoft.
69. Villani; Vet. Script.; Bernard, old French.
70. Martenne; Villani.

military Orders, and about twelve thousand men, being joined by the King of Cyprus, resolved to undergo a siege. The greater part of the useless inhabitants were sent away by sea, and the garrison prepared to defend themselves to the last. This was the final blaze of chivalric valour that shone on the Holy Land. The numbers of the Moslems were overpowering, and after a breach had been made in the walls by the fall of what was called the *Cursed Tower*, a general assault took place.

The King of Cyprus made a dastardly flight, but the Templars and the Teutonic knights died where they stood, and the Hospitallers only left the city to attack the rear of the besieging army. Here they met with infinite odds against them, and fell man by man, till the news came that the Grand Master of the Temple was killed and that the city was taken. The Hospitallers then, reduced to seven in number, reached a ship, and quitted the shores of Palestine. About an equal number of Templars fled to the interior, and thence fought their way through the land, till they gained the means of reaching Cyprus. The inhabitants of the city who had not before departed fled to the sea;[71] but the elements themselves seemed to war against them, and ere they could escape, the Saracen sword died the sands with their blood. The Moslems then set fire to the devoted town, and the last vestige of the Christian power in Syria was swept from the face of the earth.

---

71. Martenne, Vet. Script.; Villani; Sanutus.

CHAPTER 15

Fate of the Orders of the Temple and St. John

From the period of the fall of Acre crusades were only spoken of;
but the spirit of chivalry was perhaps not the less active, though it had
taken another course: nor did it lose in purity by being directed, mod-
erated, and deprived of the ferocity which always follows fanaticism.
The Holy Land had become a place of vice and debauchery, as well as a
theatre for the display of great deeds and noble resolution; and we find,
that however orderly and regular any army was on its departure from
Europe, it soon acquired all the habits of immorality and improvidence
which seemed some inherent quality of that unhappy climate. This was
peculiarly apparent in the two Orders of the Hospital and the Temple,
the rules of which were particularly calculated to guard against luxury
of every kind; yet, the one, till its extinction and both, during their
sojourn in Palestine, were the receptacle of more depravity and crimes
than perhaps any other body of men could produce.

After the capture of Acre the knights of these two Orders retreated
to Cyprus; and when some ineffectual efforts had been made to excite
a new crusade for the recovery of Palestine, the Templars retired from
that country, and, spreading themselves throughout their vast possessions in Europe, seem really to have abandoned all thought of fighting
any more for the sepulchre. With the rest of Europe they spoke of
fresh expeditions, it is true; but in the meanwhile they gave themselves
up to the luxury, pride, and ambition which, if it was not the real
cause of their downfall, at least furnished the excuse. Philip the Fair
of France, on his accession to the throne, showed great favour to the
Templars,[1] and held out hopes that he would attempt to establish the

1. Raynouard.

Order once more in the land which had given it birth.

But the Templars were now deeply occupied in the politics of Europe itself: their haughty Grand Master was almost equal to a king in power, and would fain have made kings his slaves. In the disputes between Philip and Boniface VIII., the Templars took the part of the Pope, and treated the monarch, in his own realm, with insolent contempt; but they knew not the character of him whose wrath they roused. Philip was at once vindictive and avaricious, and the destruction of the Templars offered the gratification of both passions: he was also calm, bold, cunning, and remorseless; and from the vengeance of such a man it was difficult to escape. The vices of the Templars were notorious,[2] and on these it was easy to graft crimes of a deeper die. Reports, rumours, accusations, circulated rapidly through Europe; and Philip, resolved upon crushing the unhappy Order, took care that on the very first vacancy his creature, Bertrand de Got, Archbishop of Bourdeaux,[3] should be elevated to the papal throne. Before he suffered the ambitious prelate to be elected, he bound him to grant five conditions, four of which were explained to him previously, but the fifth was to be kept in secrecy till after his elevation.

Bertrand pledged himself to all these terms; and as soon as he had received the triple crown, was informed that the last dreadful condition was the destruction of the Order of the Temple. He hesitated, but was forced to consent; and after various stratagems to inveigle all the principal Templars into France, Philip caused them suddenly to be arrested throughout his dominions,[4] and had them arraigned of idolatry, immorality, extortion, and treason, together with crimes whose very name must not soil this page. Mixed with a multitude of charges, both false and absurd, were various others too notorious to be confuted by the body, and many which could be proved against individuals.

Several members of the Order confessed some of the crimes laid to their charge, and many more were afterward induced to do so by

---

2. For the history of the Templars, see Raynouard and Du Puy, Vertot, William of Nangis, Historia Templariorum, &c. Almost all the modern writers are more or less in favour of the Templars, while every contemporary authority condemns them. As to Mills's assertion, that they were loyal and virtuous, it is perfectly untenable. All the historians of the Holy Land, many of whom died while the Templars were at the height of their power, declare that they were a corrupt, proud, perfidious body. Mills himself shows that such was the opinion entertained of them by the Saracens; and all the general letters of the popes accuse them of manifold vices and depravities.
3. Vertot.
4. Will. of Nangis.

torture; but at a subsequent period of the trial, when the whole of the papal authority was used to give the proceeding the character of a regular legal inquisition, a number of individuals confessed, on the promise of pardon, different offences, sufficient to justify rigorous punishment against themselves, and to implicate deeply the institution to which they belonged. James de Mollay, however, the Grand Master, firmly denied every charge, and defended himself and his brethren with a calm and dignified resolution that nothing could shake.

It would be useless as well as painful to dwell upon all the particulars of their trial, where space is not allowed to investigate minutely the facts: it is sufficient to say, that the great body of the Templars in France were sentenced to be imprisoned for life, and a multitude were burned at the stake, where they showed that heroic firmness which they had ever evinced in the field of battle. Their large possessions were of course confiscated. In Spain, their aid against the Moors was too necessary to permit of similar rigour, and they were generally acquitted in that country. In England, the same persecutions were carried on, but with somewhat of a milder course: and the last blow was put to the whole by a council held at Vienne, which formally dissolved the Order, and transferred its estates to the Hospitallers. James de Mollay and the Grand Prior of France were the last victims, and were publicly burned in Paris for crimes that beyond doubt they did not commit. To suppose that the Templars were guilty of the specific offences attributed to them would be to suppose them a congregation of madmen; but to believe they were a religious or a virtuous Order would be to charge all Europe with a general and purposeless conspiracy.

In the meanwhile, the Knights Hospitallers confined themselves to the objects for which they were originally instituted; and, that they might always be prepared to fight against the enemies of Christendom, they obtained a cession of the island of Rhodes, from which they expelled the Turks. Here they continued for many years, a stumbling block in the way of Moslem conquest; but at length, the chancellor of the Order, named d'Amaral,[5] disappointed of the dignity of Grand Master, in revenge, it is said, invited the Turks to the siege, and gave them the plan of the island with its fortifications. Soliman II. instantly led an army against it; but the gallant knights resisted with a determined courage, that drove the imperious *sultaun* almost to madness. He commanded his celebrated general, Mustapha, to be slain with

5. Vertot.

arrows,[6] attributing to him the misfortune of the siege; and at length had begun to withdraw his forces, when a more favourable point of attack was discovered, and the knights were ultimately obliged to capitulate.

The city of Rhodes was by this time reduced to a mere heap of stones, and at one period of the siege, the Grand Master himself remained thirty-four days in the trenches, without ever sitting down to food, or taking repose, but such as he could gain upon an uncovered mattress at the foot of the wall. So noble a defence well merited an honourable fate; and even after their surrender, the knights were the objects of admiration and praise to all Europe, though Europe had suffered them to fall without aid. The *sultaun*, before he allowed the Order to transfer itself to Candia, which had been stipulated by the treaty, requested to see the Grand Master: and to console him for his loss, he said, "The conquest and the fall of empires are but the sports of fortune." He then strove to win the gallant knight who had so well defended his post to the Ottoman service, holding out to him the most magnificent offers, and showing what little cause he had to remain attached to the Christians,[7] who had abandoned him; but Villiers replied, that he thanked him for his generous proposals, yet that he should be unworthy of such a prince's good opinion if he could accept them.

Before the Order of St. John could fix upon any determinate plan of proceeding, it was more than once threatened with a complete separation, by various divisions in its councils.

At length motives, partly political, partly generous, induced the emperor Charles V. to offer the island of Malta to the Hospitallers. This proposal was soon accepted,[8] and after various negotiations the territory was delivered up to the knights, who took full possession on the 26th of October, 1530. Thirty-five years had scarcely passed, when the Order of St. John, which was now known by the name of the Order of Malta, was assailed in its new possession by an army composed of thirty thousand veteran Turkish soldiers. The news of this armament's approach had long before reached the island, and every preparation had been made to render its efforts ineffectual. The whole of the open country was soon in the hands of the Turks, and they resolved to begin

---

6. He was afterward pardoned when the *sultaun's* wrath had abated but Soliman would never see him more.

7. Vertot.

8. Watson; Vertot; Nic. Villagagnon.

the siege by the attack of a small fort, situated at the end of a tongue of land which separated the two ports.

The safety of the island and the Order depended upon the castle of St. Elmo—a fact which the Turkish admiral well knew, and the cannonade that he soon opened upon the fortress was tremendous and incessant. The knights who had been thrown into that post soon began to demand succour; but the Grand Master, La Valette, treated their request with indignation, and speedily sent fresh troops to take the place of those whom fear had rendered weak.

A noble emulation reigned among the Hospitallers, and they contended only which should fly to the perilous service. A sortie was made from the fort, and the Turks were driven back from their position; but the forces of the Moslems were soon increased by the arrival of the famous Dragut; and the succour which the viceroy of Sicily had promised to the knights did not appear. After the coming of Dragut, the siege of St. Elmo was pressed with redoubled ardour. A ravelin was surprised, and a lodgement effected; and the cavalier, which formed one of the principal fortifications, had nearly been taken.

Day after day, night after night, new efforts were made on either part; and the cannon of the Turks never ceased to play upon the walls of the fort, while, at the same time, the ravelin which they had captured was gradually raised till it overtopped the parapet. The whole of the outer defences were now exposed: the garrison could only advance by means of trenches and a subterranean approach; and to cut off even these communications with the parapet, the *pacha* threw across a bridge from the ravelin, covering it with earth to defend it from fire.

After this, the mine and the sap both went on at once; but the hardness of the rock was in favour of the besieged, and by a sortie the bridge was burnt.[9] In a wonderfully short time it was reconstructed; and the terrible fire from the Turkish lines not only swept away hundreds of the besieged, but ruined the defences and dismounted the artillery. In this state the knights sent a messenger to the Grand Master, representing their situation, showing that the recruits they received only drained the garrison of the town, without protracting the resistance of a place that could stand no longer, and threatening to cut their way through the enemy, if boats did not come to take them off.

La Valette knew too well their situation; but he knew also, that if St. Elmo were abandoned, the viceroy of Sicily would never sail to

9. Vertot; Com. de Bel. Mel.

the relief of Malta; and he sent three commissioners to examine the state of the fort, and to persuade the garrison to hold out to the last. Two of these officers saw that the place was truly untenable, but the third declared it might still be maintained; and, on his return, offered to throw himself into it with what volunteers he could raise. La Valette instantly accepted the proposal, and wrote a cold and bitter note to the refractory knights in St. Elmo, telling them that others were willing to take their place. He said:—

> Come back, my brethren you will be here more in safety; and, on our part, we shall feel more tranquil concerning the defence of St. Elmo, on the preservation of which depends the safety of the island and of the Order.

Shame rose in the bosom of the knights; and, mortified at the very idea of having proposed to yield a place that others were willing to maintain, they now sent to implore permission to stay.

La Valette well knew, from the first, that such would be their conduct; but, before granting their request, he replied, that he ever preferred new troops who were obedient, to veterans who took upon themselves to resist the will of their commanders: and it was only on the most humble apologies and entreaties that he allowed them, as a favour, to remain in the post of peril. From the 17th of June to the 14th of July, this little fort[10] had held out against all the efforts of the Turkish army, whose loss had been already immense. Enraged at so obstinate a resistance, the *pacha* now determined to attack the rock on which it stood, with all his forces; and the Grand Master, perceiving the design by the Turkish movements, took care to send full supplies to the garrison.

Among other things thus received were a number of hoops covered with tow, and imbued with every sort of inflammable matter. For the two days preceding the assault, the cannon of the Turkish fleet and camp kept up an incessant fire upon the place, which left not a vestige of the fortifications above the surface of the rock. On the third morning the Turks rushed over the fosse which they had nearly filled, and at the given signal mounted to storm. The walls of the place were gone, but a living wall of veteran soldiers presented itself, each knight being supported by three inferior men. With dauntless valour the Turks threw themselves upon the pikes that opposed them; and after the lances had been shivered and the swords broken, they were

10. Vertot; Com. de Bel. Mel. Nic. Villag.; Watson.

seen struggling with their adversaries, and striving to end the contest with the dagger.

A terrible fire of musketry and artillery was kept up; and the Christians, on their part, hurled down upon the swarms of Turks that rushed in unceasing multitudes from below the flaming hoops, which sometimes linking two or three of the enemy together, set fire to the light and floating dresses of the east, and enveloped many in a horrible death. Still, however, the Turks rushed on, thousands after thousands, and still the gallant little band of Christians repelled all their efforts, and maintained possession of the height.

From the walls of the town, and from the castle of St. Angelo, the dreadful struggle for St. Elmo was clearly beheld; and the Christian people and the knights, watching the wavering current of the fight, felt perhaps more painfully all the anxious horror of the scene, than those whose whole thoughts and feelings were occupied in the actual combat. La Valette himself stood on the walls of St. Angelo, not spending his time in useless anticipations, but scanning eagerly every motion of the enemy, and turning the artillery of the fortress in that direction where it might prove of the most immediate benefit. At length he beheld a body of Turks scaling a rampart, from which the attention of the besieged had been called by a furious attack on the other side.[11]

Their ladders were placed, and still the defenders of St. Elmo did not perceive them—they began their ascent—they reached the top of the rampart—but at that moment the Grand Master opened a murderous fire upon them from the citadel, and swept them from the post they had gained. The cavalier was next attacked; but here also the Turks were met by those destructive hoops of fire which caused more dread in their ranks than all the other efforts of the Christians. Wherever they fell confusion followed; and at the end of a tremendous fight of nine hours, the Moslems were obliged to sound a retreat.

A change of operations now took place; means were used to cut off the communication with the town; and, after holding out some time longer, the fort of St. Elmo was taken, the last knight of its noble garrison dying in the breach. The whole force of the Turks was thenceforth turned towards the city; and a slow but certain progress was made, notwithstanding all the efforts of the Grand Master and his devoted companions. In vain he wrote to the viceroy of Sicily; no succour arrived for many days. The town was almost reduced to extremity. The

---

11. Watson; Vertot; Com.

bastion of St. Catherine was scaled, and remained sometime in the hands of the *infidels*, who would have maintained it longer, had not La Valette himself rushed to the spot; and, after receiving a severe wound, succeeded in dislodging the assailants.

A small succour came at length under the command of Don Juan de Cardonna; but this was overbalanced by the junction of the viceroy of Algiers with the attacking force. The bulwark of all Christendom was being swept away, while Christian kings stood looking on, and once more saw the knights of St. John falling man by man before the infidels, without stretching forth a hand to save them.

A large army had, in the meanwhile, been assembled in Sicily, under the pretence of assisting Malta; and at last the soldiers clamoured so loudly to be led to the glorious service for which they had been enrolled, that the vacillating viceroy after innumerable delays was forced to yield to their wishes, and set sail for the scene of conflict.[12] The island was reached in safety, the troops disembarked; and though the Turks still possessed the advantage of numbers, a panic seized them, and they fled. Joy and triumph succeeded to danger and dread, and the name of La Valette and his companions, remains embalmed among the memories of the noble and great.

This was the last important event in the history of the Order of St. John; and since that day, it has gradually descended to later years, blending itself with modern institutions till its distinctive character has been lost, and the knights of Malta are reckoned among the past.

It does not seem necessary to trace the other military fraternities which originated in the crusades to their close; but something more must be said concerning the progress of chivalry in Europe, and the effect that it had upon society in general. The Holy Wars were, indeed, the greatest efforts of knighthood; but during the intervals between each expedition beyond the seas, and that which followed, and often during the time of preparation, the knight found plenty of occupation for his sword in his own country. The strife with the Moors in Spain bore entirely the aspect of the crusades, but the sanguinary conflicts between France and England offered continual occasions both for the display of knightly valour and of knightly generosity.

The bitterest national enmity existed between the two countries—they were ever engaged in struggling against each other; and yet we find, through the whole, that mutual courtesy when the battle was over, and in the times of truce that frank co-operation, or that rivalry

12. Vertot.

in noble efforts, which belonged so peculiarly to chivalry. Occasionally, it is true, a cruel and bloodthirsty warrior would stain his successes with ungenerous rigour—for where is the institution which has ever been powerful enough to root out the evil spot from the heart of man? But the great tone of all the wars of chivalry was valour in the field and courtesy in the hall. Deeds were often done in the heat of blood which general barbarism of manners alone would excuse; and most of the men whom we are inclined to love and to admire have left some blot on that page of history which records their lives. But to judge of the spirit of the Order, we must not look to those instances where the habits of the age mixed up a vast portion of evil with the general character of the knight, but we must turn our eyes upon those splendid examples where chivalrous feeling reached its height, did away all the savage cruelty of the time, and raised human actions almost to sublimity.

Remarking these instances, and seeing what the spirit of chivalry could produce in its perfection, we may judge what the society of that day would have been without it: we may trace truly the effect it had in civilizing the world, and we may comprehend the noble legacy it left to after-years. Had chivalry not existed, all the vices which we behold in that period of the world's history would have been immensely increased; for there would have been no counteracting incitement. The immorality of those times would have been a thousand degrees more gross, for passion would have wanted the only principle of refinement; the ferocity of the brave would have shown itself in darker scenes of bloodshed, for no courtesy would have tempered it with gentleness. Even religion would have longer remained obscured, for the measures taken to darken it, by those whose interest it was to make it a means of rule, would have been but faintly opposed, had not chivalry, by softening the manners of the age, and promoting general communication between man and man, gradually done away darkness and admitted light.

Because knights were superstitious, it has been supposed that superstition was apart of knighthood; but this was not at all the case. The gross errors grafted by the Roman church on the pure doctrine of salvation often taught the knight cruelty, and disgraced chivalry, by making it the means of persecution; but the tendency of the Order itself was to purify and refine, and the civilization thereby given to the world in general ultimately produced its effect in doing away superstition. The libertinism of society in the middle ages has also been wrongly attributed to knighthood, and thus the most beneficial institutions are too often confounded with the vices that spring up around them. That the fundamental doctrine of chivalry, if I may so express myself, was decidedly opposed to every infraction of morality, is susceptible of proof. In all authors who have collected the precepts of chivalry, we find sobriety and continence enjoined as among the first duties of a knight: and female chastity was so particularly esteemed, that we are told by the Chevalier de la Tour, if a lady of doubtful virtue presented herself in company with the good, whatever were her rank, the knights would cause her to give place to those of unsullied fame. From everything that I can read or hear, I am inclined to believe that the virtues of the knights of old arose in the Order of Chivalry alone, and that their faults belonged to the age in which they lived.[13]

In common with all human institutions, chivalry presents a new aspect in every page of the book of history. Sometimes it is severe and stern; sometimes light and gay; but the qualities of valour, courtesy, and enthusiasm shine out at every period of its existence.

At the battle of Crecy, Edward the Black Prince, then fourteen years of age, fought for his knightly spurs; and his father, King Edward III., from a mound near the mill, beheld his gallant son surrounded on every side by enemies. The companions of the young hero sent to the king for succour, alleging the dangerous situation of the Prince of Wales; on which Edward demanded, "Is he dead, or overthrown, or so wounded that he cannot continue to fight?" And on being informed that his son still lived, he added, "Return to him, and to those who sent you, and tell them, whatever happens, to seek no aid from me so long as my son be in life. Further say, that I command them to let the boy well win his spurs; for, please God, the day shall be his, and the honour shall rest with him."[14]

In this instance, Edward required no more from his child than he was willing in his own person to endure. No one ever evinced more chivalrous courage than that monarch himself; and in the skirmish under the walls of Calais, he fought hand to hand with the famous De Ribaumont, who brought him twice upon his knee, but was at length vanquished by the king. After the battle, Edward entertained his prisoners in the town; and when supper was concluded the victorious monarch approached his adversary, took the chaplet of rich

---

13. Jouvencel; Ordre de Chevalerie; Fabliaux de le Grand d'Aussi; Chevalier de la Tour; Notes on St. Palaye.
14. Froissart, chap. 290.

pearls from his own brow, placed it on the head of De Ribaumont, and said, "Sir Eustace, I give this wreath to you, as the best of this day's combatants, and I beg you to wear it a year for my love. I know that you are gay and gallant, and willingly find yourselves where ladies are. Tell them, then, wherever you may be, that I gave you this token; and, moreover, I free you from your prison. Go tomorrow, if it please you."[15]

Such was the character of knighthood; and whether we read anecdotes like the above, or trace in the rolls of history the feats of an Edward the Black Prince, of a Duguesclin, of a Talbot, a Henry, or a Bayard, we find the same spirit; varied, indeed, according to the mind of the individual, but raising all his virtues to the highest pitch of perfection, and restraining all his faults as much as human errors can be restrained.

It would be endless to detail all those marvels which chivalry at various times effected; nor have I space to dwell upon Crecy, or Poitiers, or Agincourt. With respect to those great battles, where England was so eminently triumphant, it is sufficient to point out the extraordinary fact, that though the glory rested with the British, no disgrace attached to their enemies. Each knight in the French armies did everything that personal valour could do to win the field; and the honour to England consists not so much in having conquered, as in having conquered such opponents. For long, however, it appears that the French commanders were inferior to the English in skill, and that their forces were destitute of that unity which alone secures success.

At length, the son of a nobleman of Brittany, who had been much neglected in his early years, began to make head against the English. From his infancy Bertrand Duguesclin had shown the most persevering passion for arms, which had been always repressed; till at a tournament—from the neighbourhood of which he had been purposely sent away—he appeared in disguise, defeated all that encountered him, and was only discovered by refusing to meet his own father. From that hour Duguesclin rose in the estimation of the world; and after opposing, with considerable success, Edward the Black Prince himself, on the death of that noble commander he delivered the greater part of France from the domination of the English.

One of the favourite schemes of Duguesclin was to restore to chivalry its ancient simplicity, and he strove by every means to enforce the more severe and salutary laws by which it had been originally

15. *Ibid.* chap. 329.

governed. Of course, an institution which had vast privileges and obligations was not without rewards and punishments; and many of these were revived by Duguesclin after he had become Constable of France.

The custom of cutting the tablecloth with a knife or dagger before a knight who had in any way degraded himself[16] is said, by some, to have been brought into use by Duguesclin, though others affirm that he only renewed an ancient habit. Much more severe inflictions, also, were destined for those who had dishonoured the Order to which they belonged by cowardice, treachery, or any other unmanly crime. The criminal, condemned to be stripped of his knighthood, was placed upon a scaffold, in the sight of the populace, while his armour was broken to pieces before his face. His shield reversed, with the coat-of-arms effaced, was dragged through the dirt, while the heralds proclaimed aloud his crime and his sentence. The king-at-arms then thrice demanded his name; and at each time, when the *pursuivant* replied, the king added, "A faithless and disloyal traitor!" A basin[17] of hot water was poured upon the culprit's head, to wash away the very memory of his knighthood; and, being drawn on a hurdle to the church, he was covered with a pall, while the funeral prayers were pronounced over him, as one dead to honour and to fame.

Notwithstanding every means taken to uphold it, chivalry gradually declined from the beginning of the fourteenth century. In England the long civil wars between the houses of York and Lancaster called into action a thousand principles opposed to knightly courtesy and generosity. Many flashes of the chivalrous spirit blazed up from time to time, it is true; but the general character of those contentions was base and interested treachery on all parts.

The mean and avaricious spirit which seized upon Henry VII. in his latter years of course had its effect on his court and country; and the infamous extortions of his creatures Empson and Dudley, the ruin which they brought upon many of the nobility, and the disgust and terror which their tyranny spread through the land, served to check all those pageants and exercises which kept alive the sinking flame of chivalry. Henry VIII., in the vigour of his youth, made vast efforts to give back to knighthood its ancient splendour; but the spirit had been as much injured as the external form, and though he could renew the one, he could not recall the other. The wavering tyranny of his old age

---

16. Alain Chartier Le Grand.
17. La Colombiere Theatre.

also did more to extinguish the last sparks of knightly feeling, than his youth had done to revive the pomp of chivalry. Then came the Reformation, and a new enthusiasm grew up through the land.

In Germany the reign of the Emperor Maximilian was the last in which chivalry can be said to have existed. Charles V. reduced all things to calculation, and though the name of knighthood remained, it soon became nothing but a sound.

The land which had given birth to the institution cherished it long; and there its efforts were continually reawakened even in its decline. During the unhappy reign of Charles VI., France, torn by factions, each struggling for the sceptre of the insane monarch, saw chivalry employed for the purposes of ambition alone. While all parties turned their arms against their fellow-countrymen, a stranger seized on the power for which they fought, and the English house of Lancaster seated itself on the throne of France. Charles VII. succeeded to a heritage of wars; but, apparently reckless, from the desperate state of his dominions, he yielded himself wholly to pleasure, without striking a blow for the recovery of his kingdom, till Joan of Arc[18] recalled him to glory and himself. From that moment chivalry again revived, and no period of French history presents knighthood under a brighter aspect than during the wars of Charles VII. At the same time, however, an institution was founded which soon changed the character of chivalry, and in the end reduced it to a name.

The inconveniences attached to the knightly mode of warfare were many and striking; order and discipline were out of the question; and though courage did much, Charles VII. saw that courage well directed would do infinitely more. To establish, therefore, a body over which he might have some control, he raised a company of *gen-d'armerie*, which soon by its courage and its success drew into its own rank all the great and noble of the kingdom. Thus came a great change over the Order; knights became mere soldiers, and chivalry was used as a machine. Louis XI. contributed still more to do away chivalry, by depressing the nobility and founding a standing army of mercenary troops.

Charles VIII. and Louis XII., by romantic wars in Italy, renewed the fire of the waning institution; and Francis I., the most chivalrous of kings, beheld it blaze up under his reign like the last flash of an expiring flame. He, however unwittingly aided to extinguish it entirely, and by extending knighthood to civilians, deprived it of its original character. The pomps and pageants, the exercises and the games,

---

18. *Personal Recollections of Joan of Arc* by Mark Twain also published by Leonaur.

which had accompanied the Order from its early days, were now less frequent: popes had censured them as vain and cruel, and many kings had discountenanced them as expensive and dangerous: but the death of Henry II., from a wound received at a tournament, put an end to them in France; and from that time all the external ceremonies of chivalry were confined to the reception of a knight into any of the Royal Orders.

The distinctive spirit also had by this time greatly merged into other feelings. The valour was as much the quality of the simple soldier as of the knight; the courtesy had spread to society in general, and had become politeness; the gallantry had lost its refinement, and had deteriorated into debauchery. Faint traces of the lost institution appeared from time to time, especially in the wars of Henry IV. and the League. The artful and vicious policy of Catherine de Medicis did much to destroy it; the filthy effeminacy of Henry III. weakened it, in common with all noble feelings; and the iron rod of Richelieu struck at it as a remnant of the feudal power. Still a bright blaze of its daring valour shone out in Condé, a touch of its noble simplicity appeared in Turenne, but the false brilliancy of Louis XIV. completed its downfall; and chivalry is only to be seen by its general effects on society.

Thus things fleet by us; and in reading of all the great and mighty deeds of which this book has given a slight and imperfect sketch, and looking on the multitudes of men who have toiled and struggled through dangers, difficulties, and horrors for the word GLORY, the empty echo of renown, or perhaps a worse reward, I rise as from a phantasmagoria where a world of strange and glittering figures have been passing before my eyes, changing with the rapidity of light, and each leaving an impression for memory, though the whole was but the shadow of a shade.

Notes

NOTE 1.—CHAP. 1.

Menestrier enters into a disquisition on the subject of the two interpretations given to the word *miles*, which would have interrupted the thread of my discourse too much to permit of its introduction in the text. I subjoin it here, however, as a good guide for those who may be inclined to pursue the subject further.

Il ne faut pas donc confondre le titre d'ancienne noblesse, ou de noblesse militaire, avec la dignité de chevalier, par l'équivoque du terme Latin miles, qui convient à l'un et à l'autre; ce que n'ont pas assez observé quelques autheurs, qui n'ont pas fait reflexion que dans la plûpart des actes écrits en langue Latine, ce mot signifie également ces deux différentes choses.
L'Empereur Frederic avoir déjà? distingué ces deux espèces de Chevalerie, lors qu'il fit une ordonnance à Naples, l'an 1232, que personne ne se présentât pour recevoir l'ordre de Chevalerie, s'il n'estoit d'une ancienne race militaire, ou d'ancienne Chevalerie. Ad militarem honorem nullus accedat, qui non sit de genere militum; L'une de ces Chevaleries est donc genus militare, race de Chevalerie; l'autre militaris honor, honneur de Chevalerie, qui n'ont esté confondües que par quelques autheurs, qui, écrivans de cette matière sans l'entendre, n'ont fait que l'embroüiller, au lieu de la developper.
Roger, Roy de Sicile et de Naples, fit une ordonnance, que nul ne pût recevoir l'ordre de Chevalerie, s'il n'estoit de race militaire. Sancinus itaque, et tale proponimus edictum, ut quicumque novam militiam acceperit, il l'appelle nouvelle Chevalerie, pour la distinguer de celle de la naissance, sive quocumque tempore arripuerit, contra regni beatitudinem, pacem, atque integritatem, à militiæ nomine, et professione penitùs decidat, nisi fortè à militari genere per successionem duxit prosapiam.—Menestrier; Preuves, chap. 1.

St. Palaye, in the body of his admirable essays upon chivalry, names the day preceding that of the tournament as the one on which squires were permitted to joust with each other: but in a note he has the following passage, which shows that in this, as in almost every other respect, the customs of chivalry varied very much at different epochs.

Les usages out varié par rapport aux tournois, suivant les divers temps de la Chevalerie. Dans les commencements les plus anciens chevaliers joutoient entre eux, et le lendemain de cette joute les nouveaux chevaliers s'exerçoient dans d'autres tournois, auxquels les anciens chevaliers se faisoient un plaisir d'assister en qualité de spectateurs. La coutume changea depuis: ce fut la veille des grands tournois que les jeunes chevaliers s'essayerent les uns contre les autres, et l'on permit aux écuyers de se mêler avec eux. Ceux-ci étoient récompensés par l'ordre de la Chevalerie, lorsqu'ils se distinguoient dans ces sortes de combats. Ce mélange de chevaliers et d'écuyers introduisit dans la suite divers abus dans la Chevalerie, et la fit bientôt dégénérer, comme le remarque M. Le Laboureur. Les écuyers usurpèrent successivement et par degrés les honneurs et les distinctions qui n'appartenoient qu'aux chevaliers, et peu-à-peu ils se confondirent avec eux.—Note on St. Palaye.

This note is perfectly just in the statement that in after-times the distinctions between knights and squires were not so strictly maintained as in the early days of chivalry. At the famous jousts between the French and English at Chateau Joscelin, as related by Froissart, we find the squires opposed to the knights upon perfectly equal terms. The limits of this book are too narrow to admit of many long quotations; but the passage will be found well worthy the trouble of seeking, in the sixty fourth chapter of the second book of the admirable Froissart.

NOTE 3—CHAP. 2

To show the manner in which reports of all kinds were spread and collected even as late as the days of Edward III., I have subjoined the following extract from Froissart, giving an account of his reception at the court of the Count de Foix. It also affords a *naive* picture of that curious simplicity of manners which formed one very singular and interesting trait in the chivalry of old.

Comment Messire Jean Froissart enquéroit diligemment comment les Guerres s'étoient portées par toutes les parties de la France.

Je me suis longuement tenu à parler des besognes des lointaines march-
es, mais les prochaines, tant qu'à maintenant, m'ont été si fraîches, et
si nouvelles, et si inclinants à ma plaisance, que pour ce les ai mises
arrière.

Mais, pourtant, ne séjournoient pas les vaillants hommes, qui se désiroi-
ent à avancer ens [dans] on [le] royaume de Castille et de Portugal,
et bien autant en Gascogne et en Rouergue, en Quersin [Quercy], en
Auvergne, en Limousin, et en Toulousain, et en Bigorre; mais visoient
et subtilloient [imaginoient] tous les jours l'un sur l'autre comment ils
se pussent trouver en parti de fait d'armes, pour prendre, embler [en-
lever], et écheller villes, et châteaux, et forteresses. Et pour ce, je sire Jean
Froissart, qui me suis ensoingné [étudié] et occupé de dicter et écrire
cette histoire, à la requête et contemplation de haut prince et renommé
Messire Guy de Châtillon, Comte de Blois, Seigneur d'Avesnes, de
Beaumont, de Scoonhort, et de la Gende, mon bon et souverain maître
et seigneur; considérai en moi-même, que nulle espérance n'étoit que
aucuns faits d'armes se fissent ès parties de Picardie et de Flandre, pu-
isque paix y étoit, et point ne voulois être oiseux; car je savois bien que
encore au temps à venir, et quand je serai mort, sera cette haute et noble
histoire en grand cours, et y prendront tous nobles et vaillants hommes
plaisance et exemple de bien faire; et entrementes [pendant] que j'avois,
Dieu merci, sens, mémoire, et bonne souvenance de toutes les choses
passées, engin [esprit] clair et aigu pour concevoir tous les faits dont je
pourrois être informé, touchants à ma principale matière, âge, corps et
membres pour souffrir peine, me avisai que je ne voulois mie séjourner
de non poursieure [poursuivre] ma matière; et pour savoir la vérité des
lointaines besognes sans se que j'y envoyasse aucune autre personne en
lieu de moi, pris voie et achoison [occasion] raisonnable d'aller devers
haut prince et redouté seigneur, Messire Gaston, Comte de Foix et de
Berne [Béarn]; et bien sçavois que si je pouvois venir en son hôtel, et
là être à loisir, je ne pourrois mieux cheoir au monde, pour être informé
de toutes nouvelles; car là sont et fréquentent volontiers tous chevaliers
et écuyers étranges, pour la noblesse d'icelui haut prince.

Et tout ainsi, comme je l'imaginai, il m'en advint; et remontrai ce,
et le voyage que je voulois faire, a mon très cher et redouté seigneur,
Monseigneur le Comte de Blois, lequel me bailla ses lettres de famili-
arité adressants au Comte de Foix. Et tant travaillai et chevauchai en
quérant de tout côtés nouvelles, que, par la grace de Dieu, sans péril et
sans dommage, je vins en son chatel, a Ortais [Orthez], au pays de
Béarn, le jour de Sainte Catherine, que on compta pour lors en l'an

de grace mil trois cent quatre-vingt et huit; lequel comte de Foix, si
très tôt comme il me vit, me fit bonne chère, et me dit en riant en bon
François: que bien il me connoissoit, et si ne m'avoit oncques mais vu,
mais plusieurs fois avoit ouï parler de moi. Si me retint de son hôtel et
tout aise, avec le bon moyen des lettres que je lui avois apportées, tant
que il m'y plut à être; et la fus informé de la greigneur [majeure] partie
des besognes qui étoient avenues au royaume de Castille, au royaume
de Portugal, au royaume de Navarre, au royaume d'Aragon, et au
royaume d'Angleterre, au pays de Bordelois, et en toute la Gascogne;
et je même, quand je lui demandois aucune chose, il le me disoit moult
volontiers; et me disoit bien que l'histoire que je avois fait et poursuivois
seroit, au temps à venir, plus recommandée que mille autres: 'Raison
pourquoi,' disoit-il, 'beau maître: puis cinquante ans en ça sont avenus
plus de faits d'armes et de merveilles au monde qu'il n'étoit trois cents
ans en devant.'

Ainsi fus-je en l'hôtel du noble Comte de Foix, recueilli et nourri à
ma plaisance. Ce étoit ce que je désirois à enquerre toutes nouvelles
touchants à ma matière: et je avois prêts à la main barons, chevaliers, et
écuyers, qui m'en informoient, et le gentil Comte de Foix aussi. Si vous
voudrois éclaircir par beau langage tout ce dont je fus adonc informé,
pour rengrosser notre matiere, et pour exemplier les bons qui se désirent
à avancer par armes. Car si ci-dessus j'ai prologué grands faits d'armes,
prises et assauts de villes et de châteaux, batailles adressées et durs
rencontres, encore en trouverez vous ensuivant grand, foison, desquelles
et desquels, par la grace de Dieu, je ferai bonne et juste narration.—
Froissart, book iii. chap. 1.

NOTE 4.—CHAP. 2

As the Brotherhood of Arms was one of the most curious customs
of chivalry, I have extracted from the Notes on St. Palaye, and from the
Disquisitions of Ducange, some passages which will give a fuller view
of its real character and ceremonies than seemed necessary in the body
of this work.

The Notes on St. Palaye also show to how late a period the custom descended and here let me say, that of all the treatises on chivalry
which I possess, there is none in which I have found the real spirit of
knighthood so completely displayed, as in the *Essays* of Lucurne de
St. Palaye, with the elegant and profound observations of M. Charles
Nodier.

Les Anglois, assemblés peu avant la bataille de Pontvalain, tiennent conseil pour déliberer comment ils attaqueroient le connétable Duguesclin. Hue de Carvalai, l'un d'entre eux, ouvre son avis en ces termes: 'Se m'aist dieux, Bertran est le meilleur chevalier qui regne à present; il est duc, comte et connestable, et a esté long-temps mon compaignon en Espaigne, où je trouvay en luy honneur, largesse et amistié si habundamment et avecques ce hardement, fierté vasselage et emprise, qu'il n'a homme jusques en Calabre qui sceut que j'amasse autant à veoir ne accompaigner de jour ou de nuit pour moy aventurer à vivre ou à mourir ne fust ce qu'il guerrie, Monseigneur le prince. Car en ce cas je dois mettre poyne de le nuyre et grever comme mon ennemi. Si vous diray mon advis.'—(Hist. De Bert. Duguesclin, publiée par Menard, p. 407.)

Boucicaut, passant à son retour d'Espagne par le Comte de Foix, se trouva plusieurs fois à boire et à manger avec des Anglois. Comme ils jugèrent a des abstinences particulieres qu'ils lui virent faire dans ses repas, qu'il avoit voué quelque entreprise d'armes, ils lui dirent que s'il ne demandoit autre chose on auroit bien-tôt trouvé qui le delivreroit; Boucicaut leur répondit: 'Voirement estoit-ce pour combattre à oultrance, mais qu'il avoit compaignon; c'estoit un chevalier nomme Messire Regnault de Roye, sans lequel il ne pouvoit rien faire, et toutes fois s'il y avoit aucun d'eulx qui voulussent la bataille, il leur octroyoit et que à leur volente prissent jour tant que il l'eust faict à sçavoir à son compaignon.'—(Histoire du Maréchal de Boucicaut, publiée par Godefroi, p. 51.)

Lorsque le prince de Galles eut déclare la guerre au roi Henri de Castille, il manda à tous les Anglois qui etoient alors au service de ce prince de le quitter pour se rendre auprès de lui. Hue de Carvalai, qui étoit du nombre, obligé de se séparer de Bertrand, vint lui faire ses adieux: 'Gentil sire, lui dit-il, il nous convient de partir nous avons esté ensemble par bonne compaignie, comme preudomme, et avons toujours eu du vostre à nostre voulente que oncques n'y ot noise ne tançon, tant des avoirs conquestez que des joyaulx donnez, ne oncques n'en demandasmes part, si pense bien que j'ay plus reçeu que vous, dont je suis vostre tenu. Et pour ce vous pris que nous en comptons ensemble. Et ce que je vous devray, je vous paieray ou assigneray. Si dist Bertran, ce c'est qu'un sermon, je n'ay point pensé à ce comte, ne ne sçay que ce puet monter. Je ne sçay se vous me devez, ou si je vous doy. Or soit tout quitte puisque vient au departir. Mais se de cy en avant nous acreons l'un à l'autre, nous ferons nouvelle depte et le convendra escripre. Il n'y a que du bien faire, raison donne que vous (suiviez) vostre-maistre. Ainsi le doibt faire tout preudomme. Bonne amour fist l'amour de nous et aussi en fera la departie: dont me poise qu'il convient que elle soit. Lors le baisa Bertran et tous ses compagnons aussi: moult fut piteuse la departie.'—(Histoire de Bertrand Duguesclin, publiée par Ménard, c. xxiv., p. 248 et 249.)

Duguesclin tomba dans la suite au pouvoir des Anglois, qui le retinrent long-temps prisonnier. Après avoir enfin obtenu sa liberté sous parole d'acquitter sa rançon, Carvalai, son ancien frère d'armes, qu'il avoit retrouvé, et qui pendant quelque temps lui tint bonne compagnie, voulut lui parler encore du compte qu'ils avoient à regler ensemble. 'Bertran, dit-il à son ami, avant que de se separer nous avons esté compagnons ou pays d'Espangne par de la de prisons, et d'avoir (c'est-à-dire en société tant pour les prisonniers que pour le butin que nous aurions) dont je ne comptay oncques à vous et sçay bien de pieça que je suis vostre tenu (redevable, en reste avec vous) dont je vouldray avoir advis: mais de tout le moins je vous aideray ici de trente mille doubles d'or. Je ne sçay, dit Bertran, comment il va du compte, mais que de la bonne compagnie; ne je n'en vueil point compter; mais se j'ay mestier je vous prieray. Adonc baisierent li uns l'autre au departir.'—(Ibid, p. 306.)

L'adoption en frere se trouue auoir esté pratiquée en deux manieres par les peuples étrangers, que les Grecs el les Latins qualifient ordinairement du nom de Barbares. Car parmay ceux dont les mœurs et les façons d'agir ressentoient effectiuement quelque chose de rude et d'inhumain, elle se faisoit en se piquant reciproquement les veines, et beuuant le sang les vns des autres. Baudoüin Comte de Flandres et Empereur de Constantinople reproche cette detestable coûtume aux Grecs mémes, non qu'ils en vsassent entre eux: mais parce que dans les alliances qu'ils contractoient auec les peuples barbares, pour s'accommoder à leurs manieres d'agir, ils estoient obligez de suiure leurs vsages, et de faire ce qu'ils faisoient ordinairement en de semblables occasions. Hæc est, ce dit-il, quæ spurcissimo gentilium ritu pro fraterna societate, sanguinibus alternis ebibitis, cum infidelibus sæpe ausa est amicitias firmare ferales. L'Empereur Frederic I. auoit fait auparauant ce mesme reproche aux Grecs, ainsi que nous apprenons de Nicetas. Mais ce que les Grecs firent par necessité, nos François qui estoient resserrez dans Constantinople, et attaquez par dehors de toutes parts, furent contraints de le faire, et de subire la meme loy, en s'accommodant au temps, pour se parer des insultes de leurs ennemis. C'est ce que le Sire de Joinuille dit en ces termes: A iceluy Cheualier oüi dire, et comme il le disoit au Roy, que l'Empereur de Constantinople, et ses gens, se allierent vne fois d'vn Roy, qu'on appelloit le Roy des Comains, pour auoir leur aide, pour conquerir l'Empereur de Grece, qui auoit nom Vataiche. Et disoit iceluy Cheualier, que le Roy du peuple des Comains pour auoir seurte et fiance fraternel l'vn l'autre, qu'il faillit qu'ils et chascun de leur gens d'vns part et d'autre se fissent saigner, et que de leur sang ils donnassent à boire l'vn à l'autre, en signe de fraternité, disans qu'ils estoient frere, et d'vn sang, et ainsi le conuint faire entre nos gens, el les gens d'iceluy Roy, et meslérent dé leur sang auec du vin, et en beuuoient l'vn à l'autre, et disoient lors qu'ils estoient freres d'vn sang. Georges Pachymeres raconte la méme chose des Comains. Et Alberic en l'an 1187, nous fait assez voir que cette coûtume eut pareillement cours parmy les Sarazins, écriuant que la funeste alliance que le Comte de Tripoly contracta auec le Sultan des Sarazins, se fit auec cette cérémonie, et qu'ils y bûrent du sang l'un de l'autre.

Cette fraternité se contractoit encore par l'attouchement des armes, en les faisant toucher reciproquement les vnes aux autres. Cette coûtume estoit particuliere aux Anglois, auant que les Normans se rendissent maîtres de l'Angleterre, principalement lorsque des communautez entieres faisoient entre eux vne alliance fraternelle, en vsans de cette maniere, au lieu du changement reciproque des armes, qui n'auroit pas pû s'executer si facilement.

Mais entre tant de cerémonies qui se sont obseruées pour contracter vne fraternite, celle qui a esté pratiquée par les peuples Chrétiens, est la plus plausible et la plus raisonnable: car pour abolir et pour éteindre entierement les superstitions qui les accompagnoient, et qui tenoient du paganisme, ils en ont introduit vne autre plus sainte et plus pieuse en la contractant dans l'Eglise, deuant le Prétre, et en faisant reciter quelques prieres ou oraisons, nous en auons la formule dans l'Euchologium.

NOTE 5.—CHAP. 3.

The fear of Robert Guiscard was no chimera; for, after having raised himself from indigence to power and authority, he opposed successfully the whole force of two great monarchies, and defeated alternately the emperors of the east and the west.

One of the most pointed accounts of this extraordinary freebooter which I have met with I subjoin, from the *Melanges Curieux*.

Robertus Wischardi de Normania exiens, vir pauper, miles tamen, ingenio et probitate suâ Apuliam, Calabriam suæ ditioni submisit, et In-

sulam Siciliam de manu Ismaelitarum liberavit, Rotgeriumque fratrem suum ejusdem Insulæ Comitem appellavit. Demum mare transiens, Durachium urbem nobilem cepit, Dalmatiamque et Bulgariam super Alexium Imperatorem acquisivit: insuper eum ter bello fugavit, et Romanum, Henricum semel ab urbe fugere compulit, Pontificemque Romanum, quem ceperat, ab eo liberavit. Qui cum innumerabilia penè fecisset probitatis indicia, hoc de illo constans habetur, quod nisi morte præoccupatus fuisset, filium suum Boamundum Imperatorem faceret, se verò Regem Persarum, ut sæpè dicebat, constitueret, viamque Hieroso, lymorum destructâ paganitate Francis aperiret. Nunquam victus est quanquam sæpè pugnaverit. Venetos, qui contra eum omni virtute sua convenerant cum stolo suo ita profligavit, ut nec fuga, nec pelagus illis esset auxilio. Nec fuit terrarum locus ita remotus, in quo rumor, fama, timor Wischardi per omnium ferê ora non volitaret. Et ut verius de ec dici potest, nulli Regum aut Imperatorum Wischardus secundus extitit.—Pere l'Abbe.

NOTE 6.—CHAP. 3.

This cry was not the only cry of arms which the crusaders used in the Holy Land. Though it was the general battle-cry of the whole army, and each leader made use of it occasionally when he wanted to animate the whole host, by rousing up their old enthusiasm; yet when he sought to bring round him his own vassals, he used the appropriate shout of his family. Thus we find, by Raimond d'Agiles, that the battle-cry of Raimond de St. Giles was "*Toulouse!*"

The best general account of the old cry of arms which I have met with is given by Ducange.

Le cry d'armes n'est autre chose qu'vne clameur conceuë en deux ou trois paroles, prononcée au commencement ou au fort du combat et de la mêlée, par un chef, ou par tous les soldats ensemble, suivant les rencontres et les occasions: lequel cry d'armes estoit particulier au general de l'armée ou au chef de chaque troupe.

Les François que se trouuérent à la premiere conquéte de la Terre Sainte avoient pour cry general ces mots, Adjuua Deus, ainsi que nous apprenons de Foucher de Chartres, et d'vn autre ancien Auteur ou bien, Eia Deus adiuua nos, suivant l'Histoire de Hierusalem. Raymond d'Agiles rapporte la cause et l'origine de ce cry à la vision de Pierre Barthelemy, qui trouua la sainte Lance au temps que les Turcs assiegeoient la ville d'Antioche sur les nostre: car durant ce siége S. André luy estant apparu plusieurs fois, il luy enjoignit de persuader aux

Chrétiens d'auoir recours à Dieu dans les fatigues du siége, et de la faim qu'ils enduroient, et de prendre dans les combats pour cry d'armes ces motsDeus adjuua, et sit signum clamoris vestri, Devs adjuva, et reuera Deus adjuvabit vos qui sont les paroles de S. Andre, Roderic Archeuesque de Tolede dit qu'au siége et à la prise de Cordoüe sur les Sarrazins d'Espagne, les Chrétiens crierent aussi Deus adjuva.

Ils ajoustoient quelquefois à ce cry ces mots Deus vult, ou pour parler en langage du temps, et suiuant qu'ils sont enoncez en la Chronique du Mont Cassin,Diex el volt, dont l'origine est rapportée au Concile de Clermont en Auuergne, où le Pape Urbain II. ayant fait vne forte exhortation pour porter les princes Chrétiens à prendre les armes pour aller retirer la Terre Sainte demains des Infidéles, Ita omnium qui aderant affectus in vnum concitauit vt omnes acclamarent, Deux volt, Deus volt. Aprés quoy le pape ayant rendu graces à Dieu, dit entre autres paroles celle-cy, Sit ergo vobis vox ista in rebus bellicis militare signum, quia verbum hoc à Deo est prolatum, cùm in hostem fiet bellicosi impetus congressio, erit vni uersis hæc ex parte Dei vna vociferatio Deus vult, Deus vult. D'où on recueille pourquoy le cry est appelle Signum Dei dans quelques Auteurs.—Ducange, Dissertations sur l'Histoire de St Louis, Dissert. xi.

NOTE 7.—CHAP. 4.

I have used the term *Counts Palatine*, from the old writer whose name stands in the margin. The peculiar position of these *Counts Palatine,* under the ever-changing dynasties of early Europe, is a curious and interesting subject of inquiry, but one too extensive to be fully treated in this place. I hope, at some future period, to speak of it in a more comprehensive work. The learned author whose works have furnished me with the preceding note affords a good view of the original functions of the Counts of the Palace, or *Counts Palatine.*

Sovs la premiere et la seconde race de nos Rois, les comtes faisoient la fonction dans les prouinces et dans les villes capitales du royaume, non seulement de gouuerneurs, mais encore celle de juges. Leur principal employ estoit d'y decider les differents et les procés ordinaires de leur justiciables; et où ils ne pouvoient se transporter sur les lieux, ils commettoient à cét effet leurs vicomtes et leurs lieutenans. Quant aux affaires d'importance, et qui meritoient d'estre jugées par la bouche du prince, nos mémes rois auoient des comtes dans leurs palais, et prés de leurs personnes, ausquels ils en commettoient la connoissance et le jugement, qui estoient nommez ordinairement, acause de cét illustre employ,

Comtes du Palais, ou Comtes Palatins.

Il y a lieu de croire que dans la premiere race de nos Rois, et méme dans le commencement de la seconde, la charge de Comte du Palais n'estoit exercée que par vn seul, qui jugeoit les differens, assisté de quelques Conseillers Palatins, qui sont appellez Scabini Palatii, Echeuins du Palais, dans la Chronique de S. Vincent de Wlturne.

On ne peut pas toutefois disconuenir qu'il n'y ait eu en méme temps plusieurs Comtes du Palais. Car Eguinard en vne de ses Epîtres, dit en termes exprés qu'Adalard et Geboïn estoient Comtes du Palais en méme temps. Et vn titre de Louys le Debonnaire de l'an 938, qui se lit aux Antiquitez de l'Abbaye de Fulde est souscrit de ce Gebawinus, ou Gebuinus, et de Ruadbertus, qui y prennent qualité de Comtes du Palais.

NOTE 8.—CHAP. 6.

The habit of carrying a small wallet when bound on a pilgrimage is one of the oldest customs of the Christian world. This part of the pilgrim's dress was called afterward an *aumoniere,* and served either as a receptacle for containing the alms received on the journey, or, when worn by the rich, as a repository for those they intended to give away. The curious fact of Charlemagne having borne one of these wallets to Rome, and of its having been buried with him, is mentioned in the XVth Dissertation on Joinville.

Cassian traitant des habits et des vétemens des anciens Moines d'Egypte, dit qu'ils se reuetoient d'vn habit fait de peaux de chevre, que l'on appelloit Melotes, et qu'ils portoient ordinairement l'escarcelle et le baton. Les termes de cét Auteur ne sont pas toutefois bien clairs, en cét endroit-là: Vltimus est habitus eorum pellis Caprina, quæ Melotes, vel pera appellatur, et baculus. Car il n'est pas probable que cét habit de peaux de cheure ait esté appellé Pera. Ce qui a donné sujet à quelques Commentateurs de restituer Penula. Neantmoins Isidore et Papias, comme aussi Ælfric dans son Glossaire Saxon, ont écrit aprés Cassian, que Melotis, estoit la méme chose que Pera. Quant à moy j'estime que Cassian a entendu dire que ces Moines, outre ce vétement fait de peaux, auoient encore coûtume de porter vn petit sachet, et vn baton, dont ils se seruoient durant leurs pelerinages.

Ce qui ce peut aisement concilier, en restituant le mot appellatur, on le sousentendant, aprés Melotes. Tant y a que Cassian parle du baton des Moines au Chapitre suiuant; et dans l'vne de ses Collations, il fait assez, voir que lorsqu'ils entreprenoient quelque voyage, ils prenoient

l'vn et l'autre: Cum accepissemus peram et baculum, vt ibi moris est
Monachis vniuersis iter agentibus. Le Moine d'Angouléme ecrit que le
corps de Charlemagne, apres sa mort, fut inhumé auec tous ses habits
imperiaux, et que pardessus on y posa l'escarcelle d'or, dont les pelerins
se seruent ordinairement, et qu'il auoit coûtume de porter lorsqu'il alloit
à Rom: et super vestimentis Imperialibus pera peregrinalis aurea posita
est, quam Romam portare solitus erat.

D'où il resulte que le baton et l'escarcelle ont toûjours esté la marque
particuliere des Pelerins, ou comme parle Guillaume de Malmesbury
Solatia et indicia itineris.

Les Pelerins de la Terre Sainte, auant que d'entreprendre leurs peleri-
nages, alloient rcecuoir l'escarcelle et le bourdon des mains des Prestres
dans l'Eglise.

Et cela s'est pratiqué mémes par nos Rois, lorsqu'ils ont voulu entre-
prendre ces longs et facheux voyages d'outremer. Car aprés auoir chargé
leurs épaules de la figure de la Croix, ils auoient coûtume de venir en
l'Abbaye de S. Denys, et là, aprés la celébration de la messe, ils receuoi-
ent des mains de quelque Prelat le baton de Pelerin et l'escarcelle, et
memes l'Oriflamme, ensuite dequoy ils prenoient conge de S. Denys,
Patron du Royaume.

NOTE 9.—CHAP. 7.

The pretence of the Count of Toulouse for resisting the claims of
Boemond to the possession of Antioch was, that he had vowed to the
emperor Alexius to deliver up all conquests to him alone. This was but
a specious covering for his own avarice. The terms in which Baldric
mentions the cession of Antioch to Boemond are as follows; and it
will be seen that much more notice was taken of Alexius than that
contemptible usurper deserved.

Locuti sunt igitur ad invicem Christianorum duces, et sponte sua Boa-
mundo subintulerunt: Vides quo in articulo res nostra posita sit. Si
civitatem ergo istam vel prece vel pretio, nobis etiam juvantibus poteris
obtinere, nos eam tibi unanimiter concedimus: salvo in omnibus quod
Imperatori, te collaudante, fecinus sacramento. Si ergo Imperator nobis
adjutor advenerit, juratasque pactiones custodierit, perjuri vivere nolu-
mus: sed quod pace tua dictum sit, nos illi eam concedimus: sin autem,
tuæ semper sit subdite potestati. Ex Historia Hierosolymitana Baldrici,
Episcopi Dolensis.

Even in the days of Ducange the form and colour of the Oriflamme, or standard borne to battle before the kings of France, was so
far forgotten, that the learned antiquary bestowed no small research to
ascertain its texture and appearance. His erudition never left any thing
in uncertainty; but though he proved the particular banner called the
Oriflamme to have been red; yet Guillaume Guiart mentions one of
fine azure, which was carried before Philip Augustus to the siege of
Acre. Ducange speaks of the Oriflamme as follows:

*Pour commencer par la recherche du nom d'Oriflamme, la plûpart des
Ecriuains estiment, qu'on le doit tirer de sa matiere, de sa couleur, et
de se forme. Quant à sa figure, il est hors de doute qu'elle estoit faite
comme les bannieres de nos Eglises, que l'on porte ordinairement aux
processions, qui sont quarrees, fenduës en diuers endroits par le bas,
ornees de franges, et attacheés par le haut à vn baton de trauers, qui les
tient etenduës, et est soûtenu d'vne forme de pique. Ils ajoûtent que sa
matiere estoit de soye, ou de tafetas, sa couleur rouge, et tirant sur celle
du feu, et de la sandaraque, à laquelle Pline attribue celle de la flamme.
Il est vray que pour la couleur, tous les Ecriuains conuiennent qu'elle
estoit rouge. Guillaume le Breton en sa Philippide, la decrit ainsi:*

Ast Regi satis est tenues crispare per auras
Vexillum simplex, cendato simplice textum,
Splendoris rubei, Letania qualiter vti
Ecclesiana solet, certis ex more diebus
Quod cum flamma habeat vulgariter aurea nomen
Omnibus in bellis habet omnia signa preire.

*Guillaume Guiart en son Histoire de France, en la vie de Philippes
Auguste, a ainsi traduit ces vers:*

Oriflamme est vne banniere,
Aucune poi plus forte qui quimple,
De cendal roujoiant et simple,
Sans pourtraiture d'autre affaire.

*L'Oriflamme estoit l'enseigne particuliere de l'Abbe et du Monastere
de S. Denys, qu'ils faisoient porter dans leurs guerres par leur Auoüe
Car c'estoit-là la principale fonction des Auoüez, qui en qualite de de-
fenseurs et de protecteurs des Monasteres et des Eglises, entreprenoient
la conduit de leurs vassaux pour la defense de leurs droits, et portoient leurs enseignes à la guerre: d'où vient qu'ils sont ordinairement*

appellez, les porte-enseignes des Eglise, signiferi Ecclesiarum, comme
j'espere justifier ailleurs Les Comtes du Vexin et de Pontoise auoient ce
titre dans le Monastere de S. Denys, dont ils estoient les Auöiez, et les
protecteurs, et en cette qualite ils portoient l'Oriflamme dans les guerres
qui s'entreprenoient pour la defense de ses biens.

Il faut donc tenir pour constant que Louys le Gros fut le premier de nos
Rois, qui en qualite de Comte du Vexin tira l'Oriflamme de dessus
l'autel de l'Eglise de S. Denys, et la fit porter dans ses armees, comme la
principale enseigne du Protecteur de son Royaume, et dont il inuoquoit
le secours dans son cry d'armes.

Il est arriue dans la suite que nos Rois, qui estoient entrez dans les droits
de ces Comtes, s'en sont seruis, pour leurs guerres particulieres, comme
estant la banniere qui portoit le nom du Protecteur de leur Royaume,
ainsi que j'ay remarque, la tirans, de dessus l'autel de l'Eglise S. De-
nys, auec les memes ceremonies, et les memes prieres, que l'on auoit
accoûteme d'observer, lorsqu'on la mettoit entre les mains des Comtes
du Vexin pour les guerres particulieres de ce Monastere. Ces ceremonies
sont ainsi decrites par Raoul de Presle, au Traite dont je viens de parler
en cestermes: Premierement la procession vous vient à l'encontre jusques
à l'issuë du Cloistre, et apres la procession, atteints les benoists corps
Saints de Monsieur S. Denys, et ses Compagnons, et mis sur l'autel
en grande reuerence, et aussi le corps de Monsieur S. Louys, et puis est
mise cette banniere ploise sur les corporaux, où est consacre le corps de
N. S. Jesus Christ, lequel vous receuez dignement apres la celebration
de la Messe: si fait celuy lequel vous auez esleu à bailler, comme au plus
prud homme et vaillant Cheualier; et ce fait, le baisez en la bouche, et
luy baillez, et la tient en ses mains par grande reuerence, afin que les
Barons assistans le puissent baiser comme reliques et choses dignes, et
en luy baillant pour le porter, luy faites faire serment solemnel de le
porter et garder en grande reuerence, et à l'honneur de vous et de vostre
Royaume.

Note 11.—Chap. 13

Villehardouin is undoubtedly the best authority for all the particulars of the siege of Constantinople. Nicetas was extravagantly prejudiced; and though the emperor Baldwin, in his letters to the Pope, was
as frank as any man in his situation could be, it was but natural that
he should endeavour to show the causes of the warfare in the most
favourable point of view—that he should represent the conduct of
himself and his companions with every advantage—in fact that he

should see the events which raised him to the throne through a peculiar medium, and represent them tinged with the same colours that they presented to his own eyes.

Villehardouin wrote without many of these disadvantages. He did not belong to the pillaged and conquered class, like Nicetas, nor did he write to excuse himself in the eyes of the Pope. He had his prejudices, of course, like other men, but these prejudices were greatly prevented from affecting his history by the frank simplicity of chivalrous manners, which no one possessed in greater purity than he did himself.

In two points Philippe Mouskes gives a different account of the affairs of Constantinople from Villehardouin. In the first place, he states that Alexius Angelus, the brother of Isaac, commanded his nephew to be drowned; but that by entreaties the prince moved those persons who were charged with the cruel order. In the next place, he says that Murzuphlis caused Alexius the younger to be poisoned.

In regard to the destruction of the monuments of art committed by the Latins, Nicetas gives a melancholy, though somewhat bombastic account. The famous works destroyed were as follows, according to his statement:

A colossal Juno, from the forum of Constantine, the head of which was so large that four horses could scarcely draw it from the spot where it stood to the palace.

The statue of Paris, presenting the apple to Venus.

An immense bronze pyramid, crowned by a female figure, which turned with the wind.

The colossal statue of Bellerophon, in bronze, which was broken down, and cast into the furnace. Under the inner nail of the horse's hind foot, on the left side, was found a seal, wrapped in a woollen cloth.

A figure of Hercules, by Lysimachus, of such vast dimensions that the circumference of the thumb was equal in measurement to the waist of an ordinary man. From the attitude of this statue, as described by Nicetas, it is not improbable that it served as a model for that piece of sculpture, the only part of which that remains is the famous *Torso*.

The Ass and his Driver, cast by order of Augustus, after the Battle of Actium, in commemoration of his having discovered the position of Antony through the means of a peasant and his beast, the one bearing the name of *Fortunate*, and the other that of *Conqueror*.

The Wolf suckling the twins of Rome; the Gladiator in combat with a Lion; the Hippopotamus; the Sphynxes: and the famous Eagle fighting with a Serpent; all underwent the same fate, as well as the beautiful statue of Helen, which Nicetas speaks of as the perfection of statuary.

Added to these were the exquisite figure on the race-course, and a group, wherein a monster, somewhat resembling a bull, was represented engaged in deadly conflict with a serpent. Each appeared expiring under the efforts of the other; the snake crushed between the teeth of the monster, and the bull tainted to the heart by the venom of the reptile: no bad emblem of the struggle between the bold and furious valour of the Latins and the poisonous treachery of the Greeks themselves.

NOTE 12.—CHAP. 14.

That St. Louis was threatened with the torture is an undoubted fact though what that sort of torture was which Joinville calls *les Bernicles* is not so clear. Ducange fancies that it was the *Cippus* of the ancients: and whether it was or not, the resolution of the monarch in resisting showed not a little fortitude. I subjoin Ducange's observations.

Le Sire de Joinville dit que le Sultan de Babylone, ou son Conseil fit faire au Roy des propositions peu raisonables, croyant qu'il y consentiroit pour obtenir sa deliurance, et celle de ceux de sa suite, qui auoient este faits prisonniers auec luy en la bataille de Massoure. Et sur ce que le Roy refusa absolument d'y donner les mains, il le voulut intimider; et le menaça de luy faire souffrir de grands tourmens. Mathieu Paris: Cùm frequenter à Saracenis cumterribilibus comminationibus sollicitaretur Rex vt Damiatam redderet, et noluit vlla ratione, postularunt summam sibi pecuniæ persolui sine diminutione, vel diuturno cruciatu vsque ad mortem torqueretur.

Ce tourment est appelle par le Sire de Jouinville les Bernicles, lequel il decrit en ces termes. Et voyans les Sarazins que le Roy ne vouloit obtemperer à leur demandes, ils le menacerent de le mettre en Bernicles: qui est le plus grief tourment qu'ils puissent faire à nully: Et sont deux grans tisons de bois, qui sont entretenans au chef. Et quant ils veulent y mettre aucun, ils le couschent sur le couste entre ces dieux tisons, et luy font passer les jambes à trauers de grosses cheuilles: puis couschent la piece de bois, qui est là-dessus, et font asseoir vn homme dessus les tisons.

Dont il auient qu'il ne demeure à celuy qui est là cousche point demy pied d'ossemens, qu'il ne soit tout desrompu et escache. Et pour pis luy faire, au bout des trois jours luy remettent les jambes, qui sont grosses et enflees, dedens celles bernicles, et la rebrisent derechief, qui est vne chose moult cruelle à qui sauroit entendre : et la lient à gros nerfs de bœuf par la teste, de peur qu'il ne se remuë là dedans.

www.ingramcontent.com/pod-product-compliance
Lightning Source LLC
Chambersburg PA
CBHW022118080426
42734CB00006B/173